This book is due on the last date stamped below.
Failure to return books on the date due may result
in assessment of overdue fees.

FINES .50 per day

U.S. SOCIAL SECURITY

Selected Titles in ABC-CLIO's
**CONTEMPORARY
WORLD ISSUES**
Series

For a complete list of titles in this series, please visit
www.abc-clio.com.

Books in the Contemporary World Issues series address vital issues in today's society such as genetic engineering, pollution, and biodiversity. Written by professional writers, scholars, and nonacademic experts, these books are authoritative, clearly written, up-to-date, and objective. They provide a good starting point for research by high school and college students, scholars, and general readers as well as by legislators, businesspeople, activists, and others.

Each book, carefully organized and easy to use, contains an overview of the subject, a detailed chronology, biographical sketches, facts and data and/or documents and other primary-source material, a directory of organizations and agencies, annotated lists of print and nonprint resources, and an index.

Readers of books in the Contemporary World Issues series will find the information they need in order to have a better understanding of the social, political, environmental, and economic issues facing the world today.

U.S. SOCIAL SECURITY

A Reference Handbook

Steven G. Livingston

**CONTEMPORARY
WORLD ISSUES**

A B C CLIO

Santa Barbara, California
Denver, Colorado
Oxford, England

Library of Congress Cataloging-in-Publication Data
Livingston, Steven Greene.
    U.S. social security : a reference handbook / Steven G. Livingston.
        p.   cm. — (Contemporary world issues series)
    Includes bibliographical references and index.
    ISBN 978-1-59884-119-0 (hard copy : alk. paper) —
ISBN 978-1-59884-120-6 (ebook)
    1. Social security—United States.   2. Social security—United States—History.   3. Social security—Cross-cultural studies.   I. Title.
II. Title: United States social security : a reference handbook.

    HD7125.L58   2008
    368.4'300973—dc22

                                                                2008004413

13   12   11   10   09   08   1   2   3   4   5   6   7   8   9   10

ABC-CLIO, Inc.
130 Cremona Drive, P.O. Box 1911
Santa Barbara, California 93116-1911

This book is also available on the World Wide Web as an ebook.
Visit www.abc-clio.com for details.

This book is printed on acid-free paper ∞

Manufactured in the United States of America

Contents

Preface

Social Security is one of the great successes, and one of the great problems, of U.S. public policy. On the one hand, a program created more than 70 years ago continues to provide for the retirement needs of more than 40 million Americans with barely a hitch in its operations. Public opinion polls confirm that Social Security is among the most popular of the services provided by the U.S. government; it is an entitlement that most citizens expect and rely upon. On the other hand, there is a growing recognition that, within the foreseeable future, today's Social Security program will not be able to honor the promises it is making to tomorrow's retirees. Unless changes are made, it is very likely that, by the middle of the 21st century, Social Security will fall many billions of dollars short of the money it will need to pay the monthly benefits that American retirees have been promised.

This book addresses both Social Security's great success and its great problem. It is an effort to provide an overview of the U.S. Social Security system and, more specifically, how that system was developed, why it is likely to encounter difficulty, and what has been proposed to fix it. The experience of other countries is also examined to see what lessons, if any, they may offer the United States in this regard. The book offers a chronology of pensions and social security programs at home and abroad and sketches of the leading officials and personalities who have been instrumental in its development. Further, it provides an annotated guide to the many individuals and organizations, in and out of government, that are active in the U.S. Social Security debate. The objective is to provide readers with all of the information needed to understand, follow, and assess the current controversies that swirl about the U.S. Social Security program.

Social Security is currently the U.S. government's most expensive program. The total annual cost of Social Security benefits is well over $500 billion a year. Social Security may also be the most expansive government program. More Americans have a financial stake in the Social Security program than in any other program. And Social Security may be the most extensive government program. It is a promise that spans the generations: that today's workers will pay for yesterday's workers and will be, in turn, supported by tomorrow's. It is in this context of the program's enormity that any account of Social Security, or of the reform proposals in debate, must be placed.

How was such a massive program ever created in a country so suspicious of its government? From the passage of the Social Security Act of 1935 to the efforts to "save Social Security" in the 1980s and 1990s, this volume traces the program's major changes, twists, and turns, with an eye to how this history has framed the choices the United States confronts today. Certainly even the most casual observer of the current controversies over reform must be struck by the deep symbolic power that this program has attained within the U.S. political system. Social Security may not be the original "third rail" of American politics—a program too politically dangerous for politicians to want to touch—but it is hard to think of another policy that holds, year after year, such a political charge. The aim here is to provide some insight into why Social Security has become so deeply engrained in U.S. public policy.

Social Security is a mechanism to provide livable pensions to American retirees and their survivors. The details of how this program accomplishes this task are also provided here. How the program is financed, who gets benefits, and how the benefits are determined—all of these questions are carefully explained. It is from these details that one can really get a sense not only of how the program operates but of what might be its special strengths or weaknesses in coming years.

These details, moreover, go to the heart of the current debate. Why do experts believe that in 30 to 40 years Social Security will very likely not be able to fulfill its obligations, and what have they recommended the United States do about it? This issue is explained in some depth. Also explained are the many competing reforms that have been proposed to solve this problem. These reforms run the gamut from raising taxes to privatizing the Social Security system. Proponents and critics often shed more heat than light in their efforts to promote or oppose one of these re-forms. In this book, a substantial, unbiased account of each major reform proposal is presented. Both proponents and critics are given their say, so that readers can independently decide which (if any) of these reforms is worthy of support.

As the United States engages in this important discussion, very often the experiences of other countries are ignored or forgotten. Yet most of the world is facing exactly the same set of difficulties as that facing the United States, and a number of nations have already begun the painful task of reform. Have they succeeded? Are there lessons to be learned for how the United States should proceed? Probably so. *U.S. Social Security: A Reference Handbook* investigates, in some detail, the experiences of Canada, Germany, Australia, Sweden, the United Kingdom, and Chile, each a trailblazer in its own way. The reader can decide what their experiences should teach the United States.

This book offers no recommendation of the ideal reform, nor does it promise that every person, sufficiently informed, would reach the same conclusion. The huge number of Americans—one in eight—drawing a Social Security check, each with a different set of financial needs and expectations, makes the choice of reform difficult. The need to address policy to individuals at every stage of life, work, and retirement, too, makes the choice of reform challenging. Hence, while it is quite easy to recognize this coming problem, it is not so easy to decide what to do about it. The essential problem is that no reform is painless. Each involves some shift in who bears the cost of Social Security, and who bears the risk. For better or worse, this is not just a question of economics; it is a question of values. This book cannot answer this question of values, nor even of the politics that follows. But from the resources it provides, the hope is that readers will obtain the knowledge and confidence necessary to enter, from their own perspectives and values, the great debate that is now occurring over the future of a program that is so important to so many Americans.

1

Background and History

Social Security is America's largest, and many would say most important and most successful, domestic policy program. This chapter explores how and why this program was created. In spite of Social Security's near-universal popularity today, it was not easy to develop and enact a national old-age pension program in the United States. There were tremendous constitutional, political, and cultural obstacles. Because of these obstacles, the U.S. Social Security program that emerged was hardly the most rational, efficient, or transparent. It was not enacted by technocrats. Rather, its creation was intensely political, and today's program contains the compromises, horse trading, and deals that were necessary to get it passed. Even after its enactment in 1935, Social Security was not a "done deal." Continued controversy and political pressures led to changes in the program for a half century after it first became law. This chapter discusses how the initial obstacles were overcome and Social Security was first created, how the program has changed and evolved in the decades thereafter, and how the American Social Security program operates today.

The Origins and Development of Social Security

Nothing seems as obvious as a society's obligation to provide for the needs of those too aged or infirm to work. Yet true old-age pension programs are not much more than a century old. The world's first social security program was not established until

1

1889, and even then by a most unlikely individual, Otto von Bismarck, the "Iron Chancellor" of Germany. His motives were political, not humanitarian. He saw a pension program as a way to halt German socialism and increase the power of the German state against the churches, the traditional providers of aid to the indigent and elderly. Why did it take so long for any country to offer such a program? And why was the United States, a far richer country than 19th-century Germany, not the first to offer it?

Social security was late in coming because the difficulties in creating a sound and effective government old-age pension program are many. These programs are immensely expensive, and they transfer huge amounts of money from one generation to another. They require very sizable taxes on businesses or citizens, and strong and efficient governmental and legal systems to collect and administer these taxes. Since they are based on promises that are made today but paid in the future, social security programs also require political systems that are able to keep those promises. If tax revenues fail to appear, or if the program is poorly designed or administered, the government may find itself with one of two terrible choices: renege on the promises or go virtually bankrupt trying to meet them. Either choice would be disastrous. Thus it is not surprising that old-age pension systems did not arise until the emergence of strong governments and substantial, taxable societal wealth. This situation did not arise until the late 19th century. Social security is a hallmark of modernity.

Perhaps fortunately, the widespread need for these systems also was not widely felt until relatively recently. So long as most individuals worked in the fields, the need for a pension system did not appear stark. To a farmer or a peasant, there was no such thing as retirement. One worked alongside one's family almost to the day that one died. And that day frequently came well before old age. If infirmity did come, the family, and perhaps one's religious community, was expected to care for its loved one. In such a world, there was little expectation that a government would step in to help.

This world ended with the Industrial Revolution. As men and women moved to towns and began to work in factories, the old support systems came under stress. Advances in health and medicine increased life spans at the same time as the new modes of work became difficult or impossible as one aged. Either by choice or by necessity, one eventually had to leave the workforce.

Retirement became a stage of life. But these new retirees, and their families, were usually without private pensions or substantial personal savings and often faced a future of impoverishment and humiliation in their "golden years." Not surprisingly, many began to call for government action to end this plight. Whether for reasons of social justice or simply politics, most of the world's wealthy nations followed the German example by developing governmental old-age pension plans for their citizens in the first years of the 20th century.

The United States was not one of those nations. In spite of its relative wealth, it undertook no significant efforts to develop a national social security system until the Great Depression, nearly 50 years after Germany's program was established. The reasons for this delay are many. Legally, the U.S. federal government is restricted to those powers and purposes granted it by the U.S. Constitution. The Constitution is silent on the issue of social security, and for many years this was taken to mean that such a program was forbidden. Moreover, the American system of government is one of federalism. States are reserved the powers and responsibilities not explicitly granted to the federal government in the Constitution. So even if a social security program were to be contemplated, there were good constitutional reasons for thinking that such a program ought to be the responsibility of the states. However, there are tremendous difficulties with each state having its own social security system. Americans are a mobile people who do not recognize state boundaries as they move between jobs or decide where to retire. Any individual state would have an almost impossible job in taxing and apportioning benefits fairly to citizens who came and left the state at various times in their lives. There might also be a race to the bottom as states realized that the lower their social security taxes, the easier it would be to attract and keep businesses and workers. The result could be that no one state would be able to tax at a rate high enough to provide a meaningful pension. Thus a system of state-led social security programs sufficiently large to be effective would be very difficult to bring about.

These political barriers to a U.S. old-age retirement system were joined by strong American cultural beliefs. Americans have generally desired (or at least claimed to desire) a small state: "The government that governs least, governs best," in Thomas Jefferson's words. A social security system vastly increases the revenues, capacities, and, frankly, the potential intrusiveness of the government. To the extent that the program has, or appears to have, the characteristics of a welfare program or an income redistribution program, it runs against the deeply held beliefs of many Americans. Most European systems granted pensions automatically at the time an individual reached a specified age. To Americans, this reeked of giving someone money for nothing, the opposite of the American work ethic. There was little support for such an idea. In the face of these legal and cultural barriers, American reformers made little progress toward developing a social security system in the first decades of the 20th century.

This did not mean, however, that Americans had no experience with old-age pension systems. In fact, the country had a system so large that at least one expert claims that it was as generous as Bismarck's far more heralded system (Skocpol 1992). This was the system of Civil War pensions. The U.S. government paid out more than $5 billion in pensions between 1866 and the arrival of the federal Social Security program. In the last years of the 19th century, the Civil War pension program consumed more than a quarter of the entire U.S. federal budget. The program eventually reached every Union Civil War veteran over the age of 62, almost a million men and women, with rather generous payments for the time. Yet the operations, and the limitations, of the program revealed how difficult it would be to develop a more universal system of old-age pensions in the United States. For the Civil War system was clearly linked to special recognition for services rendered to the United States. This connection accounted for the political success of the program. It was not money for nothing. It was not a method of ameliorating the difficulties of old age generally. The Civil War pension system was embedded in a different moral sensibility, one still anchored in the principle that a government pension was a privilege to be earned, not a right to be had. From this principle, there was no way to expand the program to other categories of citizens. Thus the Civil War pension system expired with the veterans it supported and could not provide the foundations for a modern U.S. pension program.

As the Civil War pension system came to an end, a healthy American economy had pushed the issue of old age and poverty to the back burner. It took the shock of the Great Depression to bring it dramatically into view. The Great Depression was unlike any situation anyone had ever experienced. As banks failed and the economy contracted, both jobs and life savings were wiped out. By 1932, 38 percent of the nonfarm workforce was jobless.

Cases of starvation were reported in the press. And unlike earlier economic crashes, the United States did not quickly recover. President Herbert Hoover took the position that the Depression must be addressed without significant government help. He resisted calls for expanding or creating new federal programs, including any pension plans to help impoverished senior citizens. But his strategy to end the Depression was not successful, and he was defeated for reelection in 1932 by Franklin Roosevelt (commonly referred to as FDR).

President Franklin Roosevelt is the single most important figure in the history of the U.S. Social Security program. Roosevelt brought a dramatically different view of government to the Oval Office. He believed in strong federal action to end the Depression and was even prepared to experiment, if he must, to find programs that would work. He also had a deeper aim: to use this crisis to transform the U.S. government and its capacities to provide social services for its citizenry. This aim included the provision of pensions for the aged. But even with his immense popularity and a large Democratic majority in Congress, it still took all of his formidable political skills to accomplish this goal.

FDR's first years in office were spent enacting the many programs that became known as the "New Deal." Most were emergency responses to the unemployment and poverty that accompanied the Great Depression. A particularly severe problem was caring for the aged poor. Work programs, such as the Works Progress Administration and Civilian Conservation Corps, could not help these individuals, nor could unemployment programs. As private and public charity organizations collapsed around the country, calls grew for action to help the elderly poor. State and local governments, too, demanded that the federal government take over the provision of assistance for the poor as their own revenues disappeared. But Roosevelt responded cautiously, even rejecting a 1934 congressional bill to provide matching grants to the states to help them provide public assistance for the aged poor. Behind this caution, he was awaiting the public momentum that would allow him to enact a far broader program than simple poverty relief for aged citizens.

While he waited, others promoted their own solutions. Most argued for granting pensions to senior citizens as a mechanism to get out of the Depression. The most famous proposal among these was Louisiana governor and U.S. senator Huey Long's plan to "Share the Wealth." Claiming it would make "every man a king," Long proposed that all Americans should receive $5,000 a year to keep them out of poverty, and everyone over the age of 60 should receive a government pension. To pay for this benefit, Long suggested taxing and confiscating much of the fortunes of America's millionaires. Another, more politically potent, idea came from a retired California doctor, Francis Townsend. In 1933, Townsend published a plan to give all retired persons over the age of 60 a pension of $200 a month, with the proviso that they spend the money within 30 days. Such an "old-age revolving pension" would be financed by a 2 percent national sales tax. Townsend's plan offered a neat combination of goals: the money would support needy senior citizens and would also revive the economy as it was spent. Twenty-five million Americans signed petitions supporting the plan, and Townsend Clubs spread across the country.

FDR put off these and other programs by claiming that more study was needed. However, he was aware of the rumor that Senator Long might run for president in 1936, and, in 1934, he watched as the socialist Sinclair Lewis swept the California Democratic gubernatorial primary and nearly won the general election on a radical social platform.

Under this pressure, in June 1934, Roosevelt finally announced to Congress that he would undertake the study necessary to introduce a national social insurance program the following winter. To that end, he created the Committee on Economic Security to advise him. The committee was composed of five key administration officials: Henry Wallace, secretary of Agriculture; Henry Morgenthau Jr., secretary of the Treasury; Homer Cummings, the attorney general; Harry Hopkins, the emergency relief administrator; and, as chair, Frances Perkins, the secretary of Labor. This committee was advised by a council of 23 business and labor leaders and by a technical board of experts. In his direction to the committee, Roosevelt asked that he not receive a series of different policies or bills; he wanted *one* piece of legislation that would protect every American from *every* kind of severe economic distress. In other words, social security would be wrapped within a series of new labor, welfare, and social programs.

Roosevelt demanded a program that would be comprehensive, financially sound, and capable of passing Congress. He opposed programs such as those of Dr. Townsend and Senator Long, because he thought them fiscally irresponsible. They would saddle the U.S. government with potentially huge financial liabilities far into the future. FDR preferred a program funded by worker contributions rather than by the government's general revenues. A system based on worker contributions would also solve the potential political problems of the program. On the one hand, if pensions were not connected to worker contributions, they might be seen as welfare, pure and simple. If Americans could not distinguish the program from welfare, they would oppose it. On the other hand, if the pensions came out of the general revenues (i.e., out of the income tax) rather than contributions, they would be subject to the enduring political pressure to reduce taxes.

This understanding led Roosevelt to demand a program built around insurance principles rather than charitable principles. As he put it, "we must not allow this type of insurance to become a dole through mingling of insurance and relief. It is not charity. It must be financed by contributions, not taxes" (Rosenman 1938, 452). This rationale is the reason why the U.S. Social Security program became linked to one's job. One must work to receive Social Security, and the size of one's Social Security check is related to how long one has worked and at what salary. The program appears to operate very much like a life insurance annuity policy. One "contributes" a premium every month in the expectation of receiving an annuity when one retires. (The term "contribution" is pure politics, as the contribution is in fact a tax.)

Roosevelt also expected that if individuals associated their Social Security check with the contributions that they had made, the program would be politically impregnable. No one could ever end or reduce it without being accused of stealing the contributions that workers had already made. In his blunt words, "[w]e put those payroll contributions there so as to give the contributors a legal, moral, and political right to collect their pensions and unemployment benefits. With those taxes in there, no damn politician can ever scrap my social security program" (Schlesinger 1988, 308–9).

On January 15, 1935, the Committee on Economic Security issued its report. Though the committee had engaged in much wrangling, it unanimously proposed a legislative act composed of five major programs. The act would include a program for indigent senior citizens and dependent children; a joint federal-state program for unemployment insurance; grants for states to expand public health and child welfare services; a health insurance program; and a federal old-age insurance program. The health insurance idea was soon dropped in the face of vociferous opposition from the medical community that made its survival in Congress unlikely. Two days later, Roosevelt forwarded the remaining four recommendations to Capitol Hill.

At the time, there was great worry that any or all of these programs would be found unconstitutional. The Supreme Court had dealt harshly with many of Roosevelt's New Deal programs. The Court had already stricken eight New Deal programs on grounds that they were not constitutional. Senator Robert Wagner's pension program for railroad workers, a forerunner to Social Security, also was voided by the Court. The essential constitutional problem, as noted above, is that the Tenth Amendment appears to grant to the states all powers not given the federal government, and nowhere in the Constitution is the power to implement a social insurance program enumerated. For some of the Committee on Economic Security's proposed programs, such as aid for the aged poor, the solution was to make the programs joint federal-state undertakings. But this was not practical for Social Security. The committee optimistically identified the federal government's power to tax and the Constitution's preamble to "provide for the General Welfare" as arguments for constitutionality, but all political observers knew that the fate of these programs would rest with the Supreme Court.

It is this uncertain constitutionality that accounts for some of the complexity of the Social Security system that eventually emerged. For example, the words "pension," "annuity," and "insurance" are not to be found in the original Social Security Act (Weaver 1996). Even though the program rested on these concepts, it was feared that mentioning any of them could cause problems before the Court. In addition, the tax (or contribution) portion of Social Security was placed in a different section of the bill from the program itself so that the former could be argued as the federal government's constitutional right to raise revenue. The Social Security tax (later to become, through the Federal Insurance Contributions Act, the FICA tax) and the Social Security benefit are thus legally separate.

Social Security Act of 1935

Franklin Roosevelt was a brilliant politician. He had neatly placed himself in the middle of his opponents, dividing those who thought he had not gone far enough (the Huey Long supporters and the Townsend club members) from those who thought he had gone too far (Herbert Hoover and the Republicans). Roosevelt knew that the former would have to rally behind him as it became clear that his proposals were the best they could obtain.

Republicans were overwhelmingly in opposition to the bill. But the GOP was no threat. The Republicans had reached the nadir of their popularity by the mid-1930s. In 1936, with only 25 senators and 103 representatives in Congress, they could neither block nor even slow the legislation on their own. The question was whether conservative Democrats, especially those from the South, would join the Republicans in voting against the program. Business, broadly opposed to the bill, could be expected to pressure these members of Congress to kill, or at least gut, the bill. Interestingly, labor unions could not be expected fully to counter that pressure. The American Federation of Labor (AFL) had opposed federal old-age insurance. Samuel Gompers, the hero and longtime head of the AFL, argued that federal pensions would supplant union benefits and make it more difficult to organize. After his death, the AFL slowly shifted its position, but it never became a united force on this issue.

The old-age insurance system turned out to be the most controversial of all the programs offered in the bill. There were three points of contention. First was the issue of the contributions or tax that would be paid. To some, Roosevelt was much too conservative on this point. Many New Dealers, along with others on the left, wanted an old-age pension system built upon European lines. Such a system would be universal in coverage, generous, and well financed via, preferably, the use of the progressive income tax. Linking social security to workplace contributions, as Roosevelt wanted, would in their eyes act as a regressive tax that would limit the size of the pensions of the poorest workers. But to others, there was great unease over the size of the taxes that would be necessary to implement any form of social security. In the United States of the 1930s, only 5 percent of the population paid an income tax, and any program that would significantly increase the percentage—whether one called it a contribution or not—was politically contentious.

Second, business was opposed to the program because of the tax implications. Business wanted neither to pay a contribution itself nor collect the workers' contribution on behalf of the government. Small businesses, in particular, vociferously opposed this new taxation. Third, Representatives from the segregated South were opposed because of fears that their businesses and farms could not afford to pay for a pension plan and because social security appeared to promise a level of financial support to African Americans that they regarded as unacceptable.

Roosevelt sought compromises that would prevent these opponents from joining together. To appease those who worried about the tax implications, the initial tax for the program was revised downward to begin at a low 2 percent (1 percent each for employer and employee) on the first $3,000 of earnings, and then gradually rise to no higher than 6 percent. The first payments would not begin until 1942, five years after enactment. This modest tax also meant modest benefits. The maximum monthly payment would be $85. (Compare this amount with the $120 a month offered to retired railway workers under the Wagner bill of the previous year.) To those made unhappy by such a small pension system, Roosevelt pointed out that the options were this program, or no program. But the implicit bargain was that Social Security would be a minimal program. It would not provide a comfortable retirement or end the need for private savings; it would merely keep senior citizens out of poverty.

To further stress its financial soundness, FDR shaped the program to appear as similar as possible to that of a private pension program that a business might offer. Hence, Roosevelt unwaveringly supported the use of a reserve account, into which employers and employees would contribute equally. Social Security benefits then would be paid from the account to the employees once they had attained retirement age. This approach is very close to the manner in which a private, defined-contribution pension program operates.

To dampen opposition from small business, a very large number of Americans were excluded from the program. Farm workers, domestic labor, and "casual labor" were all exempted. Government workers and the nonprofit sector (which had vigorously opposed the system) were also left out. Thus a considerable portion of the United States was not covered under the new program. Excluding farm workers and domestic labor was also a backdoor method to meet the demands of segregationists. In hearings, representatives such as Howard W. Smith of Virginia made clear they wanted a program that allowed states to "differentiate between persons" (U.S. Congress House Committee on Ways and Means 1935, 949). They opposed a national program that mandated a minimum standard of payments to Americans in every state. Bluntly, they did not want African Americans to have access to a retirement program. Their power was such that Roosevelt did retreat by agreeing that the federal government's efforts to assist the indigent elderly should be limited to offering matching monies to state-run programs. As far as the old-age pension program itself, the workers excluded from the Social Security system constituted most of the entire rural South, which meant virtually all African Americans in that region. This shift served to diminish the strength of Southern opposition to the program.

Even with these many compromises, it was by no means clear that the program would pass. In the House of Representatives, friendly members of the Ways and Means Committee privately told Roosevelt that he should drop the old-age pension plan if he wished to see the rest of the bill become law. But the president held firm. It was in this committee that, at some point, the term "social security" was developed to replace Roosevelt's preferred "economic security," giving the name to the program that we know today. The committee also reorganized the old-age pension plan under a new agency, the Social Security Administration, in an effort to gain more support. (Roosevelt had proposed that the program be distributed among existing federal agencies.) By using House of Representatives procedures that forced an up or down vote on the entire Roosevelt package of programs, FDR's allies were able to obtain passage with an overwhelming vote of 372–33 for the bill.

The Senate was a potentially bigger obstacle because of the possibility of a filibuster. In fact, Huey Long twice initiated filibusters. Senator Thomas Gore (D-Okla.) raised yet another enduring criticism when he asked Secretary of Labor Frances Perkins, "Now, Miss Perkins, wouldn't you agree that there is a teeny-weeny bit of socialism in your program?"(Altmeyer 1966, 38). But again, the final vote showed that when Congress was presented with the choice of no program or the one FDR offered, it was no contest. The Senate passed the Social Security Act by a vote of 77–6. On August 14, 1935, Franklin Roosevelt signed the Social Security Act of 1935 into law.

As expected, the law was almost immediately challenged in court. In 1937, in two cases, *Steward Machine Co. v. Davis* and *Helvering v. Davis,* the Supreme Court, departing from earlier New Deal rulings, upheld the constitutionality of the act. Speaking for the Court, Justice Benjamin Cardozo argued that the problem of the aged may certainly be included under the Constitution's mandate to promote the general welfare and is "plainly national in area and dimensions" and thus need not be left to the states. The most expensive public program in the history of the United States was here to stay.

Clearly, the U.S. Social Security program was a political compromise. Elements such as the link of the pension to workplace taxes, the separation of the system from the U.S. government's general revenues, the use of the Reserve Account, and the scope of the occupations that would or would not be eligible for Social Security are the products of politics, not of economic necessity or financial soundness. As a product of politics, Social Security remains subject not only to economic possibilities and constraints but also to the pull and push of political pressure and the national mood. The result has been the continued reshaping of the program over the decades that have followed its initial passage. Because of its political aspects, the Social Security program of today is actually quite different from the one Roosevelt worked to enact during the years of the Great Depression. In the years after Roosevelt's presidency, the program has been expanded to encompass almost all working Americans, it has become far more generous, and it has changed from operating on insurance or annuity principles into today's "pay as you go" system.

The Expansion of Social Security: From 1935 to the Present
The Reforms of 1939
The first major bout of reform came a mere four years after the Social Security Act's passage. In the 1935 act, the old-age insurance program was a reserve or annuity-style plan, one in which an individual received back, upon retirement, his or her own contributions plus interest. (The Reserve Account was to be invested in U.S. bonds, which would generate the interest payments.) In 1939, amendments were added that began shifting the program to a pay-as-you-go plan, in which a retired individual's benefits were paid not from his or her own contributions but from the annual contributions of those currently in the workforce. The 1939 amendments also added a survivors benefit to Social Security. In the 1935 program, a worker's benefits ended with her or his death. The 1939

amendments allowed the continuation of benefits, at a reduced level, to the worker's spouse or dependent children.

The real initiative for the 1939 amendments came from Michigan Republican senator Arthur Vandenberg. Recall that the 1935 act had created a reserve account to hold the contributions paid into Social Security until they were returned as benefits. Like many Republicans, Vandenberg was deeply skeptical of how this account would be used. At best, it would be a huge temptation for those wishing to expand the federal government; at worst, it was part of a Roosevelt scheme to get the financing for more New Deal programs. Since Social Security taxes began in 1937 and benefits were not scheduled to be paid until 1942, the Reserve Account was already sizable. Vandenberg and others estimated it would grow to $47 billion by 1980. In the late 1930s this was an almost unbelievable amount of money, enough to buy every farm in the United States with $14 billion to spare. How could anyone reasonably believe that politicians could keep their hands off it? This was the gist of an article Senator Vandenberg published in an April 1937 edition of the *Saturday Evening Post* (Vandenberg 1937, 5–7). Vandenberg proposed making the program's benefits more liberal, starting the payment of benefits in 1940 rather than 1942, and postponing the tax increase scheduled for 1940, all in an effort to prevent the creation of this political menace. Of course the lack of a reserve account would mean that beneficiaries would have to be paid mostly out of that year's taxes on workers, because their own contributions had not been "stored" anywhere and could not be returned to them. Vandenberg believed, however, that this would be just as safe as a reserve account and would be less expensive to operate.

Later that year, Senator Vandenberg approached Arthur Altmeyer, the first chair of the Social Security Board, and asked if he would agree to establish a commission to examine this and other questions. Altmeyer thought it politically impossible to refuse. Although Altmeyer was not enthusiastic about making changes, he believed that some reforms would be necessary to head off the more extreme proposals of Vandenberg and others. Altmeyer suggested a fallback position to Roosevelt: get rid of the Reserve Account and increase benefits, but hold firm on the scheduled tax increases. Roosevelt agreed.

Vandenberg was not alone in criticizing the new program. Liberals who had lost the 1935 debate on financing again demanded the end of the contribution system, to be replaced by benefits paid from the general revenues. The contribution system limited the generosity of the pensions, and at the time many thought it a scandal that many senior citizens could draw higher pensions from the old-age assistance plan (i.e., welfare) than they could from the old-age pension plan. Robert LaFollette, the well-known progressive senator from Wisconsin, fought to replace the Social Security program with a flat-rate pension to all senior citizens, to be paid from the general revenues. Business representatives, too, objected to the whole idea of the Reserve Account. It was, they believed, almost a Ponzi scheme. The government was using the Social Security tax to buy U.S. bonds to place in the Reserve Account on behalf of contributing workers. But someday the bonds would come due and the U.S. government would have to raise the revenue to pay them off. Where would that money come from? The economists on the reform commission had a different problem with the account. They believed that the taxes sitting in the account constituted workers' income that could not be spent. It was idle money, and it would be better if it were put to use. The Reserve Account amounted to a reduction in American spending, served as a drag on the U.S. economy, and was a barrier to getting out of the Depression.

What all of these different groups shared was an agreement on eliminating the Reserve Account. But if this was done, how could the financial soundness of the program be guaranteed? One method, heartily endorsed by the board and liberal supporters, was to expand the number of workers paying into the program. Thus the committee recommended including agricultural workers, those working in education and the nonprofit sector, and others in Social Security. Moreover, workers over age 65 should be allowed to continue to work if they wished.

To quiet opponents' fears about the government's use of Social Security contributions, the committee suggested the creation of a trust fund, to be managed by designated, independent trustees, into which all Social Security taxes would automatically be credited and from which all benefits would be paid. In other words, contributions would not, even for an instant, pass through the operating budget of the United States.

Though "trust fund" and "reserve account" may appear to be very similar ideas, there is a vast difference. The latter provided a direct connection between an individual's contributions and her or his benefits. The benefits that one received ultimately came from one's own contributions. A trust fund provides no such connection. The money that is paid out of the Social Security Trust Fund is simply an amount that a retiree receives by statute. It has no necessary link to the amount that that individual had contributed during his or her working life. The shift from a reserve account to a trust fund amounted to disconnecting the money that came in from the money that went out. This marked the shift to a pay-as-you-go pension system. Pensions are paid out from the money that it is currently coming in from those in the workforce, not from money that is deposited somewhere from a retiree's earlier contributions.

Once this shift was accepted, the possibilities were opened for greatly increasing old-age insurance benefits. The government could now provide benefits far in excess of what a retired person had contributed during his or her working years. Thus the committee called for Social Security benefits to begin in 1940 rather than in 1942, and they were disbursed under a new formula that would give the first retirees more generous payments than contemplated under the 1935 act. It also argued for basing benefits not on lifetime earnings, as in the 1935 act, but on average monthly earnings. This proposal had the effect of boosting the payments to most retirees, who had, after all, spent the majority of their working lives before the advent of the program and had thus made no contributions to it.

The committee also proposed a second dramatic expansion of benefits, the provision of survivors' benefits. Under the 1935 law, Social Security benefits were linked to the individual who had paid the taxes. When she or he died, the benefits expired. The advisory committee suggested including the worker's family in the benefits. The surviving spouse of a married couple in which only one had worked would receive the benefit earned by the working spouse plus a supplemental allowance of 50 percent of that benefit. (The 1939 amendments actually applied only to nonworking wives. Husbands were not added until 1950.) A nonworking widow would still receive three-quarters of the benefit. Dependent children would receive one-half of their deceased parent's benefit until they reached the age of 16 (or 18 if still in school). In cases where there were no other dependents, the deceased's aged parents might be eligible for benefits as well. As a result of the implementation of survivors benefits, the Social Security program was retitled the Old-Age and Survivors Insurance Program (OASI).

Securing Franklin Roosevelt's assent to these proposals, the committee finished its business and reported its recommendations to Congress in December 1938. Congressional hearings essentially replayed the debate of 1935. A version of the Townsend plan was revived and offered on the House floor as an alternative to Social Security. It was defeated easily (by a vote of 302–97) but had the serendipitous effect of making the 1939 proposals look very minor and thus easing their passage (Solomon 1986, 16). Conservatives and Southerners were, however, able to prevent expansion of the program to cover agricultural workers. Maritime workers were the only new group allowed into the program. (An amendment to restrict Social Security benefits solely to American citizens was easily defeated.)

The 1939 amendments fundamentally recast Social Security. The favorable Supreme Court decision enabled the rewriting of the bill to develop explicitly the social insurance aspects that the 1935 drafters had feared might not pass constitutional muster. The addition of survivors' benefits, the supplemental pension for spouses, the ability to use nonpayroll taxes to finance the program, and the computation of benefits based on average monthly earnings all served to change Social Security from what had been essentially an annuity program to one in which benefits were not restricted to one's individual contributions. The 1939 amendments thus made possible the huge expansion in Social Security that was to come.

The Reforms of 1950

The reforms of 1939 did not end the debates over Social Security. In the more conservative post–World War II political environment, resistance to expanding the program remained strong. Congress repeatedly refused even to implement the Social Security tax increases that had been scheduled in the 1939 amendments. As a result, the program was starved of revenue, and the monthly benefits to retirees were not increased. The odd outcome was that, for most senior citizens, the old-age assistance poverty program remained more important than the old-age insurance program. By 1949, only one in five retired workers received a Social Security pension. The average old-age assistance payment was $42 a month, while the average Social Security check was but $25 a month. One could credibly wonder whether Social Security would survive.

But instead of collapsing, Social Security was revived, thanks to another set of expansive amendments to the Social Security Act. These amendments, passed in 1950, made four critical reforms. First, the eligibility for Social Security was greatly expanded. Most occupations previously excluded from coverage were brought into the program. Second, the 1950 amendments raised the average monthly benefit by 77.5 percent, the largest single increase in the history of the program. In effect, this redefined social security as a "livable" pension rather than as a bare minimum with which to avoid destitution. Third, the survivors' benefit was extended to new classes of Americans, including dependent husbands, dependent widowers, and children of insured women. Finally, the amendments added a modest program of public assistance for disabled Americans to the Social Security Act.

After World War II ended, President Harry S Truman attempted, unsuccessfully, to expand the Social Security program. Congress, in fact, was heading in the opposite direction. In 1948, it actually narrowed the definition of an employee under the Social Security Act, overriding a Truman veto, and cut 500,000 workers from the Social Security program. That same year, Truman was reelected president in a famous upset victory. Truman had campaigned on a platform of expanding Social Security. He thus prepared to renew his efforts. He hoped that the election would give him a more favorable political environment. The unexpected economic prosperity of the postwar years promised a better economic environment as well. Employment was high and retirement contributions to Social Security were larger than anticipated. The Social Security Trust Fund was healthy, with $13 billion in 1950. This environment gave the president room to maneuver.

On February 21, 1949, Truman transmitted to Congress the drafts of three bills to reform the Social Security Act. One bill called for the creation of national health care. This proposal produced such a storm of controversy that the other bills sailed through Congress almost without notice. And it was one of these latter bills that entailed the substantial reforms to the Social Security program that Truman wanted.

The president's requests for changes in the OASI program were ambitious. Drawing on advisory commission report recommendations and his own advisers, Truman called for ending almost all of the exclusions to eligibility written into the 1935 act. Specifically, Social Security should be extended to cover the self-employed, farm workers, domestic workers, employees in the nonprofit sector, and government workers. Qualifying for coverage would be made somewhat easier for everyone. Next, Social Security retirees should receive an immediate, large increase in benefits. Then, every year thereafter, the benefit amount should rise by 1 percent for every year of an individual's coverage in the program.

It took more than a year for Congress to act on Truman's requests. Republicans, frequently joined by Southern Democrats, fought them fiercely. They argued that the OASI program should be conceived as a basic floor of protection, not as a full pension plan. The leader of the Republicans in the Senate, Robert Taft of Ohio, argued for rolling OASI and old-age poverty assistance into one program, with no eligibility requirements and equal pensions for all retirees. This would be financed through a flat percentage of the income tax. The GOP argued this was fairer, simpler to administer, and a more honest accounting of public funds. Ironically, the proposal was similar to that offered by those on the ideological left in the debates of 1935 and 1939. The difference, of course, is that Taft and other conservatives wished to place Social Security under the income tax so as to limit, not increase, the benefits (and cost). This failed attempt marks the last time that Congress seriously considered ending Social Security as we understand it today.

The "conservative coalition" of Republicans and Southern Democrats did remove the automatic benefit increases that Truman wanted. They nearly removed farm workers once again, losing only in the final conference committee bill. Government and nonprofit workers also remained outside the program (at their own wish). But President Truman gained the rest of his desired reforms. The 1950 amendments extended Social Security coverage to 10 million working Americans, greatly increased the monthly benefit, and liberalized the eligibility and computation formulas for future benefits. To pay for this increase, Congress raised the FICA tax in increments until it reached 7.5 percent in 1969. The self-employed would have to contribute three-quarters of this amount.

The election to president of Dwight Eisenhower in 1952 was perhaps the last critical moment to the political survival of Social Security. Many Republicans had opposed the program in 1935 and in the years thereafter. With a Republican finally in the White House, would the GOP move to dismantle the program? Surprisingly, Eisenhower not only made no such move but he also used his first State of the Union address to demand that 10 million workers still excluded from the program be added to Social Security. Eisenhower's stance ended debate. Social Security was here to stay. The addition of these workers also completed the transformation of Social Security into a near-universal U.S. old-age pension program. In 1956, Congress, over the opposition of Eisenhower, also added disability benefits to Social Security. The disability plan offered monthly benefits to all totally and permanently disabled workers, to be computed in the same manner as OASI benefits. Disabled children under the age of 18 would also receive monthly benefits if their parent or guardian covered under OASI died or retired. The plan was financed by an additional one-quarter of 1 percent tax on workers and their employers (or three-eighths of 1 percent for the self-employed). To answer the worries of opponents, a special disability trust fund was created, into which this new tax would go. This fund would ensure that the OASI Trust Fund would never be "raided" for monies with which to pay disability benefits. Indeed, Social Security's disability program has grown dramatically over the years. By 2000, more than 6 million Americans received more than $100 billion a year through its auspices. It has today become the primary form of financial protection for most American workers. Perhaps ironically, the Disability Insurance Trust Fund remains financially sound even as worries over the OASI Trust Fund grow.

With the addition of the disability plan, the OASI was reorganized as the Old Age, Survivors, and Disability Insurance Program (OASDI), the current official title of the U.S. Social Security system. With one exception, the Social Security program at last looked essentially as it does today: in 1965, Medicare and Medicaid were added to the Social Security Act of 1935. While not directly affecting the operations of the OASDI program, these two health care programs have dramatically improved the lives of senior citizens and form a key part of America's compact with its senior citizens.

Completing the Package: Adding COLAs to Social Security

In 1972, Congress made a final, fundamental change to the U.S. Social Security system. At the time, this change was not much more than an afterthought. Its significance was not recognized by any but a handful of legislators, nor was it understood by many in the media or among the American public. If ever the ramshackle process of constructing Social Security was exposed, it was through the enactment of that year's Social Security legislation, when an automatic cost-of-living adjustment (COLA) was added to the program.

In the first decades of Social Security, the monthly payments that beneficiaries received were set by legislation. At any time that Congress wished, it could increase Social Security payments simply by passing a law with a new benefits schedule. During the 1940s and 1950s, years when the program still aroused controversy and the Trust Fund was very small or even in deficit, this did not happen often. But in the 1960s, mirroring the economic boom of the postwar United States, the Trust Fund grew rapidly. Existing Social Security benefits looked ever more miserly as Americans' incomes grew. And, of course, as senior citizens grew in number, politicians were not unaware of the votes that might be gained by offering them more generous pensions. The result is that Congress became increasingly active in voting in substantial Social Security benefits increases. By the early 1970s, double-digit increases were being enacted almost annually.

Federal officials and Social Security experts became concerned about these increases. Because Social Security is not means tested, every beneficiary gains from an increase in benefits, no matter how wealthy he or she may be. For that reason, one could argue that across-the-board increases of such magnitude were dubious as a matter of policy. In any event, they were extremely expensive. Peering into the future, some realized that the large increases that were occurring then could sink the program decades later. The problem, though, was a practical one: how to prevent Congress from voting large increases when these votes are so popular politically.

Many Social Security experts advanced the idea of taking the benefits decision out of the hands of Congress. As an alternative, they suggested linking the growth of Social Security benefits to the growth in the cost of living. A cost-of-living adjustment could be made annually to the Social Security benefit using the Consumer Price Index (CPI), which measures inflation. A yearly adjustment based on the CPI would be predictable and would preserve the real purchasing power of the OASI benefit. President Richard Nixon had asked the Department of Health, Education, and Welfare to study this plan early in his administration, and COLA proposals were added, unsuccessfully, as amendments to several Social Security bills. But the addition of a COLA was not uncontroversial.

The key actor in this debate was Representative Wilbur Mills (D-Ark.). Mills, the chair of the House Ways and Means Committee, was arguably the most powerful legislator of the 20th century. He jealously protected the prerogatives of his committee, but he was also beginning a rather quixotic quest for the presidency. To boost his chances, the once fiscally conservative Mills shepherded large Social Security increases through Congress in 1969 and 1971. He did not like COLAs; they would reduce his discretionary power in Congress. His ally in the Senate, Democrat Russell Long of Louisiana (the son of Huey Long) helped sneak the 1971 increase into law by placing it in a bill that raised the national debt ceiling. When the government is in deficit, it must shut down unless it can borrow the money it needs to operate. To enable this borrowing, the debt ceiling often must be raised. Because of this necessity, the bill is virtually vote proof and veto proof; it must pass. Long's wily strategy only demonstrated the difficulty of ever controlling the increase of Social Security benefits so long as it was set by Congress.

In 1972, as part of his presidential campaign, Mills introduced legislation for a 20 percent across-the-board increase in Social Security benefits. Beneath the increase, Mills had, with little notice, added the COLA provision. Strong lobbying by the American Association of Retired Persons (AARP) and other senior citizen groups had convinced candidate Mills to reverse his opposition to COLAs and to support the ending of the discretionary benefit increases that had been a major power of his own committee. President Nixon announced that he would veto such a large increase. But, having learned the trick from Senator Long, Frank Church (D-Idaho) added the increase to yet another debt ceiling bill. Nixon could not veto that bill. Church then added a second amendment to include the COLA provision. Both easily passed. Despite its profound change to the Social Security system, placing future Social Security benefits on "automatic pilot" rather than through congressional discretion, there was virtually no debate. Nixon, also needing a Social Security success on which to campaign for reelection, decided not to complain and signed the bill into law on July 1, 1972.

In 1972, Wilbur Mills was not a very keen analyst of his own presidential possibilities. But he was much better at assessing the "far reaching provisions" of his Social Security bill. Thanks to the benefits increase and the COLA provisions, poverty has declined dramatically among America's senior citizens. The United States now has virtually no need for a poverty program for the aged, once considered among the country's most pressing problems. With the addition of the COLA to Social Security, the program finally gained the appearance of the program that we have today.

The First Social Security Crisis

With the passage of the 1972 amendments, the construction of the U.S. old-age pension system was complete. Social Security appeared nothing less than a full success. However, this view was premature. Just 10 years after their passage, the entire system appeared on the brink of collapse. Social Security suddenly needed to be "saved."

Yet participants then, as now, debated exactly what they were saving the program from. The crisis, and the reforms of 1983 that followed, actually stemmed from two very different financial problems, a predicted shortfall in the OASI Trust Fund and the effects of the economic policies of the Ronald Reagan administration. The first of these problems was undoubtedly the result of the 1972 amendments that had added a cost-of-living adjustment to Social Security benefits. Benefits began to rise with the inflation rate, as measured by the CPI. At the time, this was thought to improve the process for determining Social Security benefit increases. But key assumptions turned out to be wrong. The most important was that, in the years ahead, inflation rates would remain within the historical norm. Instead, inflation raced out of control as the 1970s progressed, and by 1980, the U.S. inflation rate was four times that of the early 1970s. As the CPI exploded, so did Social Security expenditures. Even worse, the inflation rate exceeded the rate of wage increases for those still in the workforce. This unexpected situation meant that the increase in the flow of benefits paid out of the OASI Trust Fund was larger than the increase in the flow of revenues coming in. (Remember that Social Security is funded through a payroll tax on wages.) The situation was serious enough that both presidents Gerald Ford and Jimmy Carter proposed technical adjustments to remedy this problem. These measures were not enough to control the shrinkage of the OASI Trust Fund.

Soon, the Social Security Administration's Office of the Actuary, charged with making long-range forecasts of the solvency of the Trust Funds, released a prediction that all of the Trust Funds might be exhausted by the mid-1980s. By 1981, the OASI Trust Fund was expected to be in a short-run deficit. This news was all the more alarming considering the Office of the Actuary's predictions had a history of being overly optimistic. For 1980, for example, it had predicted a rise in the CPI of 4.7 percent, when in fact the rate was 13.5 percent, and it had predicted a rise in wage rates of 2.4 percent, when in fact that rate turned out to be *minus* 4.9 percent (Schieber and Shoven 1999, 184). Its projected Trust Fund shortfall of up to $200 billion thus stunned Washington.

This short-term crisis rested atop a deeper long-term crisis. As more Americans retired and lived longer, the ratio of workers paying into the OASI Trust Fund to retirees drawing out of the Trust Fund was falling. This demographic shift would inevitably drain the Trust Fund, absent reform, unless economic growth was far faster than most experts were expecting. Moreover, the growth of Social Security (and Medicare) was itself becoming a budget problem. From 1969 to 1980, the portion of the federal budget devoted to income maintenance and health care rose from 20 to 40 percent. Many questioned how long this could continue.

More sober members of Congress were already attempting to address this long-term problem. They were led by J. J. (Jake) Pickle (D-Texas), who tried to enact legislation to raise the retirement age and end the benefit penalty on those who continued to work after reaching the age of 68. Both of these changes would increase the ratio of those working to those retired. His initial efforts had little success, for one very simple reason: absent an immediate crisis, what member of Congress wanted to vote for legislation that made Social Security less generous? The Office of the Actuary's report provided that crisis.

In the spring of 1981, as members of Congress faced the necessity of Social Security reform, the Reagan administration unexpectedly dropped a bombshell: a proposed cut in Social Security benefits. This second contributor to the crisis arose out of an economic problem wholly unrelated to the Trust Fund crisis. The Reagan administration attempted to jar the U.S. economy out of its dismal performance of the 1970s through large-scale tax cuts. President Reagan's director of the Office of Management and Budget, David Stockman, recognized that the administration's program was going to produce massive federal budget deficits far into the future. He desperately needed to find programs he could cut, and cut fast. Among domestic programs, only Social Security was sizable enough to make a real difference. He thus targeted it. In addition, he recognized that the increased deficits would mean greater reliance on borrowing from the Trust

Funds in order to subsidize the current federal budget. So it was essential that the funds be as large as possible. Stockman therefore proposed a series of Social Security benefit cuts. He suggested delaying the cost-of-living increase, reducing benefits to those who choose early retirement (retirement at age 62), and tightening the rules on obtaining disability insurance, along with a variety of smaller cuts. Altogether, Stockman's reforms would have cut some $30 billion in benefits, and they affected nearly 60 million people. This plan was presented to Congress in May 1981.

The public outcry was deafening. Democrats, not believing their good luck, offered congressional resolutions condemning the proposals and, with Save Our Social Security, an umbrella lobbying organization of some 125 special interest groups in tow, ran with its attacks on Reagan's "despicable plan." Republican legislators signaled to the president that it was imperative to get the entire issue off the political agenda lest they lose the elections of 1982. The quick fix was a bill that allowed the OASI to borrow a sufficient amount from the healthier Disability and Hospital Insurance Trust Funds to keep it afloat until June 1983. But what should be done then? James Baker, Reagan's chief of staff, had the answer: create a national commission to study the issue.

In December 1981, the 15 members of the National Commission on Social Security Reform were appointed. Five were chosen by congressional Republicans, five by congressional Democrats, and five by the administration. Alan Greenspan, the future head of the Federal Reserve Bank, was made the chair. Throughout 1982, members of the commission attempted to negotiate a bipartisan package of Social Security reforms to save the system. Parallel negotiations took place between President Reagan, Speaker of the House Thomas P. "Tip" O'Neill, a Democrat, and their emissaries. Both sets of discussions nearly ended in failure. Basically, Republicans favored cutting benefits, and Democrats favored raising the FICA tax. Only after a series of intense meetings did both sides agree that Social Security must be saved by a compromise of equally cutting benefits and raising taxes. In a second important compromise, it was agreed that the Social Security benefits of high-income recipients would be taxed as personal income. Previously, all Social Security benefits had been exempt from the income tax. Following several smaller compromises, the commission voted to include these changes in its final report. (The vote was not unanimous; three conservative Republican members refused to endorse the report.)

The commission's report aroused great controversy. An alliance of interest groups, most importantly the 14-million-member AARP and the National Federation of Independent Business (NFIB), vowed to defeat the enactment of its proposals in Congress. (The AARP opposed the benefits cuts, and the NFIB opposed the tax increase.) It took a tortuous journey through Congress to enact the commission's reforms in 1983. During that journey, Representative Pickle was able to add a gradual rise in the retirement age to 67 to the reform package. For many Americans, this is probably the most important consequence of the 1983 reforms. However, those with incomes above $25,000 ($32,000 for married couples) now had to pay the income tax on one-half of their Social Security pension, while the self-employed saw an immediate rise in their FICA taxes, and all workers faced an accelerated timetable in previously planned FICA tax increases.

Defenders of Social Security breathed a sigh of relief when, following the reforms, the Social Security Administration's Office of the Actuary predicted that the Trust Funds would now last until 2063. Not only was the OASI Trust Fund saved but most observers thought that they had closed from one-half to two-thirds of the long-term Social Security deficit. However, this, too, has turned out to be an optimistic guess. The Office of the Actuary has moved forward by about 20 years the predicted date of the Trust Fund's demise. The solution to the first Social Security crisis, it turns out, actually only bought time. It did not solve the program's underlying problems.

The U.S. Social Security Program Today

Social Security has become the U.S. government's largest domestic program. More than 9 out of 10 Americans over the age of 65 receive a Social Security payment each month. Their benefits total nearly $500 billion a year, an amount that would have astounded previous generations. Though its details can at times seem fiendishly complex, the operation of today's Social Security program is fairly straightforward.

Virtually every working American can qualify for Social Security. There are a very few exceptions, mostly involving individuals who work for state and local governments or individuals who work for a number of nonprofit institutions. By statute, these employers are not obligated to join the Social Security system, although they can if they wish. Federal government workers were not brought into the system until 1984. To gain eligibility for a pension, a worker must accumulate 40 credits, or "quarters of coverage." A credit is gained each time the worker earns wages equal to a stipulated dollar amount. This amount changes each year, as it rises with an index of average American wages. In 2008, for example, the amount of earnings needed to gain one credit was $1,050. A worker is limited to accumulating four credits a year. This means, in effect, that one must work at least 10 years to gain a Social Security pension.

While individuals work, they must pay a tax, or contribution, on the covered wages that they earn until they reach what is called the "maximum earnings" limit. This tax is called the Federal Insurance Contributions Act tax. One-half of this tax is paid by the worker, the other half by the employer. If workers are self-employed, they are responsible for paying the full tax. The original Social Security law set the tax rate as 1 percent of earned income for the worker and 1 percent for the employer, but that rate has risen to 6.2 percent for each. Should workers reach the maximum earnings amount, the FICA tax ends, and those workers are not taxed on any additional income that they may earn. This amount is also set to an index of average American wages, and so it, too, rises every year. In 2008, the maximum earnings amount was $102,000. About 85 percent of the FICA tax goes into the Social Security Trust Fund, and the remaining 15 percent goes into the Disability Insurance Trust Fund. (The total FICA tax today is actually 7.65 percent each for workers and their employers, because it also includes contributions to the Medicare program, for which all Americans over the age of 65 are eligible.) Money deposited into the Trust Fund is used to pay current retirees, with any remainder invested in special U.S. Treasury bonds.

A Social Security pension begins at the date of retirement. Somewhat confusingly, the Social Security Administration defines retirement as the date at which an individual starts receiving her or his Social Security benefits, not as the date at which that person leaves the workforce. It is possible to stop working but then wait for several years or more before applying for a pension. Most workers choose to retire at their date of full retirement. This age was originally set at 65, but, as explained above, the reforms of 1983 have replaced that date with a sliding scale that incrementally increases the retirement age for younger workers. For workers born after 1960, their full retirement age will be 67. If one retires at this age, she or he will receive full Social Security benefits. One may also choose to retire early or to retire late. Early retirement may begin at age 62; workers who retire at that age will see their benefits reduced by 20 to 30 percent, depending upon their year of birth. On the other hand, one may wait until age 70 to retire. The monthly Social Security benefit for late retirees is increased 5.5 to 8 percent, again depending upon the year of birth, for each year that the retirement is delayed beyond age 65. The explanation for this scale is that the reduced benefit for early retirees and the increased benefit for late retirees are simply means to ensure that the total lifetime payments will be the same for each of these groups of retirees, but this schedule of benefits also operates as an incentive to encourage workers to postpone their retirement.

If a worker does choose to keep working past the age of 65, that individual continues to earn Social Security credits, although she or he must also continue to pay the FICA tax. If the option to retire early is taken, however, and the worker continues to be employed, she or he will be subject to an "earnings test." A portion (usually one-half) of the individual's Social Security benefit will be withheld because of the additional income that is being earned.

The monthly benefit that a worker receives depends upon the age of retirement and the Social Security benefits calculation. The calculation made to determine a worker's initial benefit is probably the most difficult part of Social Security to grasp. Basically, the calculation proceeds as follows. First, the worker's earnings for each year that she or he was employed are adjusted, or indexed, to reflect the increase in average American wages that has occurred since that time. Then, the 35 years with the highest adjusted incomes are added together. This gives the worker's lifetime earnings. By dividing this figure by the number of months in 35 years, the worker's average indexed monthly earnings (AIME) is computed. A formula then converts the AIME into a level of benefits. The formula gives more weight to lower incomes, so it has a slightly progressive effect on Social Security pensions. Individuals with low incomes do somewhat better, and individuals with high incomes do somewhat worse, than if benefits were paid strictly based on the total AIME. The benefit calculated from the AIME is called the Primary Insurance Amount (PIA). This will be the amount in the retiree's first Social Security check. By law, however, an individual's PIA cannot exceed a stipulated maximum amount. In 2008, that maximum was set at

$2,185.00 per month. The average monthly benefit is currently around $1080 per month. All PIAs are then adjusted each succeeding year by the rate of inflation, as measured by the Consumer Price Index. In 2008, for example, all benefits were raised by 2.3 percent. After the reforms of 1983, wealthier retirees are taxed on their Social Security benefits, reducing the amount that they actually receive.

Social Security benefits are given not only to the individual who earned them but potentially to the spouse as well. A nonworking husband or wife of a beneficiary receives an additional benefit equal to one-half of the primary wage earner's Social Security pension. If the spouse also works, the spousal benefit is guaranteed to equal one-half of the primary wage earner's benefit, no matter what the level of the spouse's earnings may have been. However, if the spouse's benefits would be more than one-half the primary benefit, the family is allowed to keep the full amount of both benefits, again up to a stipulated maximum.

Finally, Social Security provides survivors' benefits for family members of a deceased Social Security beneficiary. A surviving spouse can begin to collect a reduced Social Security pension at age 60 or a full pension at age 65. There are additional benefits for children under age 16 and for widows or widowers who are caring for them. In all cases, benefit conditions are somewhat liberalized if the surviving spouse or children are disabled.

The U.S. Social Security program is comprehensive and relatively generous. It must be counted as one of the country's great political successes of the 20th century. However, as discussed later in the book, absent changes or reduced expectations, the program will not continue to be so successful in the future. The United States once again must decide what to do about Social Security.

References

Altmeyer, Arthur J. 1966. *The Formative Years of Social Security*. Madison: University of Wisconsin Press.

Rosenman, Samuel Irving, ed. 1938. *Public Papers and Addresses of Franklin D. Roosevelt*, vol. III. New York: Random House.

Schlesinger, Arthur M., Jr. 1988. *The Age of Roosevelt: The Coming of the New Deal*. New York: Houghton Mifflin.

Schieber, Sylvester, and John B. Shoven. 1999. *The Real Deal: The History and Future of Social Security.* New Haven, CT: Yale University Press.

Skocpol, Theda. 1992. *Protecting Soldiers and Mothers.* Cambridge, MA: Harvard University Press.

Solomon, Carmen. 1986. Major Decisions in the House and Senate Chambers on Social Security. *CRS Report for Congress,* December 29. Congressional Research Service. Washington, D.C.: Government Printing Office.

U.S. Congress House Committee on Ways and Means. 1935. Economic Security Act. Hearings on HR 4120 before the House Ways and Means Committee, 74th Congress, 1st Session. http://www.ssa.gov/history/35house.html.

Vandenberg, Arthur H. 1937. "The $47,000,000,000 Blight." *Saturday Evening Post,* April 27: 5-7.

Weaver, Carolyne L. 1996. Birth of an Entitlement: Learning from the Origins of Social Security. *AEI Online* (May), http://www.aei.org/publications/pubID.6500/pub_detail.asp (Accessed 12/26/2007).

2

Problems, Controversies, and Solutions

More than 40 million people are receiving Social Security old-age insurance pensions. This number represents more than one out of every eight Americans. Thanks to Social Security, relatively few Americans now retire into poverty. The ending of that poverty, and the fear it created, must be credited as one of the great achievements of U.S. public policy. Whatever its controversies at the time of its founding, few would now question the value of a government old-age pension program. However, as hinted in chapter 1, unless the program is changed—or U.S. demographics change—this success is not guaranteed to continue. Within little more than a generation, Social Security is expected to encounter a severe problem. The trustees of the Social Security program currently predict that at some point during the years 2040 to 2045, there will not be sufficient funds to pay retirees all of the benefits they have been promised. At this point, it can truly be said that Social Security is in crisis.

This chapter explains the nature of the funding problem and explores the solutions that have been offered to fix it. It sketches out each major type of solution and examines what both supporters and critics have to say about it. No proposed solution is popular in all quarters or is without its opponents. Each involves trade-offs, and often the trade-offs involve personal values as well as issues of finance and economics. Some of these solutions have been tried in other countries; chapter 3 details their experience. But first the book focuses on the American debate and assesses the options that currently exist to prevent a coming Social Security crisis.

The Social Security Trust Fund

Recall that the U.S. Social Security system is what is known as a pay-as-you-go program. This means that, each month, the benefits being sent to retirees are paid out of the stream of the contributions of current workers that are coming into the program. It is *not* the case that each American worker has funds set aside under her or his name somewhere in the Social Security system. Rather, each worker's Federal Insurance Contributions Act (FICA) tax simply goes into a common pool, and the benefits are then paid out of this same pool. (The income tax that wealthier Social Security recipients have paid on some of their Social Security benefits since 1983 also goes into this pool.) When more contributions are coming in than benefits going out (as is the case today), the extra money is used to buy a special kind of U.S. Treasury bond. These bonds are held in the Old-Age and Survivors Insurance (OASI) Trust Fund. For a number of years contributions have exceeded benefits, and so, by 2008, the Trust Fund has grown to hold more than $2.2 trillion in these bonds.

However, the Trust Fund is a little more complicated and confusing than it looks. First, it does not operate like a bank account or an investment fund. There are no names or account holders in the Trust Fund. A working American earns an entitlement to Social Security benefits, but not an entitlement to any specific dollars that reside in the Trust Fund. So it is certainly possible that the amount of Social Security benefits that the government has promised to pay workers in the future can be far different from the amount that is, or will be, in the Trust Fund. Second, the Trust Fund is not a stockpile or stash of bonds that sits somewhere, like a Fort Knox of Social Security. It is merely an accounting device. Anyone who would go to Washington, D.C, and demand to see the Trust Fund would be disappointed. The Trust Fund is a piece of paper, backed by the full faith and credit of the United States to be sure, but a piece of paper nonetheless. In a typical bank account or an investment fund, one has stocks, bonds, or monies that can be sold, withdrawn, or cashed in. They are real assets that make a financial claim on a third party. The Trust Fund, however, is not composed of assets like these. The special bonds that it holds cannot be cashed. These bonds are simply a claim on future American tax revenues. They are bonds issued by the government, to the government (in the form of the Social Security Administration). In other words, the government is buying bonds from itself and so making a financial claim on itself, not a third party. Experts can thus argue over the "reality" of the assets that are in the Trust Fund. The bottom line is that the Trust Fund, despite its name, is primarily an accounting device, albeit one that earns interest. It tells us how much money the Social Security system has to pay all of its promised benefits to retirees.

Because the Trust Fund is an accounting device, it can be balanced, it can have a surplus, or it can have a deficit. If it is balanced, this means that the FICA taxes that come in exactly equal the benefits that go out. If it is running in surplus, it means, as noted earlier, that the taxes exceed the benefits and the amount of the Treasury securities in the Trust Fund is growing. But if it is running in deficit, it means that the benefits to be paid exceed the taxes that are coming in. In the case of a deficit, the Treasury securities must be liquidated to generate the extra money needed to pay the benefits that month. The Trust Fund would thus shrink. Obviously, if all of the securities were to be sold, the Trust Fund would be empty. At that point, beneficiaries could only be paid from the current stream of FICA contributions. There would be no other money available to pay them. If the benefits that were promised were greater than the contributions that were available, the government could not honor its promises within the Social Security system. It would have to renege on its obligations or find additional revenues somewhere else with which to fulfill them. It is precisely this situation in which almost all experts believe the United States will find itself within several decades.

At some point around the year 2017, Social Security benefit payments will begin to exceed the contributions and taxes coming into the system. Between 15 and 35 years later, according to the best estimates, the Trust Fund will be exhausted. Figure 2.1, produced from figures published by the Social Security Administration, illustrates the situation. As seen in the figure, the Trust Fund grew steadily after the reforms of 1983, but its size will peak before 2020. It will then steadily decline, and near the year 2042, it will be completely empty.

The magnitude of the coming Social Security deficit is stunning. According to the U.S. Treasury Department, the difference between the benefits that must be paid out and the amount of money anticipated to come in (including what is in the Trust Fund currently) is expected to amount to $4.6 trillion over the next 75 years, and $13.4 trillion over the future life of the Social

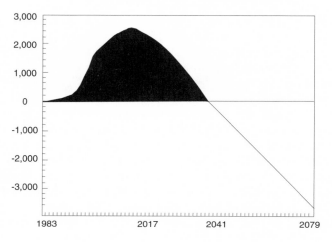

FIGURE 2.1
The Disappearing Trust Fund (in billions of dollars)

Source: Social Security Administration (2007).

Security program. As a point of reference, the entire budget of the United States was about $2.5 trillion in 2006, and the combined personal and corporate income taxes of all Americans equaled about $1.3 trillion in that year. If the United States were to close down the government and set aside every single tax dollar it received for the next three years just to prepare for the first 75 years of the Social Security deficit, that action would not be enough to close the gap.

Why Will the Trust Fund Shrink?

The Social Security Trust Fund will not be exhausted because of a simple design flaw that can be easily rectified. It will occur because of deep changes in the demographics of the United States in the 21st century. Americans are living longer, and they are having fewer children. As a result, the ratio of working to retired Americans is falling. As the number of people receiving Social Security benefits goes up and the relative number paying FICA contributions and taxes goes down, the inevitable result is the draining of the Trust Fund. This trend is exacerbated by the fact that benefits have been growing faster than the FICA tax receipts, placing additional pressure on Social Security's financing.

In 1935, the life expectancy of the average American was not much more than 65 years. Today, it is approaching 80 years. The dramatic increase in longevity has implications for Social Security because the longer one is retired, the longer he or she will be drawing benefits from the program. In 1940, the average male retiree drew Social Security benefits for a period of 12.7 years, while the average female retiree drew benefits for 14.7 years. In 2005, those periods had extended to 17.0 and 19.6 years, respectively. By 2080, the average retiree is expected receive benefits for more than 20 years, nearly half as long as the individual was in the workforce. It is also the case that a far larger percentage of people who work now live long enough to enjoy a retirement. In 1940, again, less than 60 percent of working Americans lived to the age of 65. In other words, they would have paid FICA taxes but not lived long enough to collect benefits. Today, close to 80 percent of working Americans will be alive to collect Social Security. This is a triumph for medicine, but such success means that ever more people are drawing Social Security pensions. America's retired population has grown from about 9 million in 1940 to more than 37 million today. By 2080, there will be nearly 100 million retired Americans, almost all of them receiving a Social Security benefit. The immense growth of the number who must be paid is the first reason behind the Trust Fund's future problem.

If the working population were growing as fast as the retired population, this would not be too large a difficulty, for the additional contributions of the working population would fund the additional benefits to be paid. But this is not the trend. The increase in new workers will not be close to the increase in the coming number of retirees. The primary reason is that the American birth rate has fallen. After peaking in 1960, the biggest year of the baby boom, the U.S. fertility rate has fallen substantially. The average American woman today has about two children. This is not expected to change anytime soon. Two children essentially "replace" their parents in the workforce when the latter retire; they do not represent additional workers.

In fact, as the birth rate has fallen, the largest source of new workers has been through immigration. But, though immigration has increased substantially in recent decades, the increase is not of a magnitude to make up for the smaller families of native-born

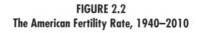

FIGURE 2.2
The American Fertility Rate, 1940–2010

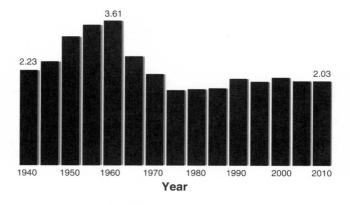

Year

Note: Fertility rate given as average number of children born to U.S. women.
Source: National Center for Health Statistics.

Americans. The result is that the number of added workers who will be joining the workforce, and paying FICA taxes, is expected to fall sharply in coming years. In recent decades, the number of working Americans has increased by 20 million or more, but in the decade of 2020, for example, the workforce is expected to increase by only 9 million and, for 2030, only 5 million. The result is stark: there will be millions of new retirees, but not the same millions of new workers. In a system where current retirees are paid from the taxes of current workers, this trend is troubling.

A neat way to summarize the problem is by looking at the dependency ratio: the number of people 65 and older divided by the number of people in the workforce (assumed to be those between the ages of 20 and 64). This ratio has grown from .135 in 1950 to .208 today. It is expected to soar to .421 by 2080 (U.S. Congressional Budget Office 1998; Social Security Administration 2007). Another way of stating this ratio is that in 1950, more than seven workers contributed to the system for every one retiree drawing from it. The number of contributing workers to retirees

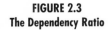

FIGURE 2.3
The Dependency Ratio

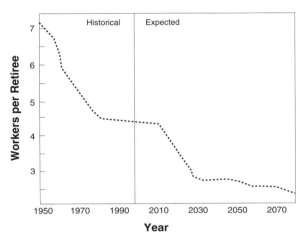

Source: Social Security Administration (2007); U.S. Congressional Budget Office (1998)

has fallen to 4.7 and is gradually falling toward 2 by the end of the 21st century. At that point, the pension of each Social Security retiree will have to be paid out of the taxes coming from only two other people. Those taxes would have to be incredibly high for the system to continue to operate.

Demographics are not the only reason for the coming exhaustion of the Trust Fund. Almost half of the expected increase in future Social Security payments is simply the result of the way in which Social Security benefits are calculated.

Because of the construction of the benefits formula, the real level of Social Security benefits is constantly rising. In 70 years, the real value of a retiree's Social Security check will be double the size of today's check. As discussed in chapter 1, an individual's initial Social Security pension is set at that person's lifetime average indexed monthly earnings (AIME). Each year of earnings before the age of 60 is adjusted upward by indexing it to the growth in American wages that has occurred since that time. (If Social Security did not make this adjustment, retirees would receive very paltry pensions indeed. In 1977, for example, the average American's income was about $10,000. If a person received a Social Security check today based on his or her earnings in 1977, it would be quite small.) This calculation appears to be necessary to achieve a fair Social Security system. The difficulty is that historically, wages have risen faster than prices. Thus, over the longer term, the real value of the Social Security check increases, and the amount of money that must be paid from the Trust Fund increases accordingly. This places a second unfavorable trend alongside the demographic problem. Together, they explain why the Trust Fund will shrink and likely disappear in a generation.

Before turning to the solutions to this problem, it is important to note one last complexity. Because all of the factors that have been discussed are projections into the future, whether fertility rates, life expectancies, dependency ratios, or wage rates, they are only estimates. They are predictions. The experts generally agree about them. The Social Security Administration and the Congressional Budget Office, for example, independently reach roughly similar conclusions about when the Trust Fund will be exhausted. But the future may not turn out as expected. The Social Security Administration also tries to estimate the worst-case and the best-case scenarios for the Trust Fund. In the worst case, the Trust Fund will be empty much sooner than thought. In the best case, it will shrink, but not hit zero, even as late as 2080. Any attempt to reform Social Security has to take into account the uncertainties of the future and the chance that the best predictions of experts might not come true. It could be worse, or better, than expected.

Saving Social Security: The Options

Solving the Social Security problem is one of America's biggest challenges. As might be expected, innumerable proposals have been made. Broadly, they can be divided into proposals that involve (a) prefunding Social Security, (b) restoring its pay-as-you-go principle, or (c) replacing Social Security with a partially or fully privatized alternative. There is always, too (d) the option of doing nothing. Each of these alternatives is considered below, describing how they would operate and the arguments for and against them. They should provide a good understanding of the menu of choices that awaits the United States in tackling this very serious issue.

Prefunding Social Security

One solution to the Social Security problem is to build up the assets of the Trust Fund before it becomes exhausted. Building up the Trust Fund adequately would enable Social Security to continue to pay out more benefits than it collects in any given year's contributions and taxes. Any potential crisis in the system would be continually pushed back into a more distant future.

Using the General Revenues

As long as the Trust Fund does not empty, Social Security can proceed without problems. An obvious solution, then, is to somehow extend the life of the fund. The easiest way to increase the size of the Trust Fund would be to increase the FICA tax or the income tax on Social Security benefits. We will consider this method later, however, because such an increase is usually placed in the context of other reforms to the operation of the program. This discussion looks at how to grow the Trust Fund by means other than raising taxes.

One recent major initiative to bolster the Trust Fund was undertaken by President Bill Clinton during his second term. This initiative serves as an example of how one might proceed. In his 1999 State of the Union address, President Clinton called for a program of "saving Social Security first." To President Clinton, part of saving Social Security was to build up the Trust Fund in anticipation of the retirement of the baby-boom generation. Thus he asked that "we commit 60 percent of the budget surplus for the next 15 years to Social Security, investing a small portion in the private sector just as any private or state government pension would do. This will earn a higher return and keep Social Security sound for 55 years" (Clinton 1999). Congress did not act on this request. But what would it entail? There are two mechanisms by which the Trust Fund could be increased without raising taxes. The first is to steer other government monies into the fund. The second is to receive a higher rate of return on the money that is already in the fund. The Clinton plan aimed to use both mechanisms.

Recall from chapter 1 that in the first years of Social Security, some lawmakers on the left, such as Wisconsin Senator Robert LaFollette, as well as skeptics on the right, like Ohio Senator Robert Taft, argued for a program that would be funded through the general revenues and not by a special "contribution."

Ironically, while both left and right had then envisaged such funding as a mechanism for *changing* the size of Social Security, today it has become an argument for *keeping* the size of the program. There is no constitutional reason why Congress cannot simply authorize the use of general tax revenues to augment the FICA tax. The idea is to begin to do this well before the Trust Fund runs out. The general revenues would be used to build up the Trust Fund to the point that it would last longer, or even indefinitely, depending upon the level of revenues that were diverted into the program. This is often called "prefunding" because the funds are put into the program before they need to be used. President Clinton specifically targeted the federal budget surpluses of the late 1990s, then expected (falsely) to last some years into the future, as the source for the prefunding. Ultimately, Clinton requested that 62 percent of the budget surplus be placed in the Trust Fund. In more general terms, Congress could stipulate that any particular amount of the general revenues go into the Social Security program.

Investing in the Stock Market

President Clinton joined this proposal with a second effort to build up the Trust Fund: he called for diversifying the investment of the money in the Trust Fund. The Trust Fund, by law, can only invest in U.S. Treasury securities. These are very safe but pay a relatively low rate of return. Historically, common stocks and corporate bonds have been substantially better investments. Many experts, and the U.S. financial services industry, have long argued that allowing the trustees of the OASDI Trust Funds to invest in the stock market would increase the rate of return and thus increase the Trust Funds for the future. Moreover, poorer Americans, who may not have the money to invest in the stock market on their own, would be able to share in the benefits of stock ownership through their participation in Social Security. Arthur Altmeyer, the first chair of the Social Security Board, had made such a proposal back in the 1930s. President Clinton's plan was to place a portion of the existing Trust Fund into common stocks and then invest 15 percent of all future FICA contributions in the stock market (while continuing to place the other 85 percent in Treasury bonds).

To manage these investments, the government would create an independent investment board that would in turn hire private fund managers to operate the investments in the U.S. stock markets. The actual investment decisions would be made by these

TABLE 2.1
Return and Risk of Financial Assets: 1955-2004

	Average Return (% per year)	Variability of return (% per year)
Treasury Bills	5.28	2.89
Corporate Bonds	6.8	10.18
Common Stocks	10.94	17.66
Small-Cap Stocks	14.56	25.64
International Stocks	20.7	56.21

*Note: Variability is measured by the standard deviation of the return.

Source: Dwyer 2005.

private managers. Supporters of this proposal maintained that the higher returns that resulted would extend the life of the Trust Fund and stave off the crisis in Social Security.

As noted, President Clinton did not succeed in getting his plan enacted. Though there was much support for both using the general revenues and investing in the stock market, there was much criticism, too. The chairman of the Federal Reserve, Alan Greenspan, was a leading critic of using the general revenues. (Recall that Greenspan was the head of the National Commission on Social Security Reform, which had examined the Social Security program in 1983 and had developed the policies that greatly increased the Trust Fund.) He voiced a common complaint, that using general revenues to fund Social Security would blur its connection to worker contributions and make it look like any other government program. This could have two negative effects. One echoes Roosevelt's fear in 1935; in Greenspan's words, many fear that "breaking the link between payroll taxes and benefits by moving to greater reliance on general revenue financing would transform social security into a welfare program" (Greenspan 2000). The other is that resorting to the general revenues would become an excuse not to engage in needed reforms. It would be another case of throwing money at a problem rather than solving it. President Clinton advanced his proposal in an era of surpluses. But in an environment of government deficits, another criticism is raised: where would the revenues to be steered into Social Security come from? Either other programs would have to be cut or the United

States would have to borrow significantly larger amounts of money. Neither option seems desirable.

Investing in the stock market is also controversial. (Note that this discussion does not refer to individual investments, to be discussed below, but to a government-owned investment.) There is both a political and an economic argument against this idea. The political argument is that allowing the government to invest in the stock market gives it too much power over U.S. companies and the U.S. economy. The size of Social Security is such that even if the government invested but a part of it, it would wind up as the legal owner of a significant percentage of the U.S. economy. (Because of this factor, Social Security could actually only invest in large companies; it would almost immediately take ownership of small companies if it started buying their stock.) For this reason, President Clinton promised that the U.S. government would not buy more than 5 percent of the total value of the U.S. stock markets. But even so, Greenspan and others claim that this would give the United States too much power over private enterprise. The government could decide to reward or punish particular companies by buying or selling their stock. This debate ultimately depends upon whether one thinks that the government could truly invest neutrally or if one thinks that that it would inevitably make investment decisions based on politics.

The economic argument is more complicated. If the Social Security program were to be invested in the stock market, two consequences would follow. First, stocks have historically had higher rates of return because they are more risky investments. The variability in their return is higher. This means that the size of the Trust Fund would fluctuate depending upon how the stock market was performing. If the stock market hit a period of an unusual or a sustained decline, the Trust Fund might actually fall and the program would be faced with raising taxes or cutting benefits to make up the difference. Though it is true that, over time, stocks have generated significantly higher returns than government bonds, there also have been periods of up to 25 years during which this trend did not take place. Different analysts reach very different conclusions over the danger of this possibility, but there is little doubt that moving from bonds to stocks would increase the risks as well as the rewards that accrue to investing in the stock market.

Second, investing in the stock market would have economic repercussions outside of the Social Security system. If Social Security reduced its purchases of government bonds, the interest rate on U.S. bonds should rise. Interest rates are set by supply and demand. The more people who wish to buy bonds, the lower is the interest rate. If one of the biggest buyers, the Social Security program, reduces its purchases while the supply remains the same, the interest rate will go up. Higher interest rates are good for investors but bad for those who wish to borrow. In orthodox economic theory, higher interest rates lead to reduced economic growth because some people can no longer borrow to build businesses or make productive investments. Moreover, because the interest rate is higher, the government will have to pay more interest on all of its debt. Where will the money to pay this extra interest come from? It would have to be from the general revenues. For this reason, some complain that moving Social Security into the stock market is but an extremely fancy way to use the general revenues without anyone noticing. Meanwhile, if Social Security starts buying stocks, this, too, may harm the economy. The huge amount of "automatic" money put into stocks every year would substantially reduce the risk of investing in those stocks. But as the risk goes down, so should the reward. As the government buys and buys, it will drive up the price of a stock. That means that other investors must pay more for the same stock, and so their return on that stock goes down. The result could be a simple transfer of wealth from individual investors to the Social Security system. Since most Americans are both investors and Social Security beneficiaries, there would be no net benefit. They would lose on one end as they were gaining on the other. Critics and supporters argue over the likelihood that these scenarios will occur. The controversy was enough to kill the Clinton plan.

However, it has not killed the support for the ideas that motivated it. Think tanks and academics continue to offer programs of reform that include both using the general revenues and diversifying the Trust Fund portfolio.

Restoring Social Security to Pay-as-You-Go Principles

Not too many years after its enactment, Social Security became a pay-as-you-go program. Building a sizable trust fund was really a later innovation. It happened only in the years after it became clear to policy makers that the retirement of the baby-boom generation was going to play havoc with the Social Security budget. A big trust fund is a preparatory measure to deal with this situation. A number of Social Security experts do not believe that a big trust fund is either the best or the most viable way of avoiding future difficulties. Instead, they argue for one or some combination of a variety of reforms that would return Social Security to a sound pay-as-you-go principle. So long as the program is devised to ensure that each year the amount going out roughly equals the amount coming in, Social Security can continue to hum along indefinitely.

Changing the Benefits Formulas

As discussed in chapter 1, the Social Security benefit is calculated by two formulas. The first uses an index of wage growth to upwardly adjust a worker's lifetime average monthly earnings in computing the size of that worker's first monthly Social Security check. The second uses an index of inflation, the Consumer Price Index (CPI), to upwardly adjust the size of the checks that follow. This second adjustment, called the cost-of-living adjustment (COLA) is made once each year. Also discussed is the notion that the wage indexing of Social Security accounts for more than 40 percent of the anticipated decline in the Trust Fund. Not surprisingly, some policy analysts call for adjusting one, or both, of these formulas to decrease the size of future Social Security payments.

Inflation is a terrible enemy of a fixed income. Even relatively modest rates of inflation can rapidly erode the real value of a pension. The COLA, added to the Social Security system in the 1970s, is an effort to ensure that Social Security benefits are not ravaged by rising prices. Every year, Social Security payments are increased at the same rate as the Consumer Price Index, the most frequently used measure of inflation in the United States. In the 1990s, however, several studies estimated that the CPI in fact overstates the rate of inflation. Moreover, some questioned the reliability of the CPI as a measure of the prices actually faced by retirees. This index includes the cost of items that are seldom, if ever, purchased by senior citizens (such as a new house). Why, critics charged, should Social Security checks be increased each year to reflect these sorts of costs? This issue has led to calls to reduce the Social Security COLA. Former senators Daniel Patrick Moynihan (D-NY) and Bob Kerrey (D-Neb.) suggested reducing the COLA increase by 1 percent each year. Others have called for smaller reductions, albeit based upon the same logic. The Boskin Commission (the Advisory Commission to Study the Consumer

Price Index), established by Congress to investigate this issue, estimated in 1995 that a 0.5 reduction in the COLA would take care of one-third of the coming Social Security shortfall. To those policy makers such as long-time Social Security advocate (and commissioner) Robert Ball, bringing the COLA into line with the true rate of inflation faced by seniors is a very modest reform that would go a long way toward restoring the soundness of the system. It would not cut benefits; rather, it would merely reduce their growth in coming years.

Others, however, have fiercely criticized this idea. One problem they cite is the automaticity of such a reduction. The U.S. Department of Labor (which is responsible for the CPI) has been working hard to improve its accuracy in measuring inflation. The higher the level of accuracy it achieves, the more accurate is the CPI. But if Social Security benefits are calculated by automatically reducing the CPI before it is applied, this improved accuracy will lead to understating the rate of inflation when making the COLA. For example, if the true inflation rate were 3.0 percent and the CPI were improved to reflect that accurately, *and* if the COLA were then to be calculated by reducing the CPI by 1 percent before applying it, as in the Moynihan-Kerrey plan, senior citizens would end up seeing a 1 percent real reduction in their benefits. Senator Bernie Sanders (D-Ver.) is one who notes that these seemingly small changes to the COLA could have big effects over time. A one-half percentage point reduction in the COLA over 30 years would produce a 15 percent difference in the size of a benefits check. And the reduction would be felt most dramatically by the oldest retirees—presumably those least able to find alternative sources of income—because the longer one draws a Social Security check, the longer one relies upon COLA increases. A final argument against reducing the COLA increase is that it is not really known whether the CPI is overstating the impact of inflation on retirees. Increasing health care costs, for example, may actually mean that inflation is more, not less, of a problem for senior citizens on a fixed income.

A counterpart to adjusting the COLA formula is to change the calculation of the Primary Insurance Amount (PIA), the Social Security benefit that will be available to a worker upon her or his retirement. The PIA is determined by computing the worker's average indexed monthly earnings, which involves indexing annual earnings to reflect the growth in wages that have occurred since that time. However, here, too, there is debate over whether this method of indexing is too generous to retirees. Some experts call for changing the indexing formula to more accurately reflect the needs of future senior citizens, especially given that this formula produces such a large part of the future Social Security deficit. The Concord Coalition, a fiscal watchdog group, has argued that changing the indexing formula is one of the best ways to keep Social Security sound. It notes that future senior citizens will be substantially wealthier than those of today. Why should they not be expected to rely less upon Social Security and more upon their own savings? Again, retirees would not see a cut in future benefits but a reduction in the *increase* of their future benefits. Given the importance of preserving the entire system, this is not an onerous demand.

President George W. Bush included a revision to the wage index as part of his plan to reform Social Security (discussed below). Indeed, it is from this portion of his plan that he expected to generate the savings that would save Social Security. In the Bush plan, the impact of wage indexing would be reduced by multiplying the AIME calculation formula by a ratio of the growth in the CPI divided by the growth in wages for that year. This reduction would be calculated each year, gradually reducing the growth in the PIA over time. Confusingly, this is sometimes called "price indexing." Essentially, earnings are adjusted more by the past increases in prices than by the past increases in wages. Consider the following example. There are currently three income levels or "bend points" in the AIME formula. A worker's initial Social Security benefits are set to be 90 percent of the income in the first level (in 2008, the first $711 earned), 32 percent of the second level ($711 to $4,288), and 15 percent of the third level (more than $4,288). Now, imagine that in the first year after the enactment of a price indexing reform, the rate of inflation (the CPI) was 2 percent and wages grew by 4 percent. Price indexing in the Bush plan is accomplished by dividing the CPI growth by the wages growth (1.02/1.04) and then multiplying each of these three percentages by that amount. If a worker had earned an average of $5,000 a month (as adjusted by the wage index), she or he would receive (0.98 × 0.90 × $711) + (0.98 × 0.32 × $3,577) + (0.98 × 0.15 × $712), or $1,853.51. Without price indexing, this same worker would have received $1,890.34 per month. For the following year, the new AIME percentages would be 88 percent (i.e., 0.98 × 0.90), 31 percent, and 14.7 percent, respectively. They would be again multiplied by that year's ratio of the CPI growth/wage index growth, and so on. The Bush plan is but one example of price indexing. One could use another ratio or another method of deflating the wage indexation. The Social Security Administration estimates that the Bush plan would eliminate the Social Security deficit over the next 75 years, and this is the order of magnitude of most reforms to the wage indexing formula.

Just as with changing the COLA formula, not everyone agrees that price indexing is a good idea. The dispute is as much philosophical as it is economic. What is the purpose of Social Security? Is it simply to provide an income floor for retirees sufficient to keep them from poverty? Should it be set to the level to their working years, so that they can continue to live as they did when they were working? Or is it to provide a level of income for retirees that grows along with the rest of the society? Should it be set to a level where they can always continue to live in a lifestyle similar to others around them? How one answers this question will likely determine how one feels about price indexing. Critics, such as the powerful seniors group AARP, note that price indexing means providing seniors with a benefit that grows at a lower rate than the earnings of the rest of society. In other words, unless they had saved a good deal of money, the standard of living of senior citizens would slowly fall behind that of the working population. It would remain linked to the income levels of their working years, not to the income levels of contemporary U.S. workers. One study calculates that, under the Bush plan, by 2085 the typical annual Social Security benefit would remain at $12,558, whereas it would be $30,689 under the current calculation (Munnell and Soto 2005, 2; the figures are in 2005 dollars).

A second criticism is that altering the wage index would disproportionately affect the poorest Social Security beneficiaries. The existing calculation formula is progressive; it is weighted to provide a larger pension to those at the bottom of the income scale. The benefit is set at 90 percent of the first (i.e., lowest) income level, but only 15 percent of the third. Those with lower incomes thus get a higher benefit compared with their lifetime earnings than do those with very high incomes. A reform such as the Bush plan that would ratchet down the benefit percentage for this first level, or indeed any reform that lowered the indexed rise of this lowest bend point, would hit those with low incomes the hardest. For this reason, supporters of price indexing, such as Senator Bob Bennett (R-Utah), have suggested using a "progressive price index" that would exempt this first income level from a change in the calculation formula and only apply it to the higher levels.

Changing the formulas used to calculate Social Security benefits is clearly one avenue of reform. However, it remains a controversial one. In large measure, the argument turns on whether one defines these reforms as benefit cuts or as reductions in benefit increases. Should the Social Security benefit reflect the current standard of living of those still in the workforce, or should it be considered as just the first part of the retirement "lifestyle" that ought to be increasingly supplemented by personal savings as society grows wealthier?

Incremental Reforms of the Social Security Program

Another approach to reforming Social Security takes Social Security's basics as given and simply aims to tweak them to extend the life of the program. This approach would include some combination of increasing the FICA contribution, reducing benefits directly, taxing more of either Social Security earnings or benefits, and/or increasing the retirement age. More rarely, "means testing" of Social Security benefits is called for. Because these changes are well understood and because similar changes have been made in the past, most recently via the 1983 amendments to Social Security, one frequently finds these sorts of incremental changes recommended in the many governmental and private commissions and reports on Social Security that have been released over the past decade. However, like every other proposal to save Social Security, these changes also have their critics.

Increasing the retirement age would be quite simple; in fact, the program is currently undergoing such an increase. The retirement age is being incrementally raised from 65 to 67. Supporters of this idea wish to continue this rise. Some would extend the age of retirement to a specified age—70 is the target age typically cited—while others would index retirement to the increase in American life expectancy, meaning the retirement age would rise in tandem with increasing life expectancy. In early 2006, Senator Bennett sponsored a bill that would have tied Social Security benefits to increases in life expectancy. Increasing this age could reduce the expected Social Security deficit by as much as a third. Later retirement would reduce the length of time a retiree draws Social Security benefits. It could also increase the dependency ratio because the number of people still in the workforce would rise as the number retired fell. Both of these changes would save substantial amounts of money.

The argument for this reform is straightforward. The American life expectancy has grown dramatically since 1935. Today's workers can expect to draw Social Security for a 50 percent longer period of time than workers in the first years of the program. Many also argue that today's work is not as arduous as in days gone by, and, in any event, the health of older Americans is much better than it was. So it is only fair that individuals who can anticipate living much longer than their parents should have to work a little longer than their parents before they can retire. Some would go so far as to say that age 65 no longer even qualifies as "old," so why should it still be treated as a magic number of retirement?

Reducing benefits is similarly easy to execute, if not the most politically popular of ideas. The COLA and price indexing reforms discussed above are backdoor methods of reducing benefits. An easier method would be to simply lower the basic PIA that a retiree can expect to receive at full retirement. If this approach was adopted immediately, a benefits cut of around 13 percent would suffice to eliminate the entire predicted shortfall in Social Security funding. If the United States waits until the early 2040s, when the Trust Fund nears exhaustion, a 27 percent cut would be needed to eliminate the shortfall. After that, as time continued to pass, the necessary cut would continue to grow. *Newsweek* and *Washington Post* columnist Robert J. Samuelson is among those who argue that, if implemented today, the reduction would be sizable but not devastating for retirees (Samuelson 2005). This is particularly so given that the program is financially unsound without it. Why not cut some now and save Social Security rather than wait until much larger changes are necessary? There is little doubt that Americans are wealthier now than they were in the Great Depression. They have many more retirement and savings options. This further justifies a necessary cut in benefits. Finally, proponents of this reform note, the brutal fact is that almost any change in the program is little more than a disguised cut in benefits. So why not at least admit up front what is happening?

The flip side to cutting benefits is increasing the taxes that support the program. This measure might be effected through raising the FICA contribution. Raising the FICA tax from 12.4 to 14.3 percent would eliminate the expected Social Security deficit. (Recall that one-half this amount would come from the employee, one-half from the employer.) If this reform is delayed until the early 2040s, the estimated FICA tax would have to be around 17.5 percent. The argument for this proposal is that Americans, again, are far wealthier than they once were. Moreover, they can antici- pate a longer retirement and more years of Social Security bene- fits. It is only reasonable, given the problems with the program, that they pay more to keep it afloat.

Alternatively, the ceiling on covered wages could be ended. Currently, there is a maximum level of earnings above which no FICA tax is paid, nor are wages above that level used to calculate the level of benefits to be received. In 2008, that level is $102,000. Removing this ceiling would be enough to end the future Social Security deficit. If an immediate removal is thought too drastic, the ceiling could be slowly increased over a period of years. Sup- porters of this reform, which included John Kerry in his 2004 run for the presidency, note that, thanks to income trends in the United States today, the percentage of total American earnings that is subject to the FICA tax has been falling over the years. Fif- teen percent of aggregate American income is today not subject to the FICA tax. This number was once 10 percent (Diamond and Orszag 2005, 15). It is not fair, it is said, that richer Americans are getting ever more of their income exempted from the FICA tax. This sentiment should justify modifying or ending the ceiling on covered earnings.

Each of these incremental changes has its critics. Opponents argue that any or all of these changes would be ineffective or un- fair. Take life expectancy, for example. Critics charge that making workers delay their retirement is a benefit cut, pure and simple. Every worker forced to retire at an older age would, over the course of his or her life, receive fewer Social Security checks. "De- layed retirement" is another name for a benefit cut. In addition, there is dispute over the health of 60- to 70-year-old Americans. Are people are really healthier, or are they just living longer? In fact, for a person who is not healthy, a rise in the retirement age is disastrous. An unhealthy individual is very likely to be forced to take early retirement. If the retirement age is extended, either the age of early retirement must be raised or the benefits paid to someone who has retired early must be substantially decreased. Either way, this worker will be hit hard. The issue quickly be- comes an argument over fairness. If higher-income workers hold the least arduous jobs (at least physically), and if these wealthier people are usually also more healthy, extending the retirement age will have its greatest impact on the poor. They have physical difficulties sooner, and will live shorter lives. They will thus suffer the most from the disguised benefits cut. Some analysts also wonder if raising the retirement age will really keep people in the workforce. If, in fact, they retire anyway and live on savings or other pensions until Social Security begins, much of the promised benefit of this reform is lost. Some have estimated that extending the retirement age might only add another four months to the average worker's career (Burtless 1998, 6–7).

A last criticism of increasing the retirement age is quite complicated, but important. Currently almost all U.S. pension and tax-deferred savings plans are established with a retirement age of 65. Unlike Social Security, they cannot be easily changed. For these other plans are specific legal promises. It would be theft, for example, for a company to offer a pension plan, based on contributions, that begins at age 65 and then suddenly to announce that it would not pay benefits until its employees reached 70. Most pension and savings plans accrue contributions into a personal account from which benefits are then taken after retirement. There is a legal connection between individuals, the money they paid into an account, and the age at which they can begin to draw it out. That connection cannot be broken by a simple policy change, as it can be for Social Security. The result would be a retirement system operating at cross-purposes. Parts of the system would encourage the worker to retire at age 65, while other parts would encourage that worker to retire later. Who knows what this worker would ultimately decide to do?

Cutting benefits is perhaps the most politically unpalatable change to Social Security. Interest groups such as AARP, often rated as the most powerful lobbying group in Washington, have made clear their opposition to benefit cuts. The reason is obvious: it is clear who would lose from this reform, and no effort would be made to hide it. Those who oppose a benefits cut usually focus on what such a reduction is: the violation of a promise. It is unfair, if not immoral, to tell the American people that they will receive a level of income at their retirement and then renege upon that promise. However, fairness is not the only complaint. To an extent, the savings generated from a benefits cut would be illusory. Retirees at lower incomes would be forced to enroll in Medicaid, Supplemental Security Income (a low-income welfare program), and other public support programs to make up for the income lost through the lowered benefits. The net effect would be only to shift some of the savings in the Social Security deficit to other federal programs. This is perceived as little more than a governmental shell game. The problem is not solved; it is merely sent elsewhere. How would seniors (and those expecting to become seniors) react to the reduced benefits? Ideally, they would increase their personal savings to make up for the anticipated lower Social Security benefits. But what if they do not? What if the result is just to bring back the old-age poverty that Social Security had earlier cured?

Raising taxes is not much more popular than cutting benefits. But again, opponents raise issues other than public support. If the FICA tax is raised on current workers, in effect those workers are paying the full price for Social Security reform. Social Security is being saved by shifting the burden from today's retirees to current and future workers. Working Americans will have to pay more taxes just to receive the same benefit. This too violates the notion of fairness. Because the FICA tax is regressive (the rate is the same at all levels of income until one reaches the earnings limit), critics charge that it will be low-income workers who will bear the brunt of the reform. They, who can afford it least, will experience the largest percentage reduction in their income. There is also suspicion about how the government would allocate this increased tax. Remember that contributions made today do not have to be paid for a number of years. If the tax is used purely to bolster Social Security, there is no problem. But if it is used for other purposes, such as to finance new government programs, the United States is in a worse position economically than if no reform had occurred. Finally, we do not know how Americans would react to the higher taxes. Specifically, would they respond to this increased tax by paying for it with money that they otherwise would have saved? Would they rather reduce their contributions to other savings programs, such as individual retirement accounts, than to cut their consumption? If so, senior citizens will be no better off at the time of their retirement. They will have saved Social Security at the cost of their other retirement investments. A last complaint about increasing the FICA tax is that, unless the dependency ratio changes, this tax will need to be continually revised upward over the life of Social Security. It is not a permanent fix. No one wants a program for which the tax must be constantly increased.

The second method of increasing taxes, raising or eliminating the ceiling on the maximum covered earnings that is taxed, also draws its critics. This reform is clearly aimed at upper incomes. To opponents such as former Republican House Majority Leader Tom DeLay and former Speaker of the House Dennis Hastert, this raises the fairness argument once more. Why should some Americans have to pay for a problem that affects all Americans? Unfairness also pops up in the problem of double taxation. A wealthier American is going to pay the FICA tax *and* the income tax on the income that is earned, and then is going to pay the income tax again on the benefits when they are received. Under realistic scenarios, the marginal tax rate on this income could be well above 50 percent. Is that fair? Even if it is, if one includes all income as covered earnings, rich Americans are going to get huge Social Security checks. These big checks are going to eat up a portion of the savings expected from raising the coverage maximum. A draconian response would be to make wealthier Americans pay the taxes but deny them the benefits that with go with it. But this might make these Americans oppose the whole program, and erode its political support. And, equally likely, an industry would grow up around helping these Americans find loopholes and other methods of hiding their income so as to not pay such a disagreeable tax. A final, not inconsiderable, criticism of ending the ceiling is that, in the American system, the employer has to pay half of the FICA tax. When the earnings ceiling is raised, a large tax bill goes to the companies that employ these individuals. The cost of doing business goes up. Is that good for these companies, or for America's economy and global competitiveness?

A Sidelight: Means Testing—The Reform No One Wants

Before moving to the more dramatic reforms that have been proposed for Social Security, one incremental reform that has proved almost uniformly unpopular must be mentioned: building means testing into the Social Security program. Social Security is an entitlement; every American who qualifies gets a benefit. There is no judgment of whether the recipient deserves it or not. Other American programs, such as Medicaid, are linked to income. This is called "means testing." To receive benefits under a means-tested program, one must have an income below a specified threshold. If one makes too much money, one is ineligible for the benefits. There is no reason that Social Security could not be made a means-tested program, wherein only those below a certain income would get monthly checks. In fact, however, very few people urge this reform.

One reason for the unpopularity of a means-tested program is that wealthier people currently do not get gigantic Social Security benefits, thanks to the earnings ceiling. Removing them from the rolls might not save enough to justify the reform. Another reason is that it is unclear what unit of measure should be used in means testing, income or wealth. In either case, incentives are created to hide or disguise assets in order to qualify for benefits under the means test. Furthermore, means testing creates negative incentives. Workers who prepare for their retirement by building up their own savings are likely to find themselves disqualified under the means test. Discouraging an individual from saving is not a message that the government or anyone else wishes to send. But by far the most important reason why almost everyone is reluctant to endorse means testing reflects a fear of President Franklin Roosevelt at the start of the program: to means test Social Security is to give the perception that it is a welfare program, that it is meant for poor people only. Ultimately, this conception could mean the political death of Social Security. Thus, even though means testing is feasible and perhaps even fair, it has very few supporters.

Privatizing Social Security

Many observers believe that the flaws of the current Social Security system are essentially beyond repair. Restoring the program to pay-as-you-go principles is impossible, undesirable, or both. Incremental reforms and short-term fixes will only put off the day of reckoning. None of the reforms discussed above would permanently solve Social Security's financing problem. They would only extend the life of the current program. The continuing change in demographics and the automatic increases in Social Security payments that occur under the program's benefit calculations would eventually force another crisis, and another round of reforms. In the meantime, the United States has a retirement program that is increasingly unsound and an ever worse deal for those who contribute to it. What the United States needs, in the eyes of these reformers, is an altogether new retirement system. It needs a permanent fix. This new retirement system should be fiscally sound and should allow Americans to maximize their own retirement benefits through the management of their own retirement portfolios. American workers should be allowed to place a portion of their FICA contributions into their own, individual investment accounts. The money earned in these accounts would then be used to help support them during their own retirement. This, after all, is the way that many private pensions and government tax-advantaged savings programs work. And these programs have been very successful. They have encouraged savings, and they have typically offered high rates of return on those savings. Changing Social Security to a program that operates on these principles has become known as "privatizing Social Security." A number of those who support this idea go so far as to say that this reform will actually make a better America. It will shrink the size of government as its largest social program withers and will encourage Americans to take "ownership" of their economic future, building a more responsible and more entrepreneurial citizenry. Needless to say, this view is not universally held. A fierce debate over whether, how, or how far Social Security should be changed toward this path has been the result.

Bush's Personal Retirement Accounts
The biggest endorsement of partially privatizing Social Security has come from President George W. Bush. In his 2005 State of the Union Address, President Bush, noting that the current Social Security system "is headed for bankruptcy," called for solving the "problems of Social Security once and for all" through a comprehensive reform of Social Security centering upon the development of voluntary personal retirement accounts for each working American born after 1950 (Bush 2005). Under this plan, workers could elect to place up to 4 percent of their payroll taxes into their own personal retirement accounts. (A transition period would be in place during which the allowable contributions to the account would gradually increase from $1,000 to the full 4 percent.) The money in this account would be used for living expenses during one's retirement, but any amount left at death could be passed on to the worker's heirs. Workers who opted for these accounts would pick a private investment fund from a government-approved list to manage their accounts. The program would offer a set of investment plans and would otherwise place limits on how the money could be invested to prevent unwise speculation or investment choices. At the time of retirement, workers would have several options as to how to withdraw their money to use during their senior years.

The plan is voluntary. Workers who chose not to open a personal retirement account would continue to draw all of their benefits from traditional Social Security. However, their benefits would be reduced so that the program would be permanently sustainable. Workers who did opt into the new program would still draw a Social Security check, too, because they would still place three-quarters of their FICA contributions into the old program. But the size of their benefits from traditional Social Security would also be reduced to reflect their smaller contributions. This simple overview of the proposal is enough to suggest that moving from today's program to one that is partially privatized would be quite complex. Some of the details are discussed below.

Breaking It Up Is Hard to Do

The fundamental complexity with privatizing Social Security is that there is no easy way to dismantle all or part of the current program without imposing substantial costs on some Americans. American society is a continuum, stretching from its most elderly, well into retirement, to its youngest, not yet in the workforce. Any attempt to "retire" today's Social Security program will affect each point in this continuum differently. Finding a way to shift out of Social Security into a new program seamlessly, that is, without placing anyone at a disadvantage, is immensely difficult. Here is an example: Imagine three individuals. One is a retired worker, say, 75 years old. The second is a 50-year-old worker. The third is a 25-year-old worker. Now, try to shift mind-sets from today's Social Security to a program based on each individual taking responsibility for his or her own retirement. The first problem is obvious. The 75-year-old retiree is unable to take this responsibility. This individual is no longer working and must rely on the promises that were made years earlier through the existing Social Security system. Remember that today's system operates by transferring current contributions to current retirees. If the program is changed so that current contributions now go into the "private" accounts of the workers who made them, and not into a general trust fund, where does the money come from to pay the benefits promised to this individual? There are only three possibilities: the government can raise taxes, it can cut other programs and use the money saved to make Social Security payments, or it can attempt to borrow the money. As there are more than 40 million retired Americans, the amount of money this would involve would be immense.

The scenario does not get much easier regarding the other two workers. The 50-year-old exemplifies another difficulty. This individual has paid into Social Security, perhaps for more than 30 years. If the program is ended, what does that person get for three decades of taxation? So long as the Trust Fund is extant, one could entertain the possibility of dividing what is left after paying all current retirees by the number of working Americans, and then sending each a check. But this check would be very small compared with the contributions paid or the benefits that were promised. In addition, a person with perhaps 15 years until retirement could hardly hope to save enough money to replace the expected Social Security benefits in that amount of time. In retirement terms, the situation for this worker would not be all that different from the 75-year-old retiree. At first glance, the 25-year-old should be in the best financial shape. With 30 years or more of working life ahead of them, this individual has time to build up contributions in the new program. This assessment is accurate, but only so long as the younger worker is not required to take care of the first two individuals through extra taxes or reductions in other programs (e.g., education, health, transportation, or defense) that matter a great deal. In that case, the younger worker would see her or his disposable income drained away to enable the payments to the older workers and retirees.

This example illustrates the general problem: it is very difficult to maintain benefits while changing the nature of contributions. This problem is widely understood, but difficult to resolve. The U.S. Government Accountability Office has estimated that the transition costs of moving to a partially privatized Social Security system will be between $1 and $2 trillion, over the next 75 years, depending upon the specifics of the program (GAO 2005, 45.). Advocates for partial privatizing argue that eventually the savings made via the lower benefits schedules will repay this money. But in the meantime, where does the money come from to fund this transition? The reason that many privatization programs sound so complicated is that they must accommodate this cost if they are going to work. Politics aside, the economics of privatization is tricky. FDR was quite right in his prediction that the program he was creating would be very difficult to get rid of.

The Choice of Choices
The transition cost is the major financial obstacle to privatizing Social Security. But once past this obstacle, there are a number of choices that must be made as to how the partial privatization will work. Each choice is yet another opportunity for debate between

advocates and opponents. Should the new program be added on top of Social Security, or should it replace a part of the existing program? Should the privatization be voluntary or mandatory? How much of the existing program should the new system absorb? What if some workers wind up with a smaller retirement income than if they had stuck with the old program? Should there be an effort to guarantee a minimum monthly payment, no matter what? Finally, should the new program attempt to maintain the progressivity of the existing program?

President Clinton, as part of his effort to reform Social Security, asked for the creation of "universal savings accounts" (USA accounts) for each working American. Americans could use their USA account to invest as they saw fit to help prepare for their retirement. As a further inducement, those with the lowest incomes would receive a match of federal money when they opened their account, much in the same way that employers match employee savings in a 401(k) or other tax-deferred pension account. This is an example of an "add-on," an individual investment account that is added on top of the existing Social Security system. It is perhaps the simplest form of partial privatization. Add-ons are claimed to have a number of advantages as a way of reforming Social Security. Transition costs are minimized because the financing of the traditional Social Security program is not touched. Workers are encouraged to prepare, through the add-on, for the reduced benefits that are likely to be paid in future years. As they contribute to their add-ons, national savings are increased, better enabling the United States to handle the coming entitlement crunch, in Medicare as well as in Social Security. The growth in savings has other beneficial effects on the American economy, such as lower interest rates and faster economic growth. Add-ons appear to be a low-cost method of accomplishing these desirable goals.

To critics, one of those goals would not be rescuing Social Security. An add-on, by itself, would in no way affect the coming Social Security crisis. Since an add-on does not change the existing system, it cannot solve its problems. It would accomplish nothing, unless coupled with substantial Social Security benefit cuts. There is also skepticism that an add-on would actually lead to increased savings. The evidence from private and government tax-deferred programs suggests that very few people take advantage of these programs, perhaps as few as 5 percent. Incentives would have to be offered to get Americans into the program.

(President Clinton's incentive was the match of government money, but this was offered during the time of large budget surpluses. This option is not available today.) The typical incentive is to shelter the money placed into the add-on from the income tax. Money placed into the program either would not be taxed in the year it was deposited or would not be taxed when withdrawn. The difficulty is that the loss of tax revenue from such an incentive could be quite large. One estimate is that the federal government would lose $600 billion in tax revenues over the next 75 years (Furman 2005, 18). This loss of tax revenue immensely worsens the U.S. budget deficit. Also at issue is whether anyone's savings would actually increase. Many of the people who would utilize the program would likely just be shifting money from existing savings to the new program in order to capture the tax advantages. If private companies then dropped their existing 401(k) programs in response to a new, and similar, governmental alternative, the effect on savings could even be worse.

The alternative to an add-on program is what is now known as a "carve-out." Rather than placing a second program on top of Social Security, carve-outs steer a portion of the contributions now going into the Trust Fund into individual retirement accounts instead. President Bush's plan, discussed above, is a carve-out, allowing Americans to divert about a third of their FICA contributions into their own accounts (4 percentage points of the 12.4 percent payroll tax). The idea is that the portion going into the individual account will help provide for that worker's retirement, while the remainder still going into the old program will pay a smaller benefit to that worker and also continue to pay benefits for those who, for whatever reason, must continue to draw from it exclusively. Sometimes, reformers speak of the new Social Security as having a Part A and a Part B, like the Medicare program, to differentiate these two streams of contributions and benefits. A carve-out does not need incentives to get Americans to join the program or to save, since it is simply using a portion of their current payroll taxes. It should not have any significant new effect on the American economy. However, the issue of transition costs moves front and center. The old, now reduced, Social Security program will not have enough money to pay those still expected to draw from it, and so over a lengthy period of 20 years or more the government must find other money to fill the gap. As noted earlier, the proposal of President Bush offers personal retirement accounts only to those born after 1950. The reason is that one cannot reasonably expect someone before that date to have built up enough savings in their own retirement account to sustain them economically. There will have to be enough funds remaining in the old Social Security program so that they can be paid their monthly checks. Any carve-out has to face this problem of financing.

Once the issue of privatizing via an add-on or a carve-out has been addressed, a second decision awaits. Should the new program be voluntary or mandatory? Voluntary add-on programs are expected to be underutilized without incentives to join. A mandatory add-on, on the other hand, could increase savings at lower cost to the government (but not at *no* cost, if the add-on were given any tax-advantaged status). However, it also has potentially grave economic side effects and could be a real burden for lower-income individuals. Someone who needs all of his or her income just to make ends meet could suffer a genuine decline in quality of life if forced to place a portion of that income into a new retirement savings vehicle. For the entire economy, the effect of a mandatory program might be to reduce spending generally as people were forced to save more for retirement. Lower spending could translate into lower economic growth and, ultimately, lower employment and incomes. This, obviously, would not be in Americans' long-term interest. As is so often the case, balancing the gains of increased savings against the cost of decreased spending depends very much on one's economic assumptions. Experts disagree about which effect would be greater under a mandatory add-on.

Moving to a carve-out plan does not remove the choice of whether to make it voluntary or mandatory. President Bush's proposal, for example, was voluntary. If a worker prefers, she or he could opt to continue in the old program, albeit with reduced benefits. The primary justification for a voluntary program is choice. Those who fear the uncertainties of leaving the existing Social Security program do not have to do so. Those who remain in the old program also ease the transition costs of the new one. Not all experts are enamored with a voluntary plan, however. Voluntary plans are much more difficult for government budgeting, because federal budget planners will not know how many workers will choose the plan, and for individual budgeting, because a worker must decide whether to choose the plan many years before the date of retirement. Someone just entering the workforce is not in a position to know the trajectory of his or her life: how much money will be earned and how many years one's career will last. Yet knowing these outcomes is vital to a wise choice. A mandatory program at least ends uncertainty about how many individuals will join and about whether a specific individual should join.

"Adverse selection" is the other potential problem of a voluntary program. It is unlikely that a random selection of Americans would choose the carve-out. One might predict that the most likely participants would be workers who had other retirement savings and were thus able to take on the extra risk of managing their own Social Security investments, and those workers who reasonably expect they will not have to retire early, before they have the time to build up their investments. Workers falling under both of these scenarios will be disproportionately those with relatively high incomes. Workers with lower incomes may be more inclined to remain with the existing system. If this happens, any gains that accrue to private accounts will go mostly to those who are already better off. Meanwhile, the reduced benefits and extra political risk of a more weakly financed traditional Social Security program will fall upon those with lower incomes. A mandatory program would not suffer from adverse selection. On the other hand, it has a larger exposure to the risks associated with the next decision that must be made; what happens if the promised greater returns of an individual account do not materialize?

The promise of a partially privatized Social Security system is a higher rate of return for its participants. But if workers are allowed complete freedom in how they choose to invest their retirement funds, there is no guarantee that in fact they will earn more than if they had stayed with the original program. For this reason, most proposals limit the options of those in the program to a set of approved stock and bond funds. This is to prevent workers from placing their money in unusually risky or unsound investments. The Bush proposal, for example, was based on a relatively safe, conservative investment program into which participants are automatically enrolled. They may then, at their option, move the funds in their retirement accounts to other investment programs, but only under strict limits.

Even so, what if a worker, thanks to bad investments or just bad luck, winds up with a smaller retirement nest egg than if he or she had stayed in the old Social Security program? Should that worker be guaranteed a pension that is just as large as if he or she had not opted for an individual account? Some say no. Risk is part of retirement, and part of choice. The existing system provides no true guarantees of how large a pension will be. Why should individual retirement accounts provide such guarantees? Others say that if such a guarantee is not made, workers with lower incomes, those most dependent upon Social Security for their retirement, will not be able to take the risk of opting for an individual account. They will be stuck with the reduced benefits of traditional Social Security.

How might such a guarantee be made? One could demand that government approval for a private investment fund to manage individual accounts be made contingent upon that fund offering such a guarantee itself. If a company markets personal retirement accounts, it must guarantee a monthly benefit at least equal to what the old Social Security program pays. Or one could use complicated systems that would use calculation formulas to transfer monies from the Social Security program or from other workers who had exceeded the guaranteed amounts to those who had come up short. The decision of whether to offer guaranteed benefit levels would be a critical factor to the operations of a partially privatized system. It would undoubtedly have a large impact upon how many workers choose to enter the new system, if the choice was made a voluntary one.

The next choice is to decide how much of the existing FICA contributions should be steered into the individual accounts. Observers agree that anything less than 2 percentage points of the current 12.4 percent of earnings would not allow workers to build a large enough nest egg to provide for their needs in retirement. Anything over 10 percentage points would have overwhelming transition costs. So the viable range of the payroll tax to be shifted into the new accounts is somewhere between these two figures. The trade-off would be between increasing the size of the individual accounts and decreasing the transition costs of the shift. Note that the smaller the remaining pay-as-you-go portion of Social Security, the greater is the impact of any risk or difficulty with the individual retirement accounts and the burden of providing benefits for those who can or must remain in the original program. As with any trade-off, there is no "best choice" to this decision. It is a question of personal values and best guesses of the future.

The final major question in designing a partially privatized Social Security program is whether one wishes to continue the progressivity of the current program. As explained above, today's Social Security provides relatively greater retirement benefits for those with lower incomes. It does this through the calculation formula for the worker's initial PIA. Partial privatization potentially threatens this aspect of the program. FICA contributions shifted into personal accounts are not then available to redistribute to other workers. The whole point of a personal account is that the money placed in an account belongs to that worker. The larger the percentage of the FICA contribution placed into these accounts, the larger is the reduction in the program's progressivity. If one wishes to maintain this aspect, the only options are to substantially alter the benefit formula within what remains of the old Social Security program or to add new rules that enable the program to redistribute the investments earned through the individual accounts. Because these accounts would be notional, and not actually held by the worker until the date of retirement, this would not be impossible to do. One could also redistribute the benefits through taxation. But this is another difficult choice that any plan to partially privatize the program must make.

Clearly, there are a number of choices to be made when devising a program to partially privatize Social Security. This is why the plans that have been offered often appear so complex. While the major choices have been explored here, there are still others to be considered. Any program that includes individual accounts must develop new institutional mechanisms to manage those accounts; create procedures to pick and oversee the private companies that will actually do the investing; and formulate the methods by which workers will exchange their retirement accounts for the income, annuity, or other form of benefits that they will begin receiving at the time of their retirement.

The Benefits of Partial Privatization: Real or Illusory?

Given the complexity of partially privatizing Social Security, is it worth it? To many, the answer is an emphatic yes. The complexity of designing a program is a small obstacle to overcome when set against the huge advantages it can provide. Topping the list of advantages is honesty. Social Security is going broke. Even the Social Security Administration estimates that the cost of fixing it will run to more than $10 trillion. The existing system cannot continue. Partially privatizing the program acknowledges this reality up front. Drastic action must be taken if Social Security is to survive permanently. Partial privatization, unlike the reforms considered above, is a permanent fix; this problem will not have to be revisited again and again in the coming years.

But equally important, to advocates, is the fact that a partially privatized system will be a better deal for retirees. The rate of return on workers' investments (i.e., the FICA tax) will be far superior if they can control those investments themselves. First, it is argued, the existing system is a very bad deal for those who expect to retire in the years ahead. The rate of return under today's program is very low; some even claim that it will eventually be negative. The first generations to draw upon Social Security had a very good deal indeed. Over the course of their retirement, they received far more Social Security benefits than the contributions they had made. In part this was because many spent a portion of their working lives before the advent of Social Security, and thus paid little or no FICA taxes. But it is also due to the rapid rise in benefits that occurred in the decades after World War II. Recall that these benefits were not linked to equally large rises in contributions. Workers who retired in 1960 received back all of the FICA contributions that they and their employers had made in only 2.8 years. After that, their benefits were, in effect, coming from someone else's contributions. The legacy of this generosity is that future generations cannot expect such largesse when they retire. It is matter of simple accounting that the net value of the Social Security transfers of the past (the extent to which benefits exceeded contributions) must be borne by later generations. That debt does not just disappear. Not surprisingly, then, it will take someone who retired in 2000 much longer, around 17 years, to receive back all of his or her contributions, and by 2020, that length of time will be up to 21.6 years. At some point, people just will not be able to live long enough to get back all that they paid into the system. This is but another way of saying that the rate of return on the FICA contribution is falling. How much this rate will fall depends upon a number of assumptions, both about the economy and about how the United States will decide to reform Social Security at the time the Trust Fund runs out. But one study has calculated that if the government raises the revenue necessary to keep the Trust Fund solvent, a typical 35-year-old male with an average income should expect to see a lifetime loss of $133,600 in wealth because of his participation in the current Social Security program (Murphy and Welch 1998).

If workers were allowed to invest as they wished, not only would they be (partially) relieved of this dire prospect but also they would be able to capture the higher rates of return available by investing in something other than U.S. Treasury securities. This, of course, is the same argument for diversifying Social Security's investments that we examined earlier. However, advocates of partial privatization claim that giving this investment choice to the individual eliminates the political and economic problems associated with having the Social Security system invest a portion of the entire Trust Fund into stocks or other assets.

The honesty of acknowledging the program's problems and the possibility of earning a better investment through individual retirement accounts combine to produce a third positive aspect of partial privatization. The benefit reductions needed to truly save Social Security can be made. The benefits available under the old program can be scaled back because workers will have a better alternative through which to more than make up for this loss. This alternative, the individual retirement account, will make the necessary benefit reductions politically possible.

Proponents of this reform also argue that it will provide a series of additional gains for Americans. Allowing each working American to have ownership of his or her retirement funds enables far more flexibility than today's system. A worker who reasonably anticipated, for example, early disability or death would be able to cash in her or his retirement early and receive the money when it could be of use. Those with other retirement savings may be able to coordinate them with the utilization of their Social Security account to better manage their retirement. There might be a variety of ways by which to receive this new benefit beyond the standard monthly payment of today's program. In short, partial privatization would end the "one size fits all" mentality of the current program in favor of one that can be tailored to the specific needs of each retiree. Another benefit would be that workers who died before retiring, or retirees who died with income still available, could leave the income in their account to their heirs. Americans could use these accounts to help their children. Some advocates of partial privatization say that such a program would actually lead many to put off the day of their retirement because they could clearly see the advantages of continuing to build up their retirement accounts. This powerful incentive could thus ease the demographic pressures on all U.S. retirement plans, including Social Security. There are even those who maintain that ownership of private accounts, and the knowledge that they were successfully preparing for their own retirement, could produce a number of positive effects on the health, social behaviors, and emotional lives of those in the program. Giving people a stake in the system reinforces and energizes the qualities of entrepreneurship and hard work that have made the United States so economically successful.

Thus, great claims are made for the effects of partial privatization. But even those new to the Social Security debate are probably aware of how controversial these plans are. President Bush received so much opposition to his idea that he did not introduce his proposals for congressional consideration, even a full two years after he initially proposed it. Why is there such an argument over partial privatization?

Opponents of individual retirement accounts reject virtually every claim made for them. Partial privatization will not save Social Security, it will not offer participants a better return on their contributions, and it will not offer Americans a safe alternative to the current system.

Individual retirement accounts will not affect Social Security's financing shortfall. Add-on accounts clearly have no impact on the program one way or the other. But even carve-outs will not solve the problem. The benefit reductions in the old program that will come with the individual accounts will not occur for decades. Until those reductions are seen, diverting a portion of new contributions to individual accounts does not affect the promises that the program has already made to beneficiaries. The money has to be found to pay them. Losing a portion of the existing FICA taxes only makes the problem worse. As one example, it has been charged that the Bush proposal would have added $4.9 trillion to U.S. debt between 2009, the first year of its operation, and 2028 (Furman and Greenstein 2005, 1). (The developers of the Bush plan have estimated the costs at $754 billion.) This is the gap between the promises made and the amounts still in the Trust Fund (along with the expected future FICA contributions) that would be available to honor them. At some point, far in the future, the individual retirement accounts may begin to pay for themselves and make Social Security sustainable. But the intervening years would saddle the United States with an unconscionable level of debt, one that would have real economic consequences. Critics deride the supposed honesty of individual retirement accounts, noting the savings included in such plans

are generally gained through the reduced benefits offered to retirees in the Social Security program, not through the operation of
the accounts themselves. This is the case with the Bush proposal,
where the savings actually occur through a combination of benefit reductions and changing from wage indexing to price indexing in the calculation of the PIA.

The opponents of partial privatization also dispute that Social Security yields a lower rate of return than would individual
accounts. A minor but still significant point is that individual accounts would necessitate higher administrative costs and the
payment of fees to the private firm that handled the investments.
These costs reduce the rate of return and should be incorporated
when making comparisons. The major point, though, is that comparing the rate of return of individual accounts versus existing
Social Security is unfair unless one includes the cost of transition.
An individual account may gain a substantially higher rate of return than a government bond, but this possibility ignores that the
fact that, to get this account, its holder must pay her or his share
of the transition costs for the whole program, either by higher
taxes, lower benefits from the existing Social Security program, or
the lower income that would follow from the slower economic
growth caused by increased U.S. debt. If this cost is subtracted
from an individual retirement account's rate of return, it is not at
all clear that it would be higher than that of the current program.
In fact, the most thorough investigation of this question found
that the two rates of return would not be much different
(Genakoplos, Mitchell, and Zeldes 2000).

Moreover, there is no guarantee that the promised higher
rate of return will even appear. For any investment, return is related to risk. High returns are gained by taking high risks. Risk
implies that the outcome is unknown. The higher the risk, the
more it is unknown. History is a guide to how investments have
fared in the past, but they cannot tell us how they will fare in the
future. As the Wall Street advertisements caution, "past performance is no guarantee of future results." In theory, allowing individuals to invest on their own might be a great idea. Some
investors will be wise (or lucky) and indeed build a large nest
egg. But others will be ill-advised (or unlucky) and not fare well
financially. If the latter must rely on their poor investment results for their retirement years, what happens to them? It is easy
for those who are more successful to say "tough luck." But luck
often is not involved in the outcome. If the United States today

had individual retirement accounts that were returned to the owner at the date of retirement, an individual who reached retirement age in 1999 would have received a pension 40 percent larger than an individual who retired in 2001, even if both had made the exact same investments. This simply reflects the massive fall in stock prices that occurred during those two years. It would not have been the fault of either investor. The noted economist Robert Schiller has calculated that 32 percent of the time, one should expect even a conservative life-cycle investment fund, an option recommended in President Bush's proposal, to return less money than if the individual had opted to stay entirely in the old program (Schiller 2005). If one presumes that stock markets are likely to offer lower rates of return in the future than they have in the past, which is the view of Schiller and other experts, that 32 percent increases to 71 percent. Is a safe, successful retirement system best built upon substantial risk? A senior citizen who did not do well is going to fall back upon the rest of the American social safety net, Medicaid and other welfare programs, to make up for the failed investments. Other government programs must grow to cover these retirees.

The position of many critics is that the United States already has excellent tax-advantaged savings programs in place. These include 401(k) and Keough plans. Workers are better advised to make use of these existing programs, through which they will gain all the benefits of individual accounts. They would not be well served to abandon a successful retirement program to undertake new and uncertain risks and dangerously expose their senior years to the possibility of inadequate income.

Complete Privatization of Social Security

A more dramatic alternative to partial privatization is to get rid of today's Social Security altogether. Any virtue associated with partial privatization could be claimed to be more fully realized through total privatization. The practical issue is how to achieve privatization. Most adherents of an eventually completely private national retirement system see partial privatization as a halfway house to that end. The diversion of the FICA contribution into individual retirement accounts can slowly be increased until the entire payroll tax goes into these accounts. At that point, the system is completely privatized. The arguments for and against doing this are not much different from the pros and cons of partial privatization, and they will not be revisited here.

Note, however, that once the traditional program is gone, there will be no dedicated retirement resources to augment individual accounts for any reason. But advocates of total privatization respond that the only reason for the government to increase the resources going to an individual would be an investment account that turned out to be too small to retire upon. This is a form of poverty and ought to be handled as other poverty programs. American poverty programs are generally means tested. So one method of complete privatization would be to implement individual retirement accounts plus a means-tested program to supplement those accounts for senior citizens whose retirement income is below a stipulated level. This money would come from the general revenues, as with any other poverty program. It would not involve a large, government retirement program.

The most audacious privatization plan is simply to return a portion of federal taxes each year to working Americans. The FICA tax and the income tax could be rolled together to make this calculation. Each person could then do what he or she wanted with the money received, subject to reasonable strictures on its use. Charles Murray has recently suggested such a reform. Each American over the age of 21 would receive $10,000 a year free of taxes (Murray 2007). The government would recommend, but not require, that $2,000 of this be invested for purposes of retirement. (The remainder would be used for health care and other purposes.) Individuals at higher incomes would have to return a portion of their annual grants. Murray suggests that, as retirement approaches, an annuity purchased with the 40 or more years of invested money that had been accrued would provide for a generous pension. Plans such as this also anticipate, as a result, a greatly reduced American government, which is generally claimed to be one of the strongest benefits of totally privatizing Social Security.

Supporters of today's Social Security are against these radical reforms. They remake their points that these plans blithely wave away the huge transition costs and substantially offload the risks of retirement from the U.S. government to individual American workers. Indeed, this latter complaint goes to the heart of the debate over privatizing Social Security. Those who oppose privatization say that Social Security was never intended to be a program for building private fortunes. Focusing upon rates of return and benefit amounts confuses this issue. There are other mechanisms for enhancing personal wealth. Social Security is, first and foremost, an *insurance* program. It is meant to handle the risks and vicissitudes of old age. It is a guaranteed floor, beneath which no working American can ever sink, no matter what might go wrong. Unlike private plans, it is a benefit that one can never outlive. The metaphor should not be the trampoline, from which one can jump ever higher, but the safety net, which catches you when you fall. That is why the program includes features such as survivors' benefits and spousal benefits. Those components are not about wealth, but about need. If one correctly sees what Social Security is, according to this view, one sees that the necessary reform is to repair the safety net, not build a better trampoline.

Leaving It Alone

There is one final approach to solving the Social Security crisis. It is the approach that rejects any reform. After reading everything discussed in this chapter, this may appear crazy. The program will soon in be crisis. It must be reformed, right? Not everyone agrees. The Social Security Administration's most optimistic scenario is that the Trust Fund may not empty until well after 2042. Given that all estimates of the future are but guesses, whether those of the Social Security Administration or anyone else, why not wait until we have better information? The economist Robert Gordon is one who forcefully argues that the predictions of the Social Security Administration are too pessimistic. American productivity and economic growth are likely to be significantly higher in the future than it estimates. If Gordon is right, FICA contributions will be substantially larger than anticipated, and the Trust Fund will not become exhausted until years later. In fact, any public policy that boosts economic growth will save Social Security as a by-product. So why not focus instead on the goal of economic growth? Even if productivity or growth does not turn out to be greater than forecasted, one could argue that the massive cost and complexity of reform suggest that it not be undertaken when economic uncertainty is large. Perhaps it is better to put off such reform until the contours of what is necessary are better understood. Supporters of this position further argue that the Social Security program will not break down for nearly 40 years, even under standard assumptions. Do we know that, when the time comes, reform of Social Security will have the best claim on U.S. resources? We must also remember that the United States is likely to be a substantially wealthier nation by that time.

One could argue that the richer United States of 2040 or beyond is, and ought to be, more able to carry out the necessary reforms than the United States of today. For all these reasons, some argue that the best thing to do right now is nothing.

It must be admitted that this is a minority view. Most analysts believe that the best estimates are just that, the best estimates. In fact, the Social Security Administration has historically been too optimistic in its forecasts. And even the organization itself gives its best scenario only a 10 percent probability of coming true. It would be foolish to base policy upon a hope that unlikely scenarios will rescue us from difficult decisions. The cost of reforming Social Security is thought to rise by about $600 billion each year that it is not undertaken. Putting reform off until tomorrow, never mind nearly 40 years of tomorrows, is fantastically expensive. Why burden the next generation with what we have failed to solve? It is far better to act now and make revisions if they are necessary later. In the eyes of many, with all of the knowledge that we already have, failing to act is irresponsible.

Conclusion

America's Social Security program is very likely to encounter severe problems in just a few decades. One can see that there is no lack of options to remedy the situation. We have examined the pros and cons of these options in some detail. Unfortunately, all have two characteristics. First, they become more difficult to implement as the years go by. Modest changes avoided now will become drastic changes if they are enacted 30 or 40 years later. The longer the United States waits, the greater the reforms it must make to save Social Security. Second, they are all controversial. There is no consensus on how to approach changes to Social Security. Further, the controversy operates at many levels. There is often dispute over the financial and economic impacts of specific proposals. How much will really be saved? How great will be the cost? There is dispute over fairness. Who will bear the brunt of reform? Who should bear it? Is it right that some will lose more than others? There is dispute over risk. Are the virtues of ownership worth the cost of more variable returns? Is security the paramount value of Social Security? There is dispute over the goal. Should the reforms preserve Social Security as it is? Or should the program be remade in accordance with the economic realities of the United States in the 21st century? There is dispute over purpose. Should Social Security continue to be the financial mainstay of America's senior citizens? Or should individuals in an increasingly wealthy society be prepared to take on more of the burden of their own retirement? These controversies are over values as well as fact. For this reason, they are very difficult to resolve. Responsible participants in the Social Security debate realize these difficulties. They know that the reform that does occur will likely be drawn from those bits and pieces among the entire menu of choices that can best and first command consensus. The position of the powerful AARP reflects the realities of today's debate. While clearly stating, and fighting for, their preferred reforms, AARP also takes the position that reform will be difficult. It understands that all positions need to be considered, and it accepts that some of the reforms that are ultimately made will not be desirable to its members. This is the view of many of those who are most intimately involved in the attempts to reform Social Security. We frequently see experts first critiquing a reform, admitting its weaknesses, and then recommending it as the best possible solution under the circumstances.

Tracing the controversies over the reform of Social Security does not, of course, tell us what the ultimate resolution will be. That will result from the debate that is now ongoing and will no doubt continue for years to come. For most Americans, Social Security is or will be one of the most important government programs that will ever affect them. For that reason alone, this is a debate in which every American has an interest.

References

Burtless, Gary. 1998. Increasing the Eligibility Age for Social Security Pensions. Testimony before the Senate Special Committee on Aging, July 15, 1998. Brookings Institution. http://www.brookings.edu/views /testimony/burtless/19980715.htm (accessed November 29, 2007).

Bush, George W. 2005. State of the Union Address. *GPO Access,* February 2. http://www.gpoaccess.gov/sou/index.html (accessed November 29, 2007).

Clinton, William Jefferson. 1999. State of the Union Address. *GPO Access,* January 19. http://www.gpoaccess.gov/sou/index.html (accessed November 29, 2007).

Diamond, Peter A., and Peter R. Orszag. 2005. "Saving Social Security." *Journal of Economic Perspectives* 19 (2): 11–32.

Dwyer, Gerald P., Jr. 2005. "Social Security Private Accounts: A Risky Proposition?" *Economic Review* 90 (3): 7.

Furman, Jason. 2005. *Evaluating Alternative Social Security Reforms.* Washington, D.C.: Center on Budget and Policy Priorities. http://www.cbpp.org/5-12-05socsec-test.pdf (accessed November 29, 2007).

Furman, Jason, and Robert Greenstein. 2005. *An Overview of Issues Raised by the Administration's Social Security Plan.* Washington, D.C.: Center on Budget and Policy Priorities. http://www.cbpp.org/2-2-05socsec4.htm (accessed November 29, 2007).

Genakoplos, John, Olivia S. Mitchell, and Stephen P. Zeldes. 2000. *Would a Privatized Social Security System Really Pay a Higher Rate of Return?* NBER Working Paper, No. 6713. Cambridge, MA: National Bureau of Economic Research.

Greenspan, Alan. 2000. Testimony before the Special Senate Committee on Aging. Federal Reserve Board, March 27. http://www.federalreserve.gov/BoardDocs/Testimony/2000/20000327.htm (accessed November 29, 2007).

Munnell, Alicia, and Mauricio Soto. 2005. "What Does Price Indexing Mean for Social Security Benefits?" *Just the Facts on Retirement Issues,* No. 14. Boston: Boston College, Center for Retirement Research.

Murphy, Kevin M., and Finis Welch. 1998. Perspectives on the Social Security Crisis and Proposed Solutions. *American Economic Association Papers and Proceedings* 88: 142–150.

Murray, Charles. 2006. *In Our Hands: A Plan to Replace the Welfare State.* Washington, D.C.: American Enterprise Institute Press.

National Center for Health Statistics, Centers for Disease Control and Prevention,U.S. Department of Health and Human Services. *Birth Data.* http://www.cdc.gov/nchs/births.htm#news%20releases (accessed December 31, 2007).

Samuelson, Robert J. 2005. "It's More than Social Security." *Washington Post.* January 14:A19.

Schiller, Robert. 2005. "The Life-Cycle Personal Accounts Proposal for Social Security." March. http://www.irrationalexuberance.com (accessed November 29, 2007).

Social Security Administration. 2007. *2007 Annual Report of the Board of Trustees of the Federal Old-Age and Survivors Benefit Insurance and Disability*

Insurance Trust Funds. http://www.ssa.gov/OACT/TR/TR07 (accessed November 29, 2007).

U.S. Congressional Budget Office. 1998. *Long-Term Budgetary Pressures and Policy Options,* May. www.cbo.gov/ftpdocs/4xx/doc492/ltbudg98 .pdf (accessed November 29, 2007).

U.S. Government Accountability Office. 2005. *Social Security Reform: Answers to Key Questions, May.* http://www.gao.gov/new.items/d05193sp .pdf (accessed December 26, 2007).

3

Worldwide Perspectives

Virtually every country on Earth has a public old-age pension system. Though under different names and with different features, each attempts to provide a generous, but affordable, retirement for its citizens. Not surprisingly, these systems have been carefully examined by those who worry about the fate of the U.S. Social Security program. What do the experiences of these other countries teach us? Are there ideas and policies, developed and employed abroad, that can improve, even "save," Social Security? This chapter places the American debate over Social Security in this international context. How have other nations reacted to the same problems that are anticipated for the American program? What did they do to solve them? Did those measures work? This chapter explores their reforms with an eye to how they might operate in the United States. Often experts do not always agree on the results. When this is the case, insight is provided into the reasons for their disagreement.

Many countries, either for reasons of their poverty or because of very different economic systems, do not offer broad lessons that are appropriate for the United States. So this chapter focuses, for the most part, upon those nations that offer similarly comprehensive retirement programs that can be meaningfully compared with Social Security. In fact, most countries in the advanced industrialized world have programs quite similar to the U.S. Social Security system, and they too face the same challenge as the United States. They must operate an ever more expensive retirement program in the face of unfavorable demographic trends. Under this pressure, several of these nations have embarked upon major reforms to save *their* social security programs. It is these countries that will form the core of the investigation in

75

this chapter. Six such countries, and the reforms they made, are discussed, roughly in the order of how dramatically their systems were changed by reform. Then the chapter draws lessons of those reforms for the United States.

Canada: Moderate Reforms with Big Results?

An excellent place to begin is Canada. Not only is it a familiar country and in many ways similar to the United States but its retirement program shares many of the features of U.S. Social Security. In the 1990s, Canada had the same debate as the United States over the future of its program. Unlike the United States, however, Canada's debate led to a substantial overhaul of its retirement program. As a result, the Canadian government believes that it has reestablished a sound pension system for the foreseeable future. Today, there is little continuing public debate over that system, or its reforms. Is this belief premature, or have the Canadians found a way to shore up its pension system, one that America can also take?

The Canadian old-age pension system dates back to the Roaring Twenties, although full federal funding did not occur until 1952. It does in one major respect differ from the system that was later developed in the United States: the original pension program, today called Old Age Security (OAS), is neither a contributions-based nor an earnings-based program. It is simply a flat monthly payment given to each retired Canadian that is paid out of the general revenues of the Canadian government. (We are ignoring here a great complexity of the Canadian system, the relationship between the federal government and the Canadian provinces. Essentially, the provinces have greater taxing power than the U.S. states, and greater responsibilities for social welfare. Thus the provinces were much more important in the creation and operation of the Canadian pension programs than were the U.S. states in Social Security. As this difference is not important to the development of the recent Canadian reforms, we will not expand upon this complexity.) Perhaps signaling a cultural difference with the United States, the Canadian OAS program is not means tested, as this sort of welfare-oriented program would likely be in the United States, but it is residence tested. Originally, one had to reside in Canada for 20 years to collect this monthly payment. The initial amount was quite small, $20 a month. Since its inception, it has been substantially increased and is now adjusted every three months to the Canadian consumer price index. As a result, the current monthly payment averages C$466.98, an amount equal to 16 percent of the average Canadian monthly wage. It is universally available to Canadians over the age of 65.

An interesting feature of the OAS, though, is the "clawback" provision. Beginning in 1989, wealthier Canadians have had to return a portion of their OAS checks to the government. They must repay 15 percent of the amount of their incomes over C$63,511 (using 2007 figures) against their anticipated OAS benefit. As a result, Canadians with incomes over C$102,865 do not receive any OAS money. This clawback, which affects about 5 percent of Canadian seniors, is an increasingly discussed method of reducing pension benefits to high-income retirees in an equitable manner and is now found in the retirement programs of several countries.

The OAS program operates alongside a second Canadian retirement program, the Canadian Pension Plan (CPP). This plan, initiated in 1966 and administered in Quebec as the Quebec Pension Plan (QPP), is quite similar to the U.S. Social Security system. Workers and their employers each contribute equally into the program, and, at retirement, workers receive a monthly pension equal to 25 percent of their "pensionable earnings." Full retirement was originally set at age 70 but today is 65. In the 1970s, following a resolution of jurisdictional issues between the federal government and the provinces, numerous reforms were made that resulted in the CPP resembling even closer U.S. Social Security. Survivors' and spousal benefits were begun, and a cost-of-living adjustment (COLA) was added. One interesting difference between the two systems, however, is that, in Canada, workers who leave employment or shift to part-time employment to care for a child under the age of seven can have these years of reduced earnings excluded from the calculation of their monthly benefit amounts. In other words, depending upon how one looks at it, the Canadian system does not punish those responsible for child care with lower pensions, or, alternatively, it offers a state subsidy to those who choose full-time child care over remaining in the workforce. A second difference is that *all* CPP benefits are fully taxable. In 2007, the average monthly benefit under the CPP was C$473.09. The OAS and the CPP combined, then, to an average pension of C$940, compared with the average U.S. Social Security pension of $1,044.

In the 1980s, this pay-as-you-go pension system encountered the same difficulties as its U.S. counterpart. Unexpected inflation and wage increases dramatically raised benefits, while long-term demographic trends threatened the future of the program's financing. As in the United States, the debate over how to resolve the financing problems was inconclusive. In 1981, the government called for a national conference on pensions but ultimately had to concede that no consensus could be gained on what steps to take to solve these problems. Three years later, the Conservative government of Brian Mulroney floated the question of whether Canada should continue a program of universal pension benefits (the OAS) and proposed lowering the COLA indexing formula, but the response was very similar to that which greeted the Reagan administration's cutbacks that were announced at this same time. The Canadian government also quickly backed off.

The debate began anew, though, when the chief actuary of the CPP announced in 1995 that the Canadian pension fund would be exhausted in 2015. This provoked the Reform Party to call for a privatization of the system. The ruling Liberal Party preferred the existing system, but it knew the pressure to reform would only continue to mount. Thus, after a series of consultations, the minister of Finance, Paul Martin, unveiled a reform package in 1996 to save the program. The reforms centered upon changing the CPP from pay-as-you-go financing to a prefunded pension system.

As defined in chapter 2, a prefunded system is one in which sufficient reserves are built in advance to enable the program to pay future retirees their full promised benefits. Unlike pay-as-you-go programs, it does not rely on a given year's benefits being taken from that same year's worker contributions. The object of the Canadian reforms was to redesign the CPP so that it would have the money on hand to guarantee full payment of promised pensions for the foreseeable future. In this sense, it was somewhat like the U.S. reforms of 1983, which substantially, albeit temporarily, prefunded the Social Security Trust Fund. However, the Canadian objective was to ensure a near-permanent prefunding.

The Liberal government defined the needed level of prefunding as the creation of a CPP trust fund that holds five years' worth of benefits. The boosted trust fund would then be combined with "steady state financing," a system that automatically ensures that the contributions entering into the program will be sufficient to pay the benefits that have been guaranteed. How did Canada achieve this prefunding? The government began with a standard approach of modest reforms in raising taxes and reducing benefits, along with efforts to raise the rate of return on the reserves held by the CPP.

Reform of the CPP required the consent of the provinces, and British Columbia was the most adamant against one "leg" of reform, that of cutting benefits. (Interestingly, the provincial government of Alberta continued to favor partial privatization, but could find no allies.) The failure to gain consensus led the government to drop all of its major proposed benefits cuts. This left only tax increases and higher rates of return. Prefunding would have to rest upon these. And so it did, in a package that passed the Canadian Parliament in 1998.

Steady state financing necessitated a substantial hike in the payroll tax. Experts determined that, given a healthy pension fund, a payroll tax of 9.9 percent, shared equally between worker and employer, would be sufficient to meet expected benefit claims. In 1998, that tax was 5.85 percent. The reform package thus mandated a nearly 70 percent rise in the payroll tax from 1998 to 2003, when it would reach 9.9 percent. (Note that this rate is still below the U.S. payroll tax rate, but, on the other hand, the Canadian payroll tax only pays for about half of the total pension. The other half comes from the general revenues.) To go with this increased payroll tax, the lower bound of taxable income was frozen. The CPP payroll tax has both a minimum floor and a maximum ceiling on taxed earnings. (The United States only has the ceiling.) Both previously were adjusted upward as incomes rose. But with the new reform, the floor will remain at C$3,500, even as the ceiling continues to rise. This amounts to a tax increase, and it is a particularly important one for those at low income levels. To make certain that this expanded payroll tax is always sufficient to pay for the benefits, the CPP is obligated to report if it ever appears that the payroll tax will not be able to cover promised benefits. Following such a finding, the payroll tax is automatically raised for a three-year period, and COLA increases are stopped. Only a vote of Parliament can intervene to prevent this almost homeostatic correction that ensures that sufficient revenues arrive to pay for the promised benefits.

The most innovative reform, however, was not this sizable tax increase; it was the creation of the Canadian Pension Plan Investment Board. To boost the rate of return on its pension reserves, the government of Canada decided to allow the CPP to invest those reserves just as if it were a mutual fund. No longer would it suffer restrictions such as those imposed upon the U.S. Social Security Trust Fund to invest only in government securities. Here Canada drew upon the province of Quebec, where such an investment board was already operating as part of the QPP. It had experienced a number of years of very good financial returns, often higher than 10 percent. The CPP Investment Board was given but one mandate: invest so as to gain the highest return possible without undue risk. As a result, it invests in stocks, bonds, real estate, and other assets, both Canadian and international. (Foreign investments are, however, limited to 30 percent of the total.) It has become Canada's largest investment fund. The CPP estimates that not until the year 2022 will any portion of the income earned through the Investment Board's activities need to be used to pay on benefits. Thus there are 16 years for the board to grow as large a reserve as it can to prefund that need.

In devising this board, the government was attuned to the issue that has so vexed U.S. efforts to move in this direction: how does such an instrument keep from gaining too much political influence over the market? This was the reason that the board was given no instructions other than to gain the best return. It was specifically to prevent political motivations or influence from creeping into the board's investment choices. Moreover, no government official may serve on the board. Instead the Investment Board is chosen from independent professional investment advisers. The Investment Board does not operate under the CPP; it has its own board of directors. In short, the system is actually organized very much along the lines of a private mutual fund.

To date, the Canadian government is very satisfied with its reform package (Office of the Chief Actuary 2007, 6). Over the four fiscal years from 2003 to 2007, the Investment Board's annualized rate of return was 13.6 percent (Canadian Pension Plan Investment Board 2007). This amount substantially exceeds the interest paid to the U.S. Social Security Trust Fund over the same period. In fact, if the Trust Fund had received a rate of return similar to that of the Investment Board's, it would have earned an additional $25 billion during these years. In 2006, a review of the CPP reaffirmed that the 9.9 percent payroll tax continues to sat-

TABLE 3.1
Comparing Rates of Return: Canada vs. the United States

	United States (%)	Canada (%)
1998	7.3	40.1
1999	7	3.2
2000	6.9	7
2001	6.7	4
2002	6.4	−1.5
2003	6	17.6
2004	5.7	8.5
2005	5.4	15.5
2006	5.3	12.9

Note: U.S. rates are for the calendar year. Canadian rates are for the fiscal year ending the following April 1.
Source: Social Security Administration, *Trust Fund Data* (ssa.gov/OACT/ProgData/IntRates.html), Canadian Pension Investment Board (http:www.cppib.ca/Results).

isfy the steady state financing condition and will do so for the foreseeable future.

Essentially, then, the Canadian reform approach is to hike the payroll tax significantly, using the initial years of increased revenues to prefund the system, and to make automatic any future hikes that may be needed. The prefunded contributions are then invested much as a mutual fund, so as to maximize the size of the pension fund to be drawn upon in the future.

Is this approach a good model for the United States to follow? The answer depends upon one's view of the tax increase and of the likely future of a trust fund invested across a variety of stocks, bonds, and other assets. No prominent policy analyst or interest group has propounded a steady state payroll tax in the United States along the Canadian lines, or estimated what that tax would be. Because Social Security does not rely on any general revenues, the payroll tax would be significantly higher than that in Canada. The two issues to consider are whether such a tax increase is the fairest method of solving the problem and whether this tax increase would have any negative effects on economic growth. Canada does not appear to have suffered economically from its increased payroll tax, but one could argue that this is because it is still at a lower level than the U.S. Federal Insurance Contributions Act (FICA) tax. The Canada Pension Plan Investment Board, and its investment activities, does not seem to attract great criticism in that country. There are no fears of excessive politicization or economic influence. But would the same sentiment hold in the United States? President Clinton's more limited plan to invest some of the Trust Fund in the stock market attracted great controversy, so it does seem clear that there is greater political resistance in the United States to this solution. Prefunding through broadening investments also attracts concern because of the undeniable fact that the annual rate of return varies much more when stocks and other investments are held by the pension program. A quick comparison across the two countries quickly establishes this. The great unknown, stated in any stock market prospectus, is that future returns cannot be predicted. Ultimately, the desire to emulate the Canadian decision to invest in markets depends upon the level of risk the United States is prepared to accept: the risk of poorer-than-expected returns versus the risk of whatever other reform the United States chooses to engage in. One's view of the Canadian reforms likely turns on one's views of the tax hikes and the increased risk that are entailed in the new Canadian old-age pension system.

Germany: Clamping Down on Benefits?

Not only is Germany the home of the world's first public retirement system but today it offers just about the most generous pension program anywhere on earth. The average German retiree receives a pension that equals approximately 70 percent of his or her earnings when still in the workforce. Compare this to the Social Security system in the United States, in which the average retiree obtains less than half of his or her average earnings through Social Security payments. Clearly, the German system is more expensive to fund than is Social Security. To make matters worse, demographic trends in Germany are far starker than those in the United States. Germans have significantly fewer children per family, and Germany has fewer immigrants as well. Thus the Germany dependency ratio of retirees to workers is deteriorating much faster than in North America. The result has been tremendous pressure for reform.

Because of this pressure, the German government has made some painful choices—different choices, however, than were made in Canada. Germany has focused on the benefits side—reducing the outgo—not on the contribution side, as did Canada.

The different approaches thus make for an interesting contrast in the discussion of how to reform Social Security.

The original Bismarckian pension system did not, of course, survive Germany's experiences of the 20th century. So while there has been a continuous system since the 1880s, the current program dates back only to 1957. In broad form it operates much like Social Security. Employees and employers each pay half into the program, and workers retire on full pension at age 65 (rising to age 67 by 2029). There are benefits for survivors and children. The program is almost completely pay as you go. The pension system currently has a reserve fund that amounts to only 14 days' worth of pension obligations. The system is more generous than that in the United States for several reasons. First, and perhaps more important, the goal of the German pension system is to provide retirees with a standard of living comparable to that when they were in the labor force. Early retirement is also easier to opt for and more generous, and thus the average German leaves the workforce earlier than the average American. The level of pension contributions is modestly higher (by about 1 percent of income) than in the United States. Finally, benefit growth is linked not to prices, as in North America, but to wages. The German pension rises with wage increases and not via a COLA. As discussed earlier, wages grow faster than prices, and so benefits linked to wages grow faster than if linked to the cost of living. This final generous feature was enacted during the favorable economic conditions of the early 1970s; it was then that the Germany pension was set at 70 percent of average earnings.

But, again as in the United States, by the 1980s experts were realizing that the German program was not going to be sustainable into the future. Just as across the Atlantic, reform commission after reform commission investigated what to do to ensure a viable pension program. A 1992 reform added incentives to not retire early, and Germany began basing benefit increases on net wages rather than gross wages (net wages are wages after the contributions are excluded). Even this reduced benefit remained more generous than it would have been using a COLA. The government also stiffened the incentives to not retire before the age of 65. This set of reforms, however, was quickly undone by the unification of Germany. The pension situation of the former East Germany was extremely poor, and adding that population to the West German National Pension Fund degraded the soundness of the latter, with the result that the united Germany found itself under renewed pressure to fix its retirement system.

The debates that followed produced consensus on one point: the already high contributions tax cannot be further hiked (Capretta 2007, 20). As a result, recent pension reforms have included mandatory caps on the size of future pension contributions. This decision, the opposite of that made in Canada, closes a number of options. Germany has a minuscule reserve fund. If contributions cannot be increased, the Canadian choice of raising the rate of return on that reserve fund is not available. Reform has to be either within the operations of a completely pay-as-you-go system or via dismantling that system in some substantial way. Few, so far, are prepared to contemplate the latter radical alternative. All that is logically left is to make some reform on the benefit side of the program, and this is what has happened. To make up for the benefit cuts, a new voluntary retirement account program has been created on top of the old program.

A direct cut in benefits was, not surprisingly, politically impossible. Even the more limited reforms that were offered brought a threat from some labor leaders to take the issue "to the streets." Instead, Germany adopted a system of deflating or reducing benefits in line with its worsening dependency ratio. As the ratio of retirees to workers grows, that is, as the gap between the contributions coming into the system and the benefits that must be paid out from it increases, benefits will be shrunk accordingly. In theory, this automatic adjustment in the benefits formula should save the system.

The first effort to develop such a formula actually failed. The initial idea was to add a "demographic factor" to the benefits formula. This factor would automatically lower benefits as the life expectancy of a German worker increased. Essentially, it multiplied any year's expected pension benefit by the ratio of the anticipated life expectancy two years earlier divided by the anticipated life expectancy of one year earlier. If the life expectancy increased, this ratio would be less than one, and the benefit would go down. The next year would begin with that lower benefit, again multiplied by the ratio, and so forth. So over the long haul, there would be steadily lower benefits. (In truth, the demographic factor was a somewhat more complicated mathematical formula than presented here, but this is the basic idea.) This idea was developed by a German pension reform commission in the late 1990s and adopted by the then Christian Democrat German government.

But in 1998, an election placed the rival Social Democratic party in power, and it refused to carry out this reform.

So a second reform commission was left to pick up the pieces and try again. This time it was a success. Beginning in 2005, a "sustainability factor" has been incorporated into the German pension benefit formula. The exact formula is rather complicated, but simply put, benefit payments are indexed to the state of the dependency ratio. If the dependency ratio worsens from one year to the next (i.e., the ratio of workers to retirees goes down), the increase in benefit payments is reduced accordingly. The index formula is set so that the government can intervene to alter the benefit reduction that results, if this reduction is thought too severe. Currently, the formula lowers benefits growth by 0.25 percent for every 1 percent worsening of the dependency ratio. German estimates show that the net long-term effects of this reform will be to decrease the value of German pension benefits from the current 70 percent of one's pre-retirement income to 67 to 68 percent of that amount (Börsch-Supan and Wilke 2006, 591).

This does raise the question of how to prepare for reduced benefits. The German solution is "Riester Pensions," a voluntary individual retirement pension that has been available since 2002. These pensions, named after Walter Riester, the German labor minister of the time, sit on top of the existing National Pension Insurance Plan. They are offered by a variety of private companies and operate along the lines of an individual retirement account (IRA) or a U.S. 401(k) plan, subject to a variety of government regulations. German workers are able to place up to 4 percent of their salary in one of these pensions, should they wish. To encourage use of Riester Pensions, the government offers subsidies to low-income workers and tax breaks to higher-income workers. The subsidies operate like matching funds, with the government matching up to 90 percent of the worker's own contributions, depending upon the level of income. An interesting feature is that the subsidies are also increased to mothers with children in an effort to reward fertility (and, thus, eventually, help the dependency ratio). Higher-income workers were thought to be more interested in reducing taxes than in obtaining these matching funds, and thus the Riester Pensions are sheltered from taxes for those who make more money.

These pensions, it is hoped, will more than make up for the retirement income lost because of the new benefits formula. In fact, this new income stream was made part of the revamped benefits formula. The anticipated financial gain made by the average holder of a Riester Pension is used to further index the benefits. As the return on the Riester grows, benefits are again adjusted downward. Needless to say, this should act as another incentive to enroll in one of these pensions, because individuals will see their benefits indexed whether they do or do not start their own account.

In sum, Germany has basically attacked pensions from the opposite direction as Canada. It has focused, albeit with difficulty, on the benefits side. A new benefits formula will automatically lower monthly payments both as the dependency ratio worsens and as new, voluntary supplemental retirement accounts kick in as an alternative source of retirement income. The concentration on benefits is also seen by the way Germany is handling its immediate pensions crunch (recall that there is no reserve fund to fall back on). There were no benefits increases at all between 2004 and 2006, as the country strove to continue its generous system under adverse demographic and economic conditions.

Is the German system a viable model for the United States? The answer likely revolves around three questions. The new benefits formula is such that a German born in 1985 can expect to see almost 40 percent of his or her retirement income come from the Riester Pension rather than from the existing system. In other words, as time progresses, the voluntary add-on pension plan increasingly supplements the basic pension. So an essential issue is, how many workers will in fact enroll in a plan? Those who do not may face a very limited retirement. To date, more than half of the eligible workforce have established Riester-style accounts. However, the evidence also seems to show that up to half of these accounts are merely transfers of money from other investments that the worker already had (Börsch-Supan 2005, 136). There has been no increase of net savings for retirement. Some have argued that an IRA-type add-on will only work if it is mandatory. Otherwise, the accompanying lower benefits will fall heavily upon those who do not or cannot open the voluntary account. For these groups, the future cut in their pensions could be substantial.

A second issue revolves around political will. Many observers are already saying that the new benefits formula will not sufficiently reduce German pension benefits to avoid running into the contributions cap (Börsch-Supan and Wilke 2006, 599). If this is the case, the hardest decisions are still being pushed off into the future. When the contributions cap is hit, will benefits be further slashed? When benefits cuts *are* faced, will the government lose its stomach and use its ability to reset the formula to avoid them? Perhaps this will not be a problem because, when the time comes, Germany will be better positioned to make the further reforms necessary. Or perhaps the recent reform is just passing the buck onto the next generation. A political system that cannot face a larger benefit cut today is not going to have an easier time accepting it tomorrow. The decision in 2007 to increase the retirement age to 67 indicates that there may not be complete faith in the ability of benefits cuts alone to do the job.

Finally, the German reform clearly involves a large intergenerational transfer of resources. Those currently retired are exempted from the recent reforms. This means that those still working are paying the same level of contributions as their elders but will be getting relatively lower benefits. Furthermore, those who are a number of years into their working careers will likely not ever obtain the retirement income from their Riester Pension that someone just entering the workforce can reasonably expect to receive. As a result, that middle generation will pay most of the cost of the reforms, the younger generation will pay some, and the older generation will pay none. Is this fair?

The German reforms, focused on reduction of benefits by automatically taking account of the dependency ratio and the performance of a voluntary add-on program, can be neatly contrasted with the Canadian program, which attempts to leave benefits uncut and turns to a tax increase and a more ambitious investment strategy instead. Could one of these options work for the United States, or is there a third possibility that's better than both?

Australia: Putting Means Testing to Work?

The U.S. Social Security program has shied away from employing means testing to determine the size of benefits (although a much smaller program, Supplemental Security Income, *is* used to provide means-tested benefits to low-income senior citizens). Recall that a means-tested program is one that subjects benefits to the level of wealth or income of the recipient. Only lower-income retirees receive full benefits. Beginning with President Franklin Roosevelt, most supporters of Social Security have feared that placing a means test on the program could make it appear to the public as if it were a welfare program and cause it to lose popular support. But more than 70 years after its implementation, is it time to revisit this question? Means testing is one certain way of reducing the program's cost. Australia, where means testing has become part of the strategy to preserve its old-age retirement system, serves as an example of how such a reform might work.

The Australian retirement program, called the Age Pension, was, in certain key respects, never much like the U.S. Social Security system. Begun in 1909, it was neither a contributions-based nor a pay-as-you-go program. Instead, all Australians were eligible for the program regardless of their work history, and it was paid for from the government's general revenues. The Age Pension initially had an income means test, but it was progressively loosened over time. By the 1970s, the means test was abolished altogether for those over age 70.

In spite of these key differences, Australia found itself in the same position as the United States in the early 1980s. Unfavorable demographics—the government estimates that the growth of the Australian workforce will approach zero sometime in the 2040s—and growing benefits made the existing program unsustainable. The government budget just would not be big enough to pay for all the pension outlays it would face. Since Australia has no reserve fund or other mechanism to prefund the coming retirements, this path for reform was unavailable. What to do? The problem for Australia is that any effort to shift the burden of reform onto either contributions or benefits, à la Canada or Germany, would have a huge, direct impact on its budget. The old-age program is not separately financed. So, in 1983, the Australian government decided to take a different tack. It turned to tightening its means test, expanding it to include all those over the age of 70. (Currently, the retirement age in Australia is 65 for men. It is lower for women, but that age is being gradually raised to age 65 as well.) It also closed an obvious loophole with means testing. Previously, an individual could spend down whatever is being "tested" and move his or her wealth into property or some other nontested asset. For example, someone could retire, take her or his company pension as a lump sum, and buy a vacation home. This would evade a means test on income. To prevent this movement of funds to nontested assets, Australia now places a dual means test on both income and assets.

Here is how this means-tested program works. The full benefit provided through the Age Pension program is set to provide an income equal to 25 percent of the average Australian wage. So, in 2007, an Australian couple with a monthly income of up to $256 Australian dollars (usually abbreviated as A$) would receive A$877 each month for their Age Pension. (The Australian system actually pays benefits every two weeks; here the figures are converted to monthly amounts in order to make the comparison with the U.S. system.) Above A$256 the means test is triggered. For each additional dollar the couple's income rises above this minimum, their Age Pension is reduced by 40 cents. If their income should reach A$5,765 a month, the amount they receive from the Age Pension would fall to zero. Above that figure, the couple is not given any public pension. On top of this income means test is the second test, that for assets. If our couple are homeowners, they will receive a full pension only if their total assets fall below A$161,500. Above that, they lose A$6.00 a month for every additional A$1,000 in assets that they possess. By the time they reach A$338,500, they will not receive any pension at all. (Assets are counted differently for those without homes.) Since both means tests are used, the actual monthly benefit is some combination of how the couple fares under both. Because of this means test, nearly 30 percent of retiring Australians do not receive any benefits from the Age Pension, which substantially eases the size of the pension bill that the government must pay.

Australia recognized two limitations of simple means testing, however, and has attempted to rectify both. The first is a question of responsibility. What happens to the Australian workers who can expect to receive no Age Pension and to the many who will receive a reduced pension? Should they be left to support themselves however they can, or does the government still have some obligation to ensure that they will have an adequate retirement? Second, as (or if) government pension expenditures continue to increase, how can the means test be tightened further? The current income and assets levels are chosen because of a belief that, below those levels, retirees really do need some financial help. But this means that if the government does ever need to further tighten the existing means tests, at least some individuals will be left with an inadequate retirement. These are both difficult questions.

Australia has developed "superannuation" to solve these problems. Essentially, it asks employers to pick up the slack.

Recognizing that only about half of Australian companies provided their own pension programs, in 1986 the government mandated that all do so. The idea is that private pensions will progressively augment the Age Pension, and workers will rely on those pensions for an increasing proportion of their retirement. In 1992, this proposal was further reformed as the Superannuation Guarantee. It is now all but impossible for an Australian firm to evade offering its employees a defined-contribution benefit plan. Ninety-five percent of Australian workers are enrolled in such a plan. The plans themselves, however, are portable. Workers may take their plans with them if they change employers. Every Australian company is required to place, each year, an amount equal to 9 percent of an employee's wage into a pension fund for that employee. Originally the employer chose the pension fund, but today most workers can select their own plans. There are a wide variety of superannuation funds to choose from. A company may offer its own plan, or there may be an industrywide superannuation fund. Alternatively, workers may enroll in a retail defined-contribution plan, or they may open a "retirement savings account," an investment plan specifically developed for superannuation by banks, insurance companies, and other financial firms.

Employees are not required to pay into these plans; only employers are required to do so. However, to encourage further savings, the government allows individuals to contribute into their plan the equivalent of an additional 2 to 3 percent of their income if they so wish. This contribution is tax advantaged. For those with lower incomes, the government also offers to match the contributions. Because of the expectation that this superannuation will provide an increasing share of a worker's retirement, Australia adds a final fail-safe provision to its new program. This is the "guarantee" in the Superannuation Guarantee. All retirees are guaranteed that they will receive a total retirement pension at least equal the amount they would have received under the original Age Pension, no matter how their own superannuation plan fares. If their private pension for some reason performed very poorly, the government will step in to make up the difference.

The Australian government believes its program is working well. A generation from now, one-third of Australian retirees are still expected to receive full benefits from the Age Pension, while three-quarters will still be receiving partial benefits. Superannuation is not expected to make the old plan redundant. However, the belief is that the superannuation plans will provide half of

Australia's total retirement benefits. One estimate is that it also will reduce the future cost of the government's pension obligations by one-third (Rothman 1998, 6).

How does this approach compare with the other reforms considered to fix the U.S. Social Security system? First, one big unknown must be accounted for. The success of the Australian plan will likely depend upon the success of the superannuation pensions that it is encouraging. There is an alarming disagreement among experts about how well they will work. Some estimate that Australian workers will wind up with two to three times the amount from their employer pensions that they could have expected from the Age Pension (Mitchell and O'Quinn 1997). But others claim that future retirees will have pensions that will be far less generous than this (Korczyk 2003, 21). To an extent, this is a version of the old "half empty versus half full" argument. The Age Pension only promised 25 percent of average working salary. So from one perspective, any pension that exceeded this figure would be a great improvement for most citizens. Yet about half of Australia's workforce already had private pensions before the onset of superannuation pensions, and to this group, such a performance may not be much, or indeed any, improvement over their situation before these reforms.

Much of this disagreement in evaluation is because it is not yet known what patterns of behavior will take shape. How much will the average worker place in her or his private pension? Over a working career, the difference between no contributions and a steady 2 or 3 percent contribution would be huge. Will the savings placed in superannuation pensions be new money? Or will it simply be transferred from existing savings to take advantage of the tax breaks? In the former case, workers will retire better off. In the latter, they will just be running in place. And will workers choose smart pension plans? There is some evidence that pension providers are investing their contributors' savings too conservatively (Congressional Budget Office 1999, 57). There is a fear that investment advisers are too cautious because they fear that a single quarter's bad results could stampede investors out of their fund. Finally, though easiest to remedy, Australia does allow lump-sum withdrawals from the superannuation funds at retirement. Through skillful manipulation of the system, or maybe just bad choices, a retiree can run through this lump sum payout and wind up back on the Age Pension, producing no advantage to the program.

At a deeper level, the superannuation funds do not evade the difficult trade-offs in contributions and benefits. Nor will they end the increasing financial burden on the Australian state. Even with means testing, the government will still have to double the amount it spends on the Age Pension by 2050. The addition of a 9 percent employer payment almost certainly amounts to lower wages for the employee. This is might be seen as the equivalent of an increased tax. Moreover, today's employees must experience these reduced earnings while they continue to pay the same formal taxes that provide for the Age Pensions of today's retirees. Whether an increasingly tough means test should be considered the equivalent of a benefit cut is more arguable. It will certainly reduce the benefits that some Australians receive from the Age Pension, though, as discussed, the promise is that overall benefits will not be lower. A last issue in evaluating this reform goes back to a difference between the Australian program and the U.S. program. Australia does not demand worker contributions. But the United States does. What is the ethics, or the political persuasiveness, of insisting that some pay into a pension program from which they will never receive any benefits? That is the ultimate trade-off with a means test. Perhaps that is the issue that would first rise to the fore if the United States should wish to follow the Australian example.

Sweden: Fully Funding without Privatizing?

As discussed in chapter 2, the leading alternative to pay-as-you-go pension systems, such as the U.S. Social Security program, is a fully funded system. Fully funded pensions are not drawn from a common pool of contributions or from the government's general revenues. Instead, each worker funds her or his own retirement through her or his own contributions. Because benefits are tied to the specific contributions made, the system is called a "defined contribution" program. Social Security operated along these lines before the 1939 reforms, but today fully funded pension systems are usually in the form of private IRAs. Experts agree that fully funded systems are financially sound. The problem is the transition costs of moving to such a system. How do you pay for the pensions of those who are already retired or who are too advanced in years to build up an IRA large enough to retire on, if the contributions of today's workers do not continue to pour in?

Sweden has led the way in creating a new retirement system that, it claims, solves this problem. Sweden calls its new system one of "notional defined contributions." Could this be the answer to saving Social Security?

Sweden is rightfully proud that it has the world's oldest truly universal pension system. It began in 1913. Like many systems it evolved from a fully funded program into one that was pay as you go. By the 1980s, it consisted of a flat-rate basic pension, called the "folkpension," that everyone received, and an additional benefit based on earnings. It was funded by contributions. The amount of a worker's benefit was determined by "pension points" that were accumulated over one's career. The benefit, as with the other countries we have examined, was then linked to rising wages and rising prices. The system also contained a reserve fund that held about five years' worth of benefits. An oddity of this system was that, for the earnings portion, the ceiling on taxable earnings was so low that the Swedish pension program was actually slowly evolving toward one in which everyone got the same benefit. (Essentially, everyone's income was hitting that ceiling. It would be as if every worker in the United States was earning more than the U.S. maximum earnings for calculating Social Security benefits.) Like many European systems, Sweden's benefits are quite generous. They are around 65 percent of average earnings. It is also important to note that almost every Swede has a private pension from his or her company or occupation. So the standard of living for Swedish retirees is currently very high.

In the 1980s, a parliamentary commission investigated the operations of this retirement system and found that it would not be sustainable into the future. The reserve fund was expected to be depleted around the year 2020, and the contributions rate was expected to rise dramatically after that—perhaps to 25 to 35 percent of a worker's annual income. The reasons for this rise were the same as elsewhere in the world: an increasing life expectancy and a worsening dependency ratio. Sweden received an additional shock in the early 1990s when it experienced several years of negative economic growth. How could benefits continue to increase if the economy, and government revenues, began shrinking?

In 1994, the Swedish government responded to this anticipated pension crisis by creating a new old-age benefit program. It is a novel attempt to combine the virtues of a fully funded system with the realities of a pay-as-you-go system that cannot easily be replaced. Creating this new program was not easy. While all political parties agreed on its necessity, and even on the need to move to some form of a fully funded program, they disagreed on how to do this. The right-of-center parties, which then governed the country, wanted to move to a privatized system of IRAs. The left-of-center opposition wanted to continue to use the old pension program. The result was a compromise to do both. The new pension system would have one tier drawn from the old pension program and a second tier that used IRAs. A third, means-tested tier was then added for those with low incomes. The most novel element of the new system is this first tier, which involves converting the existing pay-as-you-go program to a fully funded one.

Sweden created what amounts to an imaginary fully funded pension system that sits within its existing pay-as-you-go retirement program. This is why it is called a "notional" defined-contribution program. Underneath, the financing continues to operate as it did when it was a simple pay-as-you-go system. Contributions are made by employers and employees, and they equal 16 percent of a worker's annual earnings. (Unlike in the United States, in Sweden, contributions are not 50–50. Employers pay 62 percent and employees 38 percent.) Workers accrue pension points in the retirement program. The number of points accrued depends upon the level of income, although points are also given for years spent in military service, obtaining higher education, and caring for children. The points are indexed each year to the growth of real Swedish wages, so that the size of the eventual benefit continues to grow. So far, this is a pretty standard pay-as-you-go system.

But now comes the difference. Every year, the pension points accumulated by any individual worker equal an amount of money that is specifically credited to that worker within the pension system. Year by year, this amount grows. A worker can actually calculate how much savings he or she has in the Swedish retirement system at any point in time. It is "their" money. It is as if each worker had her or his own retirement account within the larger pension system. And it is the money that is in *that* account that will determine the size of the worker's pension.

So what is the practical difference? Why should these notional defined contributions solve the problems of a pay-as-you-go system? In essence, it is because this type of pension system will not pay out more than it takes in. In the U.S. system, a worker can receive benefits far in excess of what that worker ever contributed to Social Security. In Sweden, a worker will receive what is in his or her account at the time of retirement (plus interest). And that is all. Thus the program is financially balanced; it should never go into the red.

At retirement, in Sweden, the retiree has a total defined pension entitlement. This is the amount of money that has been contributed over that person's working career (plus interest), as indexed by wage growth. It is a matter of spreading this "notional wealth" over the rest of the retiree's life. This is done by dividing the wealth by the number of years that the person is expected to live during his or her retirement. For example, the Swedish government currently expects that someone who was born in 1960 and retires in 2025 (at age 65) will live another 17 years (Settergren 2005, 50). So, in 2025, this person's notional pension wealth will be divided by 17 (if this life expectancy has not changed by then). That will be the amount of benefits paid to that person each year for the rest of his or her life. As life expectancy increases, annual benefits must decrease because this "annuity divisor" will become larger and therefore the benefits will be lower. At least to the Swedes, this is a defensible limit on benefits since it is fairly tied to a worker's income, and it preserves the financial health of the pension system. If a worker wishes to obtain more benefits, he or she must continue to work a little longer. Because as one continues to work, the notional wealth rises and the divisor of future life expectancy goes down, making for a bigger benefit.

There is, however, one last complexity to consider. Retirees do not receive their benefits in a lump sum. They get a portion every year. What happens to the remainder of the benefits that are yet to be received? Sweden has developed a rather complicated way to handle these funds. Based on historical experience, Sweden believes that in the long run, its economy grows by 1.6 percent per year. According to economic theory, real interest rates should hover around the economic growth rate. So, to proxy the earnings from interest, at the time of retirement this 1.6 percent figure is incorporated into the life expectancy divisor in a manner that makes the divisor smaller. This results in a bigger pension. It roughly equals the effects of earning interest, although with the twist that the retiree actually gets the impact of that interest the day that retirement begins, rather than spread out over his or her remaining life.

Sharp readers may have spotted a flaw, however. What happens if the economy actually grows more or less than that 1.6 percent? The difficulty for the government is that if economic growth is more, or less, than expected, the amount of contributions coming into the system is going to be more or less than expected. If no correction is made for unexpectedly high or low economic growth, the system loses its notional full funding. For example, if economic growth is lower than expected, the contributions that come in that year will not be enough to pay for the promised benefits that year and the system will be in trouble. Therefore, pension benefits are adjusted annually if economic growth does not turn out to be 1.6 percent for the year. Benefits are reduced if economic growth is lower than that figure, and they are increased if it is greater.

This difficulty suggests a second problem, which Sweden has also had to solve. What happens if people turn out to live longer than expected, or, for that matter, if fewer new workers enter the labor force than expected? Either situation will lead to a shortfall in money available to pay the promised benefits. To prevent this shortfall, Sweden has added an "automatic balance mechanism" that is triggered when the pension system's ratio of assets to future liabilities falls below 1. Outgoing benefits are then multiplied by this mechanism, which further reduces benefits so as to restore the system to balance.

Critics have claimed that the Swedish formulas are so difficult and so uncertain that, in reality, Swedish workers cannot really see "their" money as the new program promises (e.g. Kotlikoff 2002, 207). In theory, more simple formulas could be used for a notional defined-contribution system. But in fact the combination of politics and the inherent uncertainty of the future may produce formulas similar to those used in Sweden.

The operations of the automatic balancing mechanism and the annuity divisor will almost certainly reduce Swedish pensions. This is where the second tier of the new system, the individual retirement accounts, enters the picture. Swedish workers are asked to place 2.5 percent of their earnings into an IRA. They have more than 700 investment funds to choose from. If the worker does not choose a fund, the government places that worker's 2.5 percent into a default "life-cycle" investment fund. The Swedish government is the sole provider of these investment funds and guarantees a minimum rate of return of 2.7 percent. Unlike the notional accounts in the first tier of the retirement system, the IRAs are real money. At retirement, workers have access to the funds to which they contributed during their working years. Because these funds are expected to generate higher returns than the notional defined-contribution system, Sweden anticipates that they will more than make up for the loss in benefits that a worker would otherwise suffer under the new pension program. Experts believe that these IRAs must earn between 2 and 5 percent a year to do this. Historically, Swedish stocks have returned 8.6 percent a year, and bonds have grown 3.1 percent a year.

The final tier of the new Swedish pension plan is a guaranteed retirement income for those who had no or little income over their working years. This guaranteed pension is set to the consumer price index. An individual who had no income whatsoever receives a pension that is roughly equal to $12,500 in 2007. This person would also receive a housing allowance. The guaranteed benefit is means tested. It gradually falls to zero as the earned pension of a worker rises.

The new Swedish system became fully operative in 2003. Anyone born before 1938 remains fully in the old system. Anyone born after 1953 is fully in the new system. Those in between receive some of their benefits from the old, the rest from the new. To date, the new plan seems popular. The greatest difficulties have actually been with its IRA portion. It turns out that many Swedes are overwhelmed with the choice of 700 investment funds. Only about 10 percent of entering workers actually choose a fund; the rest are content to let their money go into the government's default fund. An investigatory agency has recently recommended that Sweden sharply reduce the number of available investment funds and give workers more help in selecting among them.

But what of notional defined contributions? Is instituting them a good path for reform? There are some clear positives. Sweden is no longer under the burden of future pension liabilities that it had promised but for which it could not pay. This is the essential argument for its plan. Notional defined-contribution plans offer a way to manage the transition costs that otherwise swamp efforts to abandon unaffordable pay-as-you-go old-age retirement systems. They ensure that today's workers will not be burdened with paying for today's retirees, at an increasingly steep cost. Instead, the risk is shifted to the retirees themselves, who, after all, can choose, by the number of years they work, the size of the pension they will receive. The IRA add-ons also allow workers to obtain some of the advantages of the higher rates of return available in the stock and bond markets while remaining within the safety of a large government retirement program.

To critics, however, notional defined-contribution programs do not escape some of the worst effects of pay-as-you go programs. They only add additional risk to them. The pay-as-you-go system that hums underneath the new program maintains the relatively low rate of return that one generally finds in such systems. And it also maintains the intergenerational transfer that characterizes these systems. Today's workers must pay set defined contributions to provide for today's retirees, but in fact when they retire they will receive relatively smaller pensions than today's retirees due to the operations of the life expectancy divisor and the automatic balance mechanism. In other words, the shift of money from today's workers to current pensioners continues. But in addition, today's workers have also taken on more risk. Indeed, a notional defined-contribution plan is a way of shifting risk from the government to the workforce. The government escapes unaffordable pension claims by automatically reducing benefits when necessary. However, the burden of the reduced benefits rests entirely on those either living on pensions or planning for them. They must make up the difference out of their own savings, if they have any. The government projects that, by 2055, retirement benefits will have been cut by 18 percent (Settergren 2005, 49). Sweden argues that the generosity of the Swedish retirement, combined with the fact that almost all Swedes have a second private pension, makes this justifiable. The government also notes that this cut amounts to slightly more than two years of work. A delay in retirement of that length is all that is necessary to bring benefits back to today's level.

Americans must face the fact that U.S. retirees receive much less than their Swedish counterparts, and far fewer U.S. workers than Swedish workers have private pensions to supplement Social Security. The *average* American Social Security benefit is not all that different from the *minimum* that a Swede receives from the means-tested program available to those with little or no lifetime earnings. Even after the anticipated cuts, a Swede will receive a government pension valued at about 55 percent of his or her earnings, whereas an American's Social Security benefit will only be about 40 percent of his or her earnings.. For this reason, the benefit cuts entailed in a U.S. notional defined-contribution plan might have a far greater impact than the cuts that will occur in Sweden. (Another Swedish reform might cause some hackles to be raised in the United States, too, though it is not connected to notional defined contributions. Sweden has ended its survivor's benefits on grounds of gender equality. Everyone, it is thought, has the right to enter the workforce and earn his or her own pension; therefore, Sweden gives a surviving spouse a one-year adjustment to meet his or her new situation.)

Sweden is one of the few industrialized nations to successfully climb out from under its pension obligations. Its method of doing so has yet to attract many adherents in the United States, but many other nations are closely examining it. For a system as intimately tied to pay-as-you-go financing as is Social Security, is Sweden's approach the best way to salvage the U.S. old-age system?

The United Kingdom: Voluntary Carve-Outs?

Many proposals to reform U.S. Social Security, including that offered by President George W. Bush in 2005, involve giving workers the option to move a portion of their contributions into their own personal accounts. At retirement, they would draw on these accounts for their income, along with a smaller traditional Social Security benefit. Plans of this type are called voluntary carve-outs because they remove a portion of the contributions that were going into the old Social Security system. (Carve-outs can be contrasted with voluntary add-ons, where workers are given the option to make additional contributions into their own personal accounts. One example of this is the German Riester Pensions.) Only one nation has much experience with voluntary carve-outs: the United Kingdom. How has that reform worked out?

The United Kingdom has perhaps the most complicated old-age pension program in the world. On top of that, it is perhaps the most frequently changed old-age pension program in the world. More than a dozen major reforms have been made over the past two decades, with the last, made in 2007, yet to be implemented. Here the discussion focuses on the main details; there are many complications and regulations that will not be considered.

The United Kingdom's current old-age system really dates from the years after World War II. It is based on very different conceptions than those that animated the U.S. program. In 1946, following an influential report by William Beveridge, the United Kingdom developed a comprehensive cradle-to-the-grave social welfare system. It includes national health insurance, unemployment benefits, and old-age pensions, among other programs. The entire program is funded by one tax, called the National Insurance Contribution (NIC). This tax is paid both by the worker and the employer according to a complicated formula. A key principle of the system is equality: everyone should receive the same benefits. Thus the old-age program that was created, the Basic State Pension (BSP), is not earnings based. It is a flat-rate pension that is determined simply by how many years one has worked. To get a full pension, the retiree needs to have spent 44 years in the workforce. A recent reform will reduce that number to 30 years. (The British retirement age is 65 for men, 60 for women, although the latter is being raised to 65 as well.) As in most European systems, one can get credit for years spent engaged in child care, on disability, or if unemployed. The flip side of this universal, egalitarian pension is that it is rather small. It was conceived as offering a minimal pension on which a retiree could live. Anything above that would come from other pensions or from the worker's savings. In 2007, the full Basic State Pension amounted to £4,540 a year. This pension was originally indexed by wages, reindexed to prices during the 1980s, and now slated to be returned to wage indexation again.

The relatively small size of this pension produced political pressure to increase it. In 1959, the United Kingdom thus added a second pension program on top of the BSP that paid benefits according to lifetime earnings. This program has borne several names. It was substantially expanded in 1975 and titled the State-Earnings-Related-Pension-Scheme (SERPS). SERPS initially paid a benefit equal to 25 percent of a worker's best 20 years of NIC-taxed earnings. This benefit was reduced to 20 percent in 1986. In 2002, the State Second Pension Scheme (S2P) in turn replaced the SERPS. The S2P is weighted to provide relatively larger benefits to lower-income earners than did the SERPS, so it has a more complicated benefits formula. A significant limitation of this second pension is that it is not open to workers who are self-employed. Currently, the minimum pension that a qualifying retiree can obtain from the State Second Pension is about £3,120 a year. A high-income worker will receive close to double that amount. All this too will change again in a few years because recent legislation will impose yet another formula on the S2P that will make it, by the year 2030, a flat-rate pension, just like the Basic State Pension. After that, British workers will be receiving two flat-rate pensions, one stacked on top of the other. Each pension will pay about the same, so qualifying retirees will get a total pension of at least about £7,300 in 2007 dollars.

That is, however, if the worker elects to stay in the S2P. For here is where the innovation lies. The United Kingdom has created the option to "contract out" of the second pension program. Before describing this, the third leg of the British old-age pension system is discussed. The United Kingdom has a "pension credit" program for workers with very low incomes or who do not qualify for either of the state pensions. It includes a guaranteed minimum pension that is indexed to earnings (the Minimum Income Guarantee), and a "savings credit" through which low-income workers receive benefits on a sliding scale that takes account of their prebenefit income. The pension credit produces pension benefits similar to the low end of a pension drawn from the BSP and the S2P.

By the time a current worker retires, he or she has lived under, and made contributions to, several different pension programs. The government has an incredibly complex set of formulas to calculate how much one will get from each pension program. It is this constant churning of pension programs that has, perhaps ironically, made it easier for the United Kingdom to make large changes in its old-age pension system. For there is little political loyalty to any one pension program. After all, any one of them has only been around for a few years. Moreover, neither workers nor retirees can identify how much of their benefits are coming from which program. Unlike the U.S. Social Security system, nothing about the British system is politically, economically, or morally entrenched.

This ease of reform lay behind the United Kingdom's development of a voluntary carve-out to its second pension program. When Margaret Thatcher, the British prime minister in the 1980s, decided to reform her country's old-age system, she was able to take radical measures that U.S. reformers could only dream of (or have nightmares about). It was she who simply cut the SERPS benefit from 25 percent to 20 percent of taxed income. She was also the one who changed the BSP from being indexed to wages to being indexed to prices. Her most daring reform, though, was to encourage British workers to simply opt out of the SERPS plan altogether. When the second British pension was created, it was thought to be primarily a supplementary program for those without other retirement pensions. So the initial program allowed workers who already had an occupational pension to contract out of the new government pension. If they did, both they and their employers were given a rebate on their National Insurance Contributions.

In 1986, Prime Minister Thatcher moved to reward workers who opted out of SERPS by giving them a substantially larger NIC rebate if they did so. Workers were also allowed to move their pensions from an occupational pension plan—with typical British complexity, there are six types—into a "personal pension scheme" sold by a financial services company. One estimate is that the rebate given to workers after this reform was twice as large as the savings the government could expect to generate through the carve-out (Budd and Campbell 1998).

The SERPS program was only eight years old when these changes were made, revealing one key limitation on any U.S. attempt to follow the British example: after only eight years, the amount of contributions paid into the program, and the liabilities accrued, were still modest. As a result, the transition costs were not great. It would be a far different situation if Social Security tried to emulate this reform. Moreover, the United Kingdom handled much of its small transitions costs via the benefit cuts made by the Thatcher government.

As it turned out, millions of British workers eligible for SERPS, and later the S2P, contracted out of the program. Literally tens of thousands of private and occupational pension funds were developed by employers and the financial services industry to cater to them. However, a series of difficulties led the government to substantially reduce the choices offered workers and to significantly increase the regulation of the private pension industry.

The most serious problem involved the marketing practices of some financial service companies and the financial soundness of many of the private pension funds. The financial service industry rapidly developed many pension products and, of course, attempted to sell them to the public. Agents convinced many British workers to drop their old occupational plans in favor of a new personal pension scheme. However, bad advice was often given. Many workers were encouraged to leave their old retirement pensions and buy into replacements that would pay much lower benefits. This practice, which came to be called "mis-selling," ended in a scandal and a government order that the financial services industry pay some £13 billion in damages to harmed workers and retirees. Personal pension schemes also proved to have quite high administrative fees and charges, not infrequently five times more than that of the occupational pensions. Another government reform has capped private pension fees at 1.5 percent, but this is still much higher than the cost of government or occupational pension alternatives.

Among the large number of pensions offered, many proved not to be financially sound. Some 85,000 British workers have lost their pension contributions due to private pension plan failures (BBC News 2006). Because employers were not required to match worker contributions, many of the new occupational pension funds were also underfunded. They are pension shells that did little more than meet formal requirements. These funding issues produced a second scandal, addressed by the Pensions Act of 2004. This law increased regulation of occupational and private pensions and created the Pension Protection Fund to insure workers against their losses if their private pension plan fails.

Nevertheless, the funding of the personal pension schemes still remains a problem. In 10 years' time, less than half of the schemes will still be receiving contributions from their owners. In fact, more than a third of these plans have lapsed altogether, and this number is growing. Also, both workers and employers have responded to the opportunity to opt out in other ways that are likely to harm their future pensions. Employers saw the opportunity to move from defined-benefit plans, the mainstay before 1986, to defined-contribution plans. The latter are easier for companies to fund, but they impose additional uncertainty on workers preparing for their retirement and may offer lower benefits as well. Some workers have taken the rational but chaotic strategy of contracting out of the SERPS or S2P but then coming back in when reaching their highest earning years. Other workers simply could not figure out which of their many alternatives was their best choice.

In short, this voluntary carve-out experienced a very rocky start. So rocky, in fact, that the United Kingdom is all but ending the experiment. Upon taking power from the Conservatives in 1997, Tony Blair and his Labour Party took a series of steps to reimpose sharp limitations on the ability of British workers to contract out from their government pension program. After the S2P was created to replace the SERPS, a "stakeholder pension scheme" was first developed to offer far more regulated private pension plans than the existing personal pension schemes. Then in 2007, a final Pensions Bill was enacted that will end both stakeholder *and* personal pension schemes. Only defined-benefit employer pensions will now be allowed to contract out of the system. Everyone else must remain in what will become, as discussed above, a flat-rate pension program. Personal voluntary carve-out plans also will all but disappear. (The Labour government has also moved to return the program to one indexed to wages, not prices. This action, too, may also hold lessons for the United States.)

The British government has instead turned in a different direction. Following the recommendations of a national pensions commission, it now intends to offer not a carve-out but an add-on pension program. It has established a commission to develop such a program by 2012. Workers will contribute 4 percent of their NIC-taxed earnings, employers will contribute an amount equal to 3 percent of a worker's earnings, and the British government will add the equivalent of 1 percent of earnings in the form of a tax credit to this as yet unnamed plan. These contributions will be on top of the existing NIC tax. Workers will be automatically enrolled in this program, though they may opt out. If they do opt out, they are re-enrolled every three years. In other words, a worker must continue to express a desire not to be in the program. Within the program, workers will be able to choose from a small number of selected, regulated pension funds. It is not yet clear whether these funds will be private or government managed. The British government believes that the combination of the flat-rate Basic State Pension, this add-on plan, and existing employer pensions will produce a total retirement that is sufficiently generous while also financially sustainable (Department of Work and Pensions 2006, 41). Because the program is yet to be implemented, it is impossible to know if it will really succeed in accomplishing this goal.

What, then, is the lesson for voluntary carve-outs? Because of the problems discussed above, many organizations, including the Trades Union Congress, the United Kingdom's major labor union, had already been recommending to all workers that they not contract out of the SERPS/S2P. The number who did choose to leave began falling in the early 1990s. But perhaps the most significant measure of how little popularity the carve-outs had developed is the fact that, during the Parliamentary debates of 2007, no political party opposed the proposal to get rid of them.

Should it thus be concluded that voluntary carve-outs do not work? Against the criticisms raised above, some experts retort that the British experience does not prove this at all; it only provides a lesson of how not to implement them. A virtually unregulated carve-out program was bound to cause problems. There were too many choices, and there was too little oversight of them. The carve-outs were placed within an almost ludicrously complicated pension system. Voluntary carve-outs can and should be much simpler to understand and execute. Finally, some British pension experts have claimed that the greater financial knowledge of most Americans makes the United States better suited for a system of private retirement plans than is the United Kingdom. So whether the United Kingdom provides proof that partial privatization of government pensions does not work or just serves as a model for how not to do it remains in dispute. President Bush's 2005 initiative demonstrates that the idea, at least, is alive and well. Nevertheless, whatever position one takes, the past two decades of the British schemes of voluntary carve-outs does offer critical information about how this type of reform actually might work and what must be done if an administration wants to implement this sort of reform most effectively.

Chile: Privatization?

The most audacious, and controversial, way of reforming U.S. Social Security is simply to get rid of the program. Carve-out *all* of Social Security, if you will. This means making workers responsible for their own retirement. They have to save the money, in their own accounts, that they will need during their retirement. Most of those who favor this sort of reform continue to see the government as useful for setting guidelines and regulating how these accounts should operate, but beyond that, it should let the private sector take over. Supporters of this approach often cite the case of Chile, the first country to try such a plan. The "Chilean model" has spread to other countries in Latin America. What is this model, and how has it performed?

Prior to its current model, Chile had a standard pay-as-you-go retirement system. It was, in fact, directly based on the German program. But the system experienced a crisis in the 1970s.

The program became insolvent. Generous benefits, a worsening dependency ratio, and financial mismanagement were the main culprits. Chile had no reserve fund left, and it had to pay more benefits than it received in contributions. The government needed to pay more than a quarter of all the benefits owed out of the nation's general tax revenues. This system simply could not be sustained. A larger political crisis intervened when a military coup ousted the country's president, Salvador Allende, in 1973. The new government, led by General Augusto Pinochet, believed that restoring Chile's fiscal soundness was essential, at whatever cost. As a military dictatorship, Chile's government had certain obvious advantages in its ability to eliminate its unaffordable old program and to replace it with one that would meet the test of soundness.

The Pinochet government drew on the work of Milton Friedman, a Nobel Prize–winning economist, who argued that retirement was a personal, not a governmental, responsibility. Each individual knows her or his retirement needs better than does anyone else, including the government. Therefore, it is that individual who should make the necessary choices, not the government. The best way to help that individual is to create the legal environment to protect and support each worker's retirement savings, and then get out of the way.

This is what Chile proceeded to do. It began preparing for an end to its pay-as-you-go system in the late 1970s by cutting government spending so as to produce the large budget surpluses that would be needed to fund the transition from the old program. That achieved, in 1981, the government announced that it was closing the old program. Workers in the program could stay in, with reduced benefits, or they could move into the new program and receive government bonds, called "recognition bonds," that contained a portion of the assets of the old system. The bonds cannot be cashed until the date of retirement, but they are guaranteed to grow each year at a rate of 4 percent. New workers were not given a choice. They had to join the new system.

This new system is quite simple. Workers are required to pay 10 percent of their income into a state-approved retirement account. (If one includes the requirement to contribute to a disability program and to a survivor's pension fund, this number grows to 12.5 to 13 percent.) Because employers are no longer required to make contributions, the Chilean government passed legislation that mandated they raise the salaries of their workers who had joined the new system by the amount of their old employer contributions. This operated as a further incentive to get workers to switch into it. Today only about one in seven workers remains in the old system.

This contribution of 10 percent of earnings is placed into an individual retirement account that is managed by a private financial company approved by the government. These companies are called AFPs (*administradora de fandos de pensiones*). A company must meet a number of requirements that concern size and financial solvency, among other factors. The number of companies that seek to be AFPs has varied over the years. Currently, a worker can choose from six AFPs. Each AFP offers five funds, with each of the funds having a different level of risk. The government, through its Superintendent of Pension Fund Management, has firmly regulated what investments can be held in each of these five funds. For example, the "safest" fund holds no stocks, while the most risky fund is allowed to hold a significant percentage of its portfolio in stocks, as well in foreign assets. Since the 1980s, the government has gradually relaxed its rules on risk. In the program's first years, no stocks at all were allowed in any AFP fund. The theory behind having multiple AFPs is that they will compete with one another for the workers' accounts.

Unlike a defined-benefit plan, the AFPs cannot guarantee the size of future pensions; this will depend upon how skillfully the company has invested and how the market has fared during a worker's years of contributions. But the government still commands that AFPs return to the worker a stipulated minimum pension at the time of retirement. The AFP must draw from its own financial resources, if necessary, to meet this criterion. If the company cannot do so, for whatever reason, the government steps in and provides the resources. AFPs must also offer fairly stable rates of return. For any given year, the deviation from the average annual growth rate of an AFP fund cannot exceed either 2 percentage points or one-half of that average growth rate, whichever is the greater number. If an AFP fund grows faster than this rate, the company is obligated to put the extra money into a special reserve fund that will be used should the deviation ever be lower than that allowed. All of these regulations are intended to maximize the security and stability of the private funds into which Chilean workers will place their retirement savings.

The Superintendent of Pension Fund Management provides additional financial support for low-income workers. Originally, there was a "minimum pension guarantee" set at 27 percent of the average earnings of a worker with 20 or more years of employment. However, in 2008, a new two-tier plan replaces this guarantee. All Chilean workers, upon retirement, now receive a "basic solidarity pension." Currently, the basic solidarity pension is set at about $111 a month. (Because of a history of high inflation, Chile uses a basket of international currencies, not its peso, to denominate much of its pension system.) Then, retirees with small individual retirement accounts have their accounts "topped off" by the Chilean government until they also reach $111. In other words, the effective minimum Chilean pension is really $222 per month. This money will come from Chile's general revenues, an interesting deviation from the principle of privatization.

At the date that workers retire, they have three options for how to collect their pensions. First, they may buy an annuity from a life insurance company, using the money in their individual pension account. The annuity, which is government insured, will pay an annual benefit for the rest of their lives. However, retirees will not be able to deed any of their annuity to their heirs. Second, a retiree can choose to take programmed withdrawals from his or her existing pension fund. In this case, the Chilean government has calculated a withdrawal formula based on mortality rates and expected interest rates. The retiree can withdraw the amount each year that is stipulated by the formula. If money remains at the time of death, it goes to the heirs. The trade-off is that it is possible, if retirees are long lived, that their pension will be exhausted and they might run out of money before they die. Because of this worry, most retirees currently choose the annuity. However, a third plan, which combines the ability to leave one's money to one's estate with annuity-type guarantee that one cannot outlive the pension, has recently been developed.

Chile anticipated that its new plan would provide a generous retirement if its average individual retirement account could return 5 percent a year. In this case, someone who had worked for 40 years could expect to receive an annual pension valued at 60 percent of his or her final average wage. If these accounts could achieve a return of 10 percent, the annual pension would grow to 85 percent of the average wage. Relative to the average wages of Chile and the United States, both scenarios in Chile's pension program yield substantially larger pensions than does U.S. Social Security. Thus far, Chilean accounts have performed better than expected. The rate of return has exceeded 10 percent since the start of the program (Tamborini 2007, 14). This outcome is the genesis of the argument supporting a similar program for the United States. In addition to the solid financial performance of the Chilean system, supporters also point to the freedom of choice it allows Chilean workers and to real benefits the program has brought to the country's economy. The national savings rate has grown rapidly since the inauguration of the program. This trend is thought to have contributed to the many years of strong overall economic growth that the nation has experienced. And Chile never need worry about its government pension program again becoming insolvent or becoming a huge burden upon government finances.

So what are the negative aspects of such a system? While opponents have focused on inequalities produced by the program (e.g. Sinha 2002), in fact the largest problem, should the United States choose to move in this direction, is the cost. Unlike Chile, the United States has been running deep budget deficits. Recall that Chile had to sustain years of surpluses to pay for the costs of transitioning to the new program. (In fact, Chile is now using its surpluses to create a pension reserve fund from which it will pay for its basic solidarity pensions and for its topping up of worker pensions that fall below the minimum.) But Chile still must pay transition costs for as long as a single retiree is left in its old system, and that transition is estimated to take another 40 years. If the transition cost for the United States is similar to that of Chile's, at its peak the cost would be more than $600 billion a year. This amount is approaching half of the size of all the annual revenues gained through the personal income tax in the United States. One has to ask whether the United States could ever assemble the money it would need for such a transition.

Transition costs may be the biggest practical barrier, but most opposition turns on the more politically charged questions of the risk and fairness of privatization. So far, the Chilean program has turned in very good numbers. But were the decades of the 1980s and 1990s typical or unusual? The excellent financial returns of those years were in fact what made the Chilean program successful. If the program had been launched in a less favorable investment era, it might very well have failed. Critics charge that one cannot presume that the next decades will match the rates of return seen recently and that it is very risky to assume that they will.

Most independent observers agree that the new Chilean program has worked well for those with steady, stable jobs. They have been able to regularly accumulate enough funds for a good retirement. Those who cannot enter the program (currently the self-employed) or who do not work regularly, though, have more difficulty accumulating funds. Fifteen years into its life, half of Chile's workers had accumulated less than $1,500 in their plans (Shah 1997, 9). Why? The average Chilean worker actually contributes to a retirement fund during only 21 years of her or his career. This shortened contribution period occurs for a variety of reasons, including years of self-employment and years out of the workforce, as well as time spent working in the "informal" economy or otherwise avoiding having to make the required contributions. As a result, this average worker will wind up with benefit amounts below those offered by Chile's soon-to-be-ended minimum pension program. Whether these same problems would affect the United States would depend upon the percentage of workers brought into the system and the course of the typical American work career. A program that provides a guaranteed minimum income that many workers will not reach on their own could become surprisingly expensive for the government.

Another argument concerns the expense of the Chilean program. Critics charge that it is far too expensive. Its administrative costs are more than double those of the U.S. Social Security program. Pension fund fees strip away a quarter of the accumulation of Chilean workers. Because the fees are charged on contributions, not accounts, they are especially burdensome for newer contributors. The AFPs have been charging 10 to 15 percent of the initial contributions as fund fees and charges (Soto 2005, 5). These fees appear to many observers to be excessive. They have reduced the true rate of return that a worker actually sees by nearly 40 percent. Supporters retort that this fee structure is not much different from that used by U.S financial firms for U.S individual retirement accounts. A Chilean worker who has been employed for 40 years will actually end up paying less than 1 percent of his or her assets in fees. Furthermore, the Chilean government has taken steps to reduce the fees. It has banned flat-rate fees altogether, and it will soon begin automatically placing the accounts of new workers in the AFP with the lowest fees to encourage price competition. It has also moved to expand the pool of AFPs.

Banks, in particular, are now encouraged to enter this market. Calculating the cost of a pension program is quite technical and a little obscure, but it is of great importance, as even small differences in expenses will, over the decades, make a very large difference in the size of a pension someone will receive.

A final argument over the value of Chile's program is simply whether the average worker is financially savvy enough to succeed in the program. The Chilean president, Michelle Bachelet, has worried that he or she is not (Pension Research Council 2006, 3). Choosing a fund is the easy part. Understanding the financial effects of when one enters and leaves the workforce, how often one contributes, and how one interprets an annual rate of return takes a lot more sophistication. Perhaps U.S. workers have more experience with financial information (most Chilean workers never even read their fund statements) and are less likely to make bad choices. Perhaps not. There is much debate surrounding this issue.

Chile's program is certainly the most drastic reform yet undertaken of a major government pension program. Since it is more than two decades old, it cannot be claimed that nothing is known about how the system will perform. President Bachelet has continued to back the new system, and it is proving popular elsewhere in Latin America. But clearly many questions remain to be settled. The least that can be said is that this reform would be one of the greatest magnitude should the United States try to emulate it.

Too Many Alternatives?

The world holds a wide variety of public pension programs. There is certainly no lack of models for any country wishing to reform its own program. This discussion has considered only six countries; more than a dozen others, including Japan, France, Mexico, and several in Eastern Europe and South America, have undertaken significant reforms of their retirement programs in recent years. Perhaps this fact reinforces a point made in chapter 2: It is not that the United States has no options for reforming Social Security. Rather, it is that the number that are available is bewildering.

Beginning in the 1980s, most of the world experienced the same problems as those that afflict the U.S. program. Increasing life expectancy, a decreasing ratio of workers to retirees, and indexed benefits that grow relentlessly combine to put most retirement programs in jeopardy. As discussed above, different countries took very different paths to reform. Most of these reforms are quite recent, and it is still perhaps too early to judge the results, a fact that makes it even more difficult to determine in which direction the United States should go. But what conclusions, if any, can be drawn from the experiences of these other countries?

The first obvious point is that every reform has imposed costs upon some sector of society. Most of the difficulty of reforming pension programs is not technical; it is political. Who should pay the costs? Current workers, as in Canada, those receiving benefits, as in Germany, or wealthier individuals, as in Australia? A second point is that risk is the hallmark of any pension system. A huge element in how one views the various reforms discussed here is how one approaches the question of risk. How much is acceptable, and upon which elements of society is the risk best placed? Should the risk be borne by everyone in the system, as in Sweden, or by the individual worker, as in Chile? A third point is that the biggest difficulty that most of these nations has had to face is how to pay for the transition costs of moving from their old systems to their new ones. In many cases it was public money that made this transition possible. For the United States, too, this is likely to be the biggest practical obstacle to reform. Abandoning pay-as-you-go systems turns out to be rather difficult. The only completely successful effort took place in Chile, under a military dictatorship.

Comparing reforms across nations reveals the good news that saving Social Security is certainly possible. There are many paths. But such an exercise also demonstrates the difficult nature of taking any one of these paths. No model stands out as completely and clearly superior to any other. All those with a stake in the future of America's Social Security program should analyze each reform carefully and watch closely their successes, and their difficulties, in the years ahead.

References

Börsch-Supan, Axel. 2005. "Mind the Gap: The Effectiveness of Incentives to Boost Retirement Saving in Europe." *OECD Economic Studies.* 39:111-143 www.oecd.org/dataoecd/18/60/35664007.pdf.

Börsch-Supan, Axel, and Christina B. Wilke. 2006. "The German Public Pension System: How It Will Become an NDC System Look-Alike." In *Pension Reform: Issues and Prospects for Non-Defined Financial Contribution Schemes,* ed. Robert Holtzman and Edward Palmer, 573-610. Washington: The World Bank

BBC News (British Broadcasting Company). 2006. Q & A: Ombudsmen's Pension Report. (March 14). http://news.bbc.co.uk/1/hi/business/4764098.stm.

Budd, Alan, and Nigel Campbell. 1998. The Roles of the Public and Private Sectors in the U.K. Pension System. In *Privatizing Social Security,* ed. Martin Feldstein. Chicago: University of Chicago Press.

Canadian Pension Plan Investment Board. 2007. *2007 Annual Report.* http://www.cppib.ca/.

Capretta, James C. 2007. *Global Aging and the Sustainability of Public Pension Systems: An Assessment of Reform Efforts in Twelve Developed Countries.* Washington: Center for Strategic and International Studies. (January). http://csis.org/gai.

Capretta, James C. 2006. *Building Automatic Solvency into U.S. Social Security: Insights from Sweden and Germany.* Policy Brief #151 (March). Washington: The Brookings Institution.

Congressional Budget Office. United States Congress.1999. *Social Security Privatization: Experiences Abroad.* Washington: CBO. http://www.cbo.gov/ftpdoc.cfm?index=1065&type=0.

Department of Work and Pensions (United Kingdom). 2006. *Personal Accounts: A New Way to Save.* Presented to Parliament by the Secretary of State for Work and Pensions (December). http://www.dwp.gov.uk/pensionsreform/pdfs/PA_PersonalAccountsFull.pdf.

Korczyk, Sophie M. 2003. *Women and Individual Social Security Accounts in Chile, Australia, and the United Kingdom.* Washington: AARP. http://assets.aarp.org/rgcenter/econ/2003_09_wmnss.pdf.

Kotlikoff, Laurence J. 2002. Comments on Edward Palmer, "Swedish Pension Reform: Its Past and Its Future." In Martin Feldstein and Horst Siebert, eds. *Social Security Pension Reform in Europe.* Chicago: University of Chicago Press.

Mitchell, Daniel J., and Robert P. O'Quinn. 1997. "Australia's Privatized Retirement System: Lessons for the United States." *Backgrounder,* 1149. Washington: The Heritage Foundation (December 8). http://www.heritage.org/research/socialsecurity/.

Office of the Chief Actuary (Canada). 2007. *Optimal Funding of the Canada Pension Plan.* Ottawa: Office of the Superintendent of Financial Institutions. (April)

Pension Research Council. 2006. *Lesson from Pension Reform in the Americas*. Pension Research Council Working Paper 2006-8. Philadelphia: Pension Research Council, The Wharton School, University of Pennsylvania.

Rothman, George P. 1998. Projections of Key Aggregates for Australia's Aged—Government Outlays, Financial Assets, and Incomes. Paper Presented at the Sixth Colloquium of Superannuation Researchers, July 1998, in Melbourne, Australia. http://rim.treasury.gov.au/content /CP98_2.asp.

Settergren, Ole, ed. 2005. *The Swedish Pension System Annual Report, 2005*. Stockholm: Swedish Social Insurance Agency. http://www.fk.se/filer /publikationer/pdf/par05-e.pdf.

Shah, Hemant. 1997. *Towards Better Regulation of Private Pension Funds*. Policy Research Working Paper No. 1791, World Bank. http://www .worldbank.org/html/dec/Publications/Workpapers/WPS1700series /wps1791/wps1791.pdf.

Sinha, Tapen. 2002. "Can Latin American Experience Teach Us Something About Privatized Pensions with Individual Accounts?" *Retirement Implications of Demographic and Family Change Symposium Monograph*. Schaumburg IL: Society of Actuaries. http://ssrn.com/abstract=390720.

Soto, Mauricio. 2005. *Chilean Pension Reform: The Good, the Bad, and the In Between*. Issue Brief #31 (June). Boston: Center for Retirement Research, Boston College.

Tamborini, Christopher. 2007. *Social Security: The Chilean Approach to Retirement*. CRS Report to Congress (May 17). Washington: United States Congress, Congressional Research Service.

4

Chronology

This chronology indicates the dates of significant events in the history of the U.S. Social Security program. It also provides the dates of the major reforms and innovations that have occurred elsewhere among the world's many government pension systems. These reforms and innovations may be of interest to those who wish to know more about the options available to the United States.

U.S. Chronology

1890   The Disability Pension Act of 1890 (also called the Dependency Pension Act) becomes law. The United States will now pay every Union Civil War veteran over the age of 62 a monthly pension. The act breaks the link between having suffered a disability during the war and receiving a pension. All veterans are eligible. Pensions are also given to widows of veterans. This is America's first large-scale government pension program. Two-thirds of the nonimmigrant males in the North who are over the age of 65 will draw pensions under this program, roughly the same percentage as under the German program.

1909   The first old-age pension bill is introduced in the U.S. Congress. It does not pass.

1914   Arizona becomes the first state to pass an old-age pension law. The law is declared unconstitutional by the Arizona Supreme Court in 1916.

1915   The territory of Alaska enacts a limited old-age pension program. It is not challenged in court. This is the first public pension program in the United States.

1929   The Great Depression begins. Unparalleled unemployment and financial distress lead to calls for new U.S. programs to remedy old-age poverty.

1932   Franklin Delano Roosevelt is elected president. Roosevelt is the first president to support an old-age pension program and becomes the key actor in the development and passage of such a program in the United States. He appoints Arthur Altmeyer, a Wisconsin academic and administrator, to be assistant secretary of labor. Altmeyer goes on to become the commissioner of the Social Security Board.

1933   Francis Townsend, a retired doctor in Long Beach, California, publishes his Townsend Old-Age Revolving Pension Plan. The plan, which offers a pension to every retired American over age 60, provided that the pension is spent within a month, is to be funded by a national sales tax. Within months, thousands of Townsend clubs are organized around the United States to pressure for the Townsend Plan's adoption.

1935   Senator Huey Long (D-La.) delivers a speech in which he offers a plan to "share the wealth." The plan includes a guaranteed pension for all retired Americans, to be financed by greater taxation on the wealthy.

The Social Security Act of 1935 is signed into law. This massive bill includes unemployment insurance and income assistance programs for the aged, the blind, the disabled, and poor mothers and their children, as well an old-age pension plan. The pension plan, which later becomes known simply as "Social Security," is a fully funded program based on equal employer and worker contributions and pays monthly benefits based on the worker's average earnings. The retirement age is set at 65.

1936   The Social Security Administration issues the first Social Security number.

1937   By a vote of 7–2, the Supreme Court rules that the U.S. Social Security program is constitutional.

1939   The United States enacts the Social Security amendments of 1939. These amendments significantly increase the number of eligible workers and increase both benefit and contribution levels. Benefits will now also be provided to the survivors of a deceased worker. Significantly, following the Swedish example, the program is shifted to pay-as-you-go financing.

1940   Ida M. Fuller, of Ludlow, Vermont, receives the first monthly benefit paid under the U.S. Social Security program. Her check is for $22.54.

1944   One million Americans are receiving benefits under Social Security.

1945   President Harry S Truman proposes adding a comprehensive medical insurance plan to the Social Security system. Congress does not act on his proposal.

1950   The Social Security Amendments of 1950 again significantly expand the U.S. Social Security system by liberalizing eligibility and adding more than 10 million workers to the program. The amendments also include a large increase in benefits.

1954   The U.S. Social Security program is extended to the self-employed in specified professions, most importantly including farmers, and, on a voluntary basis, to members of state and local government.

1956   The Social Security Amendments of 1956 add a program for disabled workers between the ages of 50 and 64, with its own trust fund. Children of eligible workers who become disabled before the age of 18 are also included in the program.

1961   Male workers are allowed to opt for early retirement, at age 62. Workers who elect early retirement will, however, receive lower monthly Social Security benefits. (Most women had gained this right in 1956.)

1965   Medicare and Medicaid are added to the Social Security Act. Medicare is given its own trust fund, from which it will pay most hospital-related medical expenses for all Americans over the age of 65. Medicaid is established to pay for the medical care of those with low incomes. These programs are administered separately from the old-age pension program but are financed by a portion of the Federal Insurance Contributions Act (FICA) tax that also supports Social Security.

U.S. Social Security benefits are extended to divorced wives.

1968   The Social Security Amendments of 1967 begin a series of double-digit annual increases in pension benefits under the U.S. Social Security program.

1972   The United States increases Social Security benefits by 20 percent but also changes the system of future benefit increases. Instead of congressional vote, the Consumer Price Index (CPI) will be used to adjust future benefit levels. Pensions are linked to the CPI and will be increased each January in line with the rise of that index. This increase is called a cost-of-living adjustment (COLA).

1974   Congress passes the Employee Retirement Income Security Act. This act creates tax-deductible "individual retirement accounts" [called IRAs or 401(k)s] that workers may utilize to save for their retirement needs. The funds accrued through IRAs will provide retirement income in addition to that received under Social Security.

1981   Because of the rapid deterioration of the Social Security Trust Fund, President Ronald Reagan establishes the bipartisan National Commission on Social Security Reform. The commission is headed by the future chair of the Federal Reserve Board, Alan Greenspan.

1983   Following the report of the Greenspan committee and faced with the looming exhaustion of the Social Security Trust Fund, the United States revises the Social Security system. The United States raises the retirement age, increases the FICA tax, and taxes some Social Security benefits, along with a series of smaller reforms.

1986   U.S. federal government workers hired after 1983 are brought into the Social Security system.

1994   The Social Security Advisory Board is created to replace the program's Advisory Council, which had periodically met in previous years.

1995   The shutdown of the U.S. government, following a budget impasse, briefly stops the issuance of Social Security checks.

1997   The last Advisory Council on Social Security issues its final report. It offers three different options for bolstering the Social Security program, but there is no unanimous agreement for any of them.

1998   In his State of the Union Address, President Bill Clinton exhorts the United States not to spend any of its expected budget surplus before it is able to "save Social Security."

          The National Commission on Retirement Policy, sponsored by the Center for Strategic and International Studies, issues its report. It recommends raising the retirement age to 70, ending the retirement earnings test, and placing a portion of the FICA tax into IRAs. A bill to enact these reforms is offered in Congress but is not voted upon.

1999   President Clinton calls for voluntary "universal savings accounts" (USA accounts). Each American worker would contribute an additional contribution above the current FICA tax into an IRA. The government would guarantee a small contribution for lower-income workers and would match contributions for those with middle incomes. At retirement, income from the USA accounts would supplement Social Security. Congress does not act on this plan.

2000   Congress passes the Senior Citizens Freedom to Work Act, the last major change to Social Security as of the time of this book's publication. The act ends the earnings test for workers who retire at age 65 or later. (Previously, the Social Security benefit had been reduced for individuals who continued to remain in the workforce while they drew a Social Security check.)

2001   President George W. Bush establishes a bipartisan study group, the Commission to Strengthen Social Security, to examine possible reforms for the Social Security program which include its partial privatization. The commission offers three different plans to add private accounts to Social Security, but it does not officially endorse any.

2005   In his State of the Union Address, President George W. Bush states that Social Security is "headed for bankruptcy" and calls for partial privatization of the system. He urges the United States to allow workers to place a portion of their FICA tax into an individual account to be invested in stocks and bonds. Their retirement pension would then be composed of the return on their individual account along with a reduced payment from the Social Security Trust Fund. Amidst much controversy, President Bush does not submit specific legislation to Congress, and the proposal is not acted upon.

2007   The Social Security Trustee's Report estimates that the Trust Fund will be exhausted in 2041.

World Chronology

1889   Germany enacts the world's first old-age pension system. Called the Law on Invalidity and Old Age Insurance for Workers, Journeymen and Apprentices, it provides a pension for all German workers, regardless of their income. The program is funded by a combination of government revenues and payroll taxes on workers and their employers.

1908   The United Kingdom enacts the Old Age Pensions Act, a means-tested old-age pension program. The program is supported by general revenues, not worker contributions, and the pension begins at age 70. Benefits are set at a minimal level.

1909   Australia creates the Age Pension, a plan that offers monthly benefits to aged Australians that is paid from the government's general revenues.

1913   Sweden passes the National Pension Act, the world's first universal pension system. All Swedes will receive a basic retirement pension based on the level of their earnings. The program is fully funded from worker contributions. A second supplemental pension, financed by government revenues, is given to those who are permanently disabled.

1925   The United Kingdom enacts the Widows', Orphans and Old Age Contributory Pensions Act of 1925. Promoted by Neville Chamberlain, who would later become prime minister, this act reduces the retirement age to 65 and adds a widow's benefit.

1926   Chile enacts a pension program entitled the Workers Security Fund. The program operates on the same principles as German chancellor Otto von Bismarck's program.

1927   The Canadian government enacts the Old-Age Pension Act, agreeing to pay half of the cost of each

1927
(cont.)

province that participates in the system. All Canadian residents who earn less than $365 a year are eligible.

1935

Sweden becomes the first major country to adopt a pay-as-you-go pension system. The system is based on employer and employee contributions, from which current retirees are given pensions. The level of pensions is substantially increased, and a retired worker no longer need be invalided to receive the supplemental pension.

1942

Japan establishes the Workers Pension System, a fully funded pension program and the precursor to the country's current retirement system.

1943

Mexico enacts its first pension system. Called The Mexican Institute for Social Security, the system requires a minimum number of weeks worked before a pension can be drawn. The pension is based on average earnings and begins at age 65. The system is funded by employer and worker contributions, as well as general revenues. However, it is limited to workers in the mining, transportation, and commerce industries. Other workers are allowed to join on a voluntary basis.

1946

The United Kingdom's new Labour government passes the National Insurance Act, a universal system of retirement pensions for the United Kingdom. The program is jointly funded by government revenues, employer contributions, and worker contributions. Beneficiaries receive pensions based upon years of contribution, regardless of earnings level. The act follows proposals outlined in William Beveridge's influential report that argue for a "cradle to the grave" social welfare system that includes pensions, unemployment insurance, and national health care. Together, the programs ensure a minimum standard of living for all people in the United Kingdom. Many date the birth of the modern "welfare state" to the passage of this act together with its sister Family Allowance Act (1945) and the National Health Care Act (1948).

1952   Canada enacts the Old Age Security (OAS) Act, its first fully national pension program. The program is financed out of the general revenues, not worker or employer contributions. Retirement can begin at age 70 (reduced to 65 in 1965). The size of the basic benefit is determined by how long one has lived in Canada. For those with little or no additional income, there is a supplementary allowance based on marital status and income.

Chile amends its pension program, now titled the Social Insurance Service. The operations of the program differ depending upon the occupational status of the worker.

1954   Japan rebuilds its pension program, creating a two-tiered system. All retirees receive a flat, basic pension and then a second pension that is based on earnings.

1955   The Central Provident Fund is designed in Singapore. This is a compulsory savings account for citizens of Singapore. Workers and their employers must make annual contributions to individual workers' accounts, which are then used to fund workers' retirement. However, the accounts are also used to fund health care and disability insurance. They are later made available for certain other economic activities, such as purchasing a house, in addition to retirement payments. At age 55, an account holder must set aside a portion of the funds in the account for his or her retirement and may take the rest as a lump-sum payment. Similar provident funds are later adopted for the retirement systems of other Southeast Asian nations, such as Indonesia.

1959   The British National Insurance Act is amended to add a second level of contributions and pensions, based upon earnings, to the existing flat-rate system created in 1946. However, employers can opt out of this new system if they offer their own pensions. This program creates the first partial privatization of a Social Security system.

1959
(cont.)
Sweden adds a second earning-related pension benefit, called the Allmän Tillägspension (ATP), to its retirement program.

1966
The Canadian Pension Plan (CPP) comes into force. It is a new retirement and disability pension program based on worker and employer contributions. The resulting benefit is set at 25 percent of "pensionable earnings." (The plan is operated as the Quebec Pension Plan in that province.)

1972
Canada adds a cost-of-living adjustment to its Old Age Security program. A COLA is added to the CPP two years later.

Japan adds a cost-of-living adjustment to its National Pension Law.

Switzerland becomes the first country to add compulsory private accounts to its pension program. This structure is added to its existing pay-as-you-go program. (However, the private accounts are not actually introduced until 1985.)

1975
The United Kingdom passes the Social Security Pensions Act. This act substantially raises pension benefits by adding the State Earnings-Related Pension Scheme (SERPS) and indexes future benefits to the higher of the growth in wages or prices (changed to prices only in 1980). British employers can still opt out of SERPS, keeping the system partially privatized.

1979
Switzerland introduces a new form of indexation that it uses in its calculation formula for both earnings and benefits increases. Called "Swiss indexation," it revalues lifetime earnings and increases annual pension benefits using an index created by taking the average of the increase in the consumer price index and the increase in the wage index. Other countries also adopt this form of indexation.

1981
Chile becomes the first nation to create a fully privatized pension system. The Augusto Pinochet govern-

ment ends contributions to the national system. All new workers must establish retirement accounts with a private pension fund company. Existing workers are encouraged to move their retirement investments to one of these companies as well. Employers no longer make any contributions.

1985   Japan becomes one of the first nations to reduce its overall benefits through changing its benefits calculation formula. It begins to calculate benefits based on 40 years of employment rather than on 25 years, as was previously done.

1986   Australia demands that all employers offer a pension program for their workers. This program is called "superannuation."

Under Prime Minister Margaret Thatcher, the United Kingdom engages in a major overhaul of its pension system. Employers as well as individual employees are allowed to opt out of the SERPS. Workers who opt out must instead place their contributions in a tax-deferred "approved personal pension," a type of IRA. Benefits are cut for those who remain in the old program.

1989   The Berlin Wall is torn down and the countries of Eastern Europe gain their freedom. Most of these countries suffer from poorly constructed, socialist-era pension programs that are financially threatened. As a result, these countries design a series of new pension programs, and countries such as Poland, Slovakia, and Hungary become among the first to adopt the new pension ideas that have been developed in the 1980s and 1990s.

Canada adds a "clawback" provision to the OAS program.

Mexico indexes its pension system to the minimum wage. As the minimum wages increase, pensions increase by the same amount.

1992   Australia creates the Superannuation Guarantee, clos-
             ing loopholes in the superannuation system and
             promising all workers that the government will en-
             sure a pension at least equal to the old state pension
             no matter how their own superannuation fund may
             have fared.

1993   Peru reforms its pension system to offer its workers
             the choice of entering either a traditional pay-as-you-
             go pension program or a Chilean-style system of fully
             privatized personal retirement accounts. The two
             pension programs compete for workers. This variant
             of Chile's privatization system encounters problems
             and must be relaunched in 1995, but it has since been
             adopted by several other countries.

1994   Sweden develops a new pension system composed of
             three pillars: notional defined contributions, individ-
             ual retirement accounts, and a means-tested guaran-
             teed pension.

             Japan passes a law mandating that the country re-
             view the actuarial soundness of its pension program
             every five years. The retirement age is raised to 65 for
             any kind of government pension.

1996   Latvia becomes the first country to adopt a pension
             system based on notional defined accounts. (While it
             is the first, it drew heavily on the debates then occur-
             ring in Sweden for the specifics of its reform.)

1997   Mexico begins major reforms of its pension system.
             The state pension system is replaced by a system of
             private retirement accounts similar to that in Chile.
             However, Mexican workers who contributed to the
             old system are still able to draw benefits from that
             system. All Mexican workers choose a privately run
             pension company to handle their contributions, but
             they must also contribute to a publicly owned hous-
             ing fund that offers a safe, but small, basic pension.

Kazakhstan goes even further than Chile in its efforts to privatize old-age pensions. On January 1, it closes its old pay-as-you-go system and all citizens are required to move into a new system of private individual accounts. Moreover, the government does not offer any guarantees on the rate of returns that will be provided through the new IRAs, nor does it offer a minimum level of benefits. (In 2005, "citizens pensions," a flat-rate payment to all retirees, is added.)

Singapore allows its citizens to place a portion of the money in their accounts within the Central Provident Fund (CPF) into the new Central Provident Investment Scheme. The latter allows for investment of this money into a wider variety of assets (such as stocks or real estate) than simply government bonds, to which the CPF is restricted.

China establishes its Unified Pension System. It remains available to only a modest percentage of Chinese workers and is not yet implemented nationally. Building from its older system, the first pillar is a pay-as-you-go system with employee and employer contributions. The second pillar is individual retirement accounts for each eligible worker, into which the employee and employer contribute. The third pillar is private employer–provided pensions. This system is broadly in line with World Bank recommendations.

1998   Canada reforms the CPP, moving to prefund a substantial portion of the Canadian retirement system. It does this through greatly increasing the payroll tax and creating the CPP Investment Board, an investment body that is given the mandate to invest tax receipts in stocks, bonds, or other assets so as to maximize the rate of return on its holdings.

Sweden reforms its pension system. The program is changed from a defined-benefit to a notional defined-contribution program. Though the program is still a pay-as-you-go system, it now holds each worker's contributions in a separate account, and the amount

1998
(cont.) in the account at the time of retirement is used to purchase an annuity for the worker. A portion of each individual's pension tax also goes into an IRA of the individual's choosing. Individuals can choose from up to five different private companies from a list of government-approved IRA funds, or they may keep their contributions in a state-operated fund. The retirement age is made flexible, starting as early as age 61.

1999 British Prime Minister Tony Blair introduces "stakeholders pension" schemes and broadens retirement pensions to include widowers. Stakeholders pensions are available to lower-income workers as an alternative to SERPS or to personal pensions.

Ireland begins a program to prefund a portion of its future pension obligations. The government will deposit the equivalent of 1 percent of the country's gross national product in a reserve fund each year until the year 2026. The reserve fund will be allowed to invest in a wide variety of assets, such as stocks, bonds, and real estate. By 2026, the fund is expected to be able to pay one-third of the amount of the country's pensions. This program is enacted as the National Pensions Reserve Fund in 2000.

2000 Japan reduces its earnings-related pensions benefits by 5 percent and shifts the calculations formula from using wage indexation to using price indexation. (This shift results in a lower benefit as well.)

2001 Japan creates a national defined-contribution pension program as a third tier to its pension system. Employer-funded accounts are created, in which employers deposit retirement monies on behalf of their workers, as well as personal accounts, into which workers can contribute up to 4 percent of their annual earnings.

2003 Sweden's notional defined-contribution system comes fully into force.

The Dominican Republic becomes the sixth Latin American nation to fully privatize its pension program along the lines established by Chile.

2004   Japan reforms its pension system. It substantially increases the contribution rate for both workers and employers and lowers benefits from 59 percent of annual salary to no less than 50 percent. An automatic adjustment mechanism is added to further reduce benefits, if necessary, based upon trends in the country's economic growth and population projections.

Nigeria becomes one of the first African countries to develop a pension program based on mandatory personal retirement accounts. The program has yet to be fully implemented.

2005   Germany adds a "sustainability factor" to its old-age pensions system. This factor reduces benefits if and when the dependency ratio of retirees to workers worsens. "Riester Pensions" are offered to German workers as a voluntary add-on to make up for the expected benefits cut.

Slovakia becomes the seventh, and most recent, country to adopt a pension system based on notional accounts.

2006   New Zealand creates a system of voluntary private retirement accounts called KiwiSaver. Workers are automatically enrolled into an account, from which they can opt out if they wish. If they remain in the program, each payday 4 or 8 percent of their pay (the worker chooses the figure) is automatically deducted and placed into their account. Their employer will make an additional annual contribution to their account. Under a 2008 reform, employers are mandated to contribute the equivalent of 1 percent of a worker's income to that individual's KiwiSaver account. This amount will grow to 4 percent by 2011. KiwiSaver accounts offer a variety of investment choices and will provide retirement income supplemental to the

2006
(cont.)
country's basic, flat-rate pension. However, the accounts can also used to finance the purchase a first home or for other purposes in cases of financial hardship.

2007
The United Kingdom passes the Pensions Act, which turns its state pension into a flat-rate pension, returns the program to being indexed on wages, and sharply curtails the ability of workers to "contract out" of the system by opening personal retirement accounts. The act also includes the creation of voluntary individual retirement accounts that can be added on top of the state pension.

Germany passages legislation to raise its retirement age to 67 by the year 2029.

Argentina becomes one of the first countries to allow workers to shift from being in a mandatory personal retirement account program back into the country's pay-as-you-go program. Previously, and consistent with other countries following Chilean-type reforms, it had only allowed workers to transfer from the latter into the former. Argentina also reverted to automatically placing new workers in the pay-as-you-go program rather than in the private accounts program. Argentina's measures may represent the first serious backtracking among those countries that have chosen to partially or fully privatize their pension programs.

South Africa announces its intent to develop its first full government pensions program by 2010. The program will feature the creation of a pay-as-you-go pension program that all workers must join, mandatory private or occupational pensions for wealthier South Africans, and voluntary private accounts for those who wish to enroll in them.

2008
Chile has plans in place to replace its pension guarantee program with a new two-tier program. The first

will offer a flat, guaranteed minimum pension to all Chilean workers. The second will commit the government to add monies into all private accounts up to the level necessary for those accounts to pay a monthly benefit equaling the same sum as the flat pension.

5

Biographical Sketches

Arthur Altmeyer (1891–1972)

Sometimes referred to as "Mr. Social Security," Arthur Altmeyer was a key developer of the U.S. Social Security program. Altmeyer began his career as a high school teacher before returning to the University of Wisconsin to complete a doctorate. At Wisconsin, he was deeply influenced by his professors, who had been important figures in the development of the progressive social policies for which the state was then famous. In the 1920s, he rose to become the secretary of the Wisconsin State Industrial Commission. In this capacity he often went to Washington, D.C., where he made a mark as a consistent supporter of policies to expand the U.S. social welfare system. Based on this reputation, President Franklin Roosevelt (also known as FDR) first asked him to help organize his new administration and then selected him to become an assistant secretary of Labor. FDR then appointed Altmeyer to be a member of the 1934 committee that drafted Roosevelt's Social Security legislation. Altmeyer was chair of the committee's Technical Board and perhaps the primary figure in crafting the new program. In 1937, he was asked to serve as the second chair of the Social Security Board. In 1946, when the Social Security Administration was developed to replace the board, Altmeyer became its first chair, serving until 1953. In these positions, he continually argued for expanding the Social Security program. It was his idea to add survivors' benefits to the Social Security program. Altmeyer was the vital force behind both the 1939 and the 1950

133

Amendments to the Social Security Act. These two sets of amendments largely achieved his goal of a universal system with relatively generous benefits. He was also behind the push to develop a worker's disability program within Social Security. On the other hand, he failed in his desire to keep Roosevelt's reserve account intact, and he had to oversee the change to a pay-as-you-go program, in spite of his warnings that the change would lead to a financing crisis in the future. In acknowledgment of his contributions to the development of Social Security, the national headquarters of the Social Security Administration, in Baltimore, is named after him.

Robert Ball (1914–)

Credited as the most important administrative figure to the development of Social Security in the years after 1950, Robert Ball joined the Social Security program in 1939 and rose to become the Commissioner of Social Security from 1962 to 1973. Perhaps his most important influence was in the early 1950s, when he played a critical role in expanding both the number of workers included under Social Security and the size of the program's monthly benefits. This accomplishment, obtained through skillful management of the 1947–1948 Social Security Advisory Council, made Social Security a truly universal retirement program and completed the shift from its earlier emphasis on public assistance to that of being a contributions-based social insurance program. Ball, working with labor groups, later spearheaded the addition of a disability program (1956) as well as Medicare (1965). After his retirement, Ball remained active in Social Security's politics, serving on independent reform committees and on a Social Security Advisory Council through the 1990s. Personally aligned with the Democratic Party, Ball was one of the de facto leaders of the Democrats on the Greenspan Commission (1981–1983). Ball continues to offer his ideas on Social Security reform and has written several books on the subject. His most recent plan focuses upon raising the amount of income subject to the income tax, devoting a portion of the estate tax to Social Security, and investing the Trust Fund in the stock market. These measures, he states, will solve the funding problem for at least the next 75 years.

William Beveridge (1879–1963)

As much as any individual, William Beveridge may be called the intellectual father of the welfare state. Born in Bengal, India, Beveridge was trained as a lawyer but achieved influence as a writer on social insurance. Because of his expertise, in 1908 he was asked to join the United Kingdom's Board of Trade, and his ideas were used to develop that country's National Insurance Act (1911), its first old-age pension plan. Beveridge later became the director of the London School of Economics. During World War II, he was asked to lead a study examining how the United Kingdom should rebuild after the war. Known as the Beveridge Report, his resulting study argued for the development of a "cradle to the grave" social security system, including free health care, for all citizens. This approach is the major alternative to a means-tested welfare system, such as that found in the United States. In 1945, the United Kingdom's Labour Party, upon its election victory, announced that it would enact the major provisions of the Beveridge Report. This led to the significant liberalization of the British old-age pension program. After briefly serving in the House of Commons, in 1946 Beveridge was made a peer of the House of Lords.

Carl Bildt (1943–)

In the relatively consensual world of Swedish politics, it is difficult to identify a single individual who was primarily responsible for that country's pension reform. However, former Prime Minister Nils Daniel Carl Bildt has as good a claim as any to that status. The leader of a coalition government from 1991 to 1994, Bildt launched the negotiations that led to the major Swedish reform that included the new notional defined-contribution accounts. From a distinguished Swedish family, Bildt entered the Swedish parliament in 1979 and rose to become the leader of the Moderate Party in 1986. Sweden, then as now, was dominated by the Social Democrat party, which has held power for most of the past century. The Social Democrats were the creators of Sweden's famous welfare state, including its generous pension program. In the late 1980s, Sweden entered a recessionary period that imperiled this pension program. Political leaders generally recognized the need for reform, but the Social Democrats, in particular, were reluctant to attack their own creation. Promising policies to liberalize the economic system and return growth, Bildt led four nonsocialist parties to victory in the elections of 1991. Somewhat surprisingly, Bildt immediately focused upon pensions and used his inaugural address to invite all of Sweden's parties to hold negotiations on reforming the system. Outside interest groups were excluded. A parliamentary committee of these parties, headed by Bo Könberg, minister of Health and Social Affairs, then produced successfully a reform package that was enacted into law in 1994. That same year, though, new elections returned the Social Democrats to power. Bildt later resigned as leader of his party to engage in various diplomatic missions. In 2006, following another victory by the nonsocialist parties, Bildt was appointed minister of Foreign Affairs.

George W. Bush (1946–)

The most powerful advocate to date of partially privatizing U.S. Social Security, George W. Bush, the 43rd president of the United States, proposed such a plan during his second term in office. After a career in the Texas oil industry, Bush, the son of President George H. W. Bush, advised his father in Washington and then returned to Texas to become the managing partner of the Texas Rangers Major League Baseball club. In 1994 he became governor of Texas and served until his very narrow victory in the presidential race of 2000. He had campaigned on entitlement reform and quickly appointed a bipartisan commission to examine the Social Security program. However, the September 11, 2001, terrorist attacks took the administration in a very different direction. Bush did not return his attention to Social Security until after his reelection in 2004. He then used the report of the earlier bipartisan commission to develop a series of reforms. From a programmatic standpoint, the most important may have been a change in the wage indexing formula. But both the administration and its critics devoted nearly all of their attention to the "personal retirement accounts" that were the centerpiece of the plan. These were to be voluntary private accounts into which workers could place a portion of their FICA contributions. The workers would control the money themselves, subject to federal guidelines. In exchange, there would be a reduced traditional Social Security benefit. The

Bush package did not fare well politically, suffering from low popular support and the administration's difficulties with the war in Iraq. As a result, Congress did not take it under consideration. In 2006, under even more unfavorable circumstances, President Bush again included the plan, with more detail, in his proposed budget to Congress.

Benjamin Cardozo (1870–1938)

In May 1937, U.S. Supreme Court Associate Justice Benjamin Cardozo wrote the Court's opinion that established the constitutionality of Social Security. Considered one of the greatest jurists of the United States, both for the acuity of his analyses and the clarity of his prose, Cardozo advocated the principle that U.S. common law was not fixed but grew and changed to meet the demands of the times. Previously serving as chief justice of the New York Court of Appeals, he was a virtually unanimous choice to replace Supreme Court Justice Oliver Wendell Holmes upon the latter's death in 1932. The Court he joined was soon factionalized by a succession of New Deal cases. Cardozo was among the three "progressive" members who supported the New Deal laws, which, one by one, were ruled unconstitutional by the majority. In this environment, a shareholder of Boston's Edison Electric Illumination Company brought suit claiming that the Social Security tax on his company was illegal. The Constitution did not enumerate a power to devise national insurance systems; they were unconstitutional under the Tenth Amendment. The U.S. Circuit Court of Appeals agreed, and the case, *Helvering v. Davis,* went to the Supreme Court. The drama was intensified by the politics of the day. President Roosevelt had announced a plan to "pack" the Court with more justices, ostensibly on grounds that the existing Court was too aged. The plan met a firestorm of controversy, but it greatly ratcheted the pressure on those justices opposing his policies. By a margin of 7–2, the Court would find that Social Security was indeed constitutional. Cardozo's opinion followed the administration's brief: the magnitude of the problem, and its national scope, justified the program under Congress's authority to "provide for the general welfare." This accorded with his principle that the very meaning of "general welfare" must change with the times. Social Security had survived. Only a year after writing this decision, Cardozo died of a stroke.

William J. Clinton (1946–)

The 42nd president of the United States, Bill Clinton proposed the most significant changes to the funding of the Social Security program since it became a primarily pay-as-you-go program in 1939. Clinton rose from difficult circumstances to become governor of Arkansas in 1978. After being defeated for reelection, he was again elected in 1982 and served for another 10 years. In 1992, he gained the presidency in a three-way race with George H. W. Bush and H. Ross Perot. The 1990s were years in which worries over the future of Social Security rose to the fore. After his reelection in 1996, President Clinton asked his advisers to develop a reform plan to extend the life of the program. These advisers recognized that the large government budget surplus that had emerged could form the backbone of reform. In his 1998 State of the Union address, Clinton announced a program to "Save Social Security First" by dedicating the surplus to Social Security. In his 1999 address, he offered the specifics for reform: 62 percent of the surplus would be steered into the Trust Fund, and a portion of the Trust Fund would then be used to purchase stocks. This measure would "prefund" future benefits payments and extend the life of the program. Moreover, a second portion of the surplus would be used to create "universal savings accounts" for all Americans. These accounts, which would operate like 401(k) or other tax-advantaged savings plans, would further boost retirement savings. The government would match the monies placed in their accounts by poorer Americans. While this ambitious proposal placed both the use of the stock market and the use of add-on retirement accounts firmly on the political agenda, the combination of a hostile Congress and Clinton's impeachment difficulties doomed its passage.

Wilbur Cohen (1913–1987)

Another "Mr. Social Security" (this time so named by President John Kennedy), Wilbur Cohen was a key behind-the-signs actor for many of the U.S. Social Security program's most significant changes. Cohen, the son of immigrants, studied at the University of Wisconsin when it was considered the preeminent institution for the development of new social programs. He went to Washington, D.C., in 1934 to join his professor, Edwin Witte, who had been named a member of President Roosevelt's Committee on

Economic Security, charged with designing Social Security. In 1935, Cohen became the first employee of the Social Security Board and later served as the program's chief legislative liaison for 20 years. Cohen provided the staff work behind the 1939 Amendments, advised President Harry Truman on his health care plan, played a major role in the passage of the Social Security amendments in the early 1950s (bringing nearly every working American into the program), and was a leading advocate of the disability program that was added in 1956. Cohen is credited for fusing the coalition of congressional leaders with labor organizations and other supportive interests that would come to make Social Security politically impregnable. Cohen succeeded in implanting his view that Social Security was better advanced through small steps than large reforms. After a brief stint in academia, Cohen returned to Washington in the Kennedy administration, and, under President Lyndon Johnson, led the fight for Medicare. After succeeding, Cohen would become the secretary of Health, Education, and Welfare (1968–1969).

Nelson Cruikshank (1902–1986)

The U.S. labor movement has been the most powerful supporter of Social Security for much of the program's existence. For decades, its chief expert and lobbyist was Nelson Cruikshank. Numerous reforms, most importantly the addition of disability insurance in 1956, were, in significant part, due to his efforts. Cruikshank was a deckhand on Great Lakes freighters before entering college and eventually being ordained as a Methodist minister. In 1944, he joined the American Federation of Labor (AFL), becoming its director of social insurance. He then served as a member of four of the succeeding six Social Security Advisory Councils, the chief venues for policy reforms. In 1955, Cruikshank became the head of the AFL's new Department of Social Security, continuing in that position after the merger of the AFL with the Congress of Industrial Organizations (CIO) later that year. His strong belief was that many workers, because their trades did not enable them to spend their careers with one employer or even in one location, had need of a generous, national pension program. His first great success was the lobbying effort behind the 1950 amendments that expanded both the benefits and the coverage of the Social Security program. He was then an even more central player in the development and passage of the 1956 disability program. After successfully lobbying for Medicare, he retired from the AFL-CIO. However, Cruikshank went on to a second career leading retiree interest groups, first the labor-financed National Council of Senior Citizens and then, in 1980, Save Our Security, launched in association with Wilbur Cohen as an omnibus lobbying group opposed to reductions in Social Security benefits. From 1977 to 1980, Cruikshank served as chair of the Federal Council on Aging.

Marion Folsom (1893–1976)

Marion Folsom probably did more to end the antipathy of American business toward Social Security than any other person. Folsom was a pioneer in the development of pension programs. At Eastman Kodak Company, he devised one of the first private retirement plans in the United States. Because of his experience, he was asked to join the Committee on Economic Security's Business Advisory Council in 1934. There he supported a national pension plan, although he favored a small program so that private pensions would still be relevant. However, most businesses continued to oppose Social Security, even after its passage. Folsom undertook major efforts to change this sentiment. Operating through positions in the Chamber of Commerce and the National Association of Manufacturers, he developed educational materials to convince business of the program's value. Folsom served on Social Security's second Advisory Council, where he was one of the leaders in developing the recommendation that the program shift to a pay-as-you-go basis. In the 1940s, he opposed raising taxes or benefits for Social Security, but, as a member of the 1947 Advisory Council, he changed his mind. He then, once again, led the effort to bring business to support the large benefits increase of 1950. In 1953, President Dwight Eisenhower appointed him undersecretary of the Treasury, where he had responsibility for Social Security. He would later become the secretary of Health, Education and Welfare (1955–1958). Though he did oppose the disability benefits added in 1956, his support for Social Security was critical in the first days of the administration when, as the first GOP government since the Herbert Hoover administration, it faced important questions about whether it would continue to endorse the program. Folsom returned from retirement to serve again on the 1963 Advisory Council that met at the opening of the Medicare debate.

Milton Friedman (1912–2006)

One of the most influential economists of the 20th century, Milton Friedman is considered the intellectual father of efforts to privatize Social Security. The son of immigrants, Friedman earned a doctorate from Columbia University after holding a series of government jobs during the New Deal era and World War II. In 1946, he took a faculty position at the University of Chicago and was instrumental in the construction of perhaps the world's most renowned and influential department of economics. Friedman himself became the leader of "monetarism," the belief that the money supply is fundamental to inflation and economic growth. He became the major critic of the Keynesian economic theory that dominated the Western world after World War II. His contributions to monetarism, economic history, the consumption function, and the permanent income hypothesis earned him the Nobel Prize in Economics in 1976. Early in his career, Friedman became a fierce advocate of limited government, arguing that the individual should always have the freedom to choose, even on questions such as prostitution or the use of drugs. He made this argument on both moral and economic grounds. He claimed to have always opposed Social Security for this reason. He believed that a one-size-fits-all program was inevitably inferior to a program in which each citizen could make his or her own choice about how to finance retirement. He claimed that no government could know as much about the citizens as those citizens knew about themselves and that therefore any individual was better able to understand his or her retirement needs than could the government. He championed his views both in the United States and abroad and is often credited with being the inspiration for the privatization program undertaken by Chile. Friedman remained an active participant in economic debates over Social Security and other issues almost to his death from heart failure at age 94.

Alan Greenspan (1926–)

An economist, a presidential adviser, and chair of the Board of Governors of the Federal Reserve of the United States (1987–2006),

Alan Greenspan headed perhaps the most significant Social Security reform commission since the advent of the program. After a successful business career, Greenspan became an adviser to presidents Richard Nixon and Gerald Ford and served as the chair of the Council of Economic Advisors from 1974 to 1977. By the early 1980s, it was all but certain that the Social Security system would go into a small deficit within two years. Nevertheless, President Ronald Reagan aroused a storm of controversy over his proposals to thus limit cost-of-living adjustments (COLAs) and otherwise trim the Social Security program. As a result, the president suggested a bipartisan committee to study the issue and develop proposals to save Social Security. In 1981, Greenspan was chosen to chair the National Commission on Social Security Reform, soon to be generally known as the "Greenspan Commission." Though nominally a committee of 15, a smaller group of members, including Greenspan, conducted all of the hard negotiating. By 1983, they had developed a set of proposals that essentially traded off Republican and Democrat views on needed reforms. These reforms included raising the retirement age, raising payroll taxes, and subjecting higher-income recipients to an income tax on their benefits. Congress then enacted these proposals into law. Greenspan's ability to bring the commission to a successful completion (only three conservative Republicans dissented) was a tremendous relief to the Reagan administration and was one factor behind Reagan's later choice of Greenspan to head the Federal Reserve, a position in which Greenspan attained near celebrity status.

Paul Keating (1944–)

While serving as treasurer and prime minister of Australia, Paul Keating became the chief architect of Australia's superannuation program. From a trade union background, Keating was elected as a member of the Labour Party to Australia's House of Representatives in 1969. His sharp tongue and debating skills led him to the party's front benches. He became treasurer (finance minister) upon Labour's victory in the 1983 general election, inheriting a very difficult situation. Australia was deep in debt and seemingly in economic decline. Though politically on the left, Keating and his prime minister, Bob Hawke, were committed to reversing this slide through market-friendly policies. Keating engaged in a variety of reforms that together did indeed turn the country around. He approached the problem of pensions from this same perspective. The nation needed a truly universal retirement system, but it had to be achieved through a program that harnessed the efficiencies of the market. Indebted Australia could not afford a system based on government money; the ideal program would increase private savings instead. On this basis, Keating and the leader of Australia's labor unions struck a deal in 1986 in which the unions agreed to defer a wage increase in favor of having 3 percent of workers' salaries placed into private investment funds that would be available for use after their retirement. This was the birth of "award superannuation." Hawke and Keating had a falling out in 1991, and Keating was removed from the government. However, within months he had returned to defeat Hawke and to become prime minister that year. He served until his party was defeated in the election of 1996. As prime minister he continued his work on superannuation, drawing up the reforms of 1992 that created the Superannuation Guarantee, Australia's current program that mandates compulsory contributions into superannuation funds by all of the country's employers. After 1996, Keating left politics to become the chief executive officer (CEO) of an Australian investment bank. He remains an active participant in the Australian pension debate, calling, in 2007, for an increase in superannuation payments from the current 9 percent to 15 percent of wages.

Huey Long (1893–1935)

Vowing to make "every man a king," Senator Huey Long (D-La.), "the Kingfish," offered his "Share the Wealth" program as a competitor to Social Security in the 1930s. In a relatively brief life, Long became one of America's most flamboyant and controversial political figures. Long was elected governor of Louisiana in 1928 and quickly used his powers to build, by means fair and foul, an immense political machine. As governor, enacting a series of bills to build roads and hospitals, lower gas prices, and give children free textbooks made him a hero throughout rural Louisiana. In 1930, Long, still governor, was also elected to the U.S. Senate. Initially he supported Franklin Roosevelt, but the two became political enemies as Long accused the president of being too timid in attacking the Great Depression. In 1934, he unveiled his Share the Wealth plan, which entailed using the tax code to limit any individual's wealth to $50 million. It would also set ceilings on incomes and inheritances. The money taken would be redistributed to U.S. families via a minimum guaranteed income and household grants. The money would also finance an old-age pension program for every American over the age of 60. The Share the Wealth Society, created by Long to support his proposal, soon had more than 7 million members. Long fought against FDR's alternative, Social Security. Rumors grew that he would run against Roosevelt in 1936, but fate intervened. From his Senate seat, Long still essentially ran the government of Louisiana. Power struggles within the state grew more intense. Finally, in 1935, a doctor approached Long and his bodyguards in the Louisiana capitol building. What happened next is still debated, but in a barrage of bullets, Senator Long was killed.

Paul Martin, Jr. (1938–)

As the finance minister and prime minister of Canada, Paul Martin led the reform of the Canadian pension system in the 1990s. The son of a prominent Canadian politician who was an early supporter of the Canadian Pension Plan (CPP), Martin first pursued a career in business, rising to become president and CEO of the Canadian Steamship Lines Group (CSL). He left CSL to enter Parliament in 1988 as a member of the Liberal Party. In 1993, he became Canada's minister of finance. He is widely credited for restoring the country's financial footing while holding this office. He resigned in 2002 but returned to office as prime minister, serving from 2003 to 2006. In his tenure as finance minister, Martin pressed several major pension reforms. The first was unsuccessful. In 1995, he proposed a plan called "the Seniors Benefit." Essentially, it would have combined the two existing national pension programs under a new calculation formula that would reduce benefits to middle- and upper-income Canadians while somewhat increasing them for poorer Canadians. This reform would have cut the cost of the retirement system by 10 percent. However, it did not have the support of the prime minister, Jean Chrétien, and it was delayed until after the following election. By then, an improving budget combined with opposition from many interest groups doomed the idea. However, Martin was already pursuing another avenue of reform. In 1996, he opened negotiations with the finance ministers of all of the provinces to reform the financing of the Canadian Pension Plan. The reforms involved increasing the contributions rate and slightly reducing benefits in order to substantially prefund the plan. He then oversaw the creation of the CPP Investment Board to invest these monies in stocks and other assets in order to gain a higher return. These changes were enacted in 1998. As prime minister, Martin suffered the fallout of a corruption scandal that eventually led to his party's defeat in 2006. After leaving power, Martin announced his retirement from politics.

Wilbur Mills (1909–1992)

Once called "Social Security's congressional Godfather," Representative Wilbur Mills (D-Ark.) is perhaps the most significant legislator in the history of the Social Security program. Mills was elected to Congress in Arkansas' Second District in 1938 and served until 1977. From 1957 to 1975, he was the chair of the House Ways and Means Committee, then considered the most powerful committee in Congress. Mills himself was generally considered the most powerful man in Congress. Because his committee had jurisdiction over the Social Security program, he controlled the fate of any and all proposals for its change or development. His influence began even before attaining the chair. In 1955, he helped secretly craft the legislation that added a disability plan to the Social Security program. For the next 20 years, Mills set Social Security benefits increases and FICA tax rates, keeping the program fiscally sound. However, in the early 1970s, in a quixotic bid to win the presidency, he first sponsored ruinously large annual benefits increases and then supported cost-of-living adjustments, both in a bid to attract the vote of senior citizens. Mills led the passage of the 1972 COLA reform. Mills's most important contribution to the Social Security program, however, was the passage of the Social Security amendments that created Medicare and Medicaid. At first, Mills opposed the programs, but he shifted to support them in 1965. Today's Medicare is a program drafted by Mills, containing the compromises he felt desirable or necessary. Mills's career ended in scandal when he was stopped by Washington, D.C., police and an Argentine stripper ran from his car and jumped into the nearby Tidal Basin, after which Mills acknowledged a problem with alcohol. Following a second unseemly incident, he was removed as committee chair, and he retired after the next election.

Daniel Patrick Moynihan (1927–2003)

The iconoclastic Daniel Patrick Moynihan was the leading congressional expert on Social Security in the last decades of the 20th century. He offered a number of controversial reforms for the program. Moynihan served in the Kennedy, Johnson, Nixon, and Ford administrations, where he was an architect of the War on Poverty, a major supporter of a guaranteed minimum income, an ambassador to India, and an ambassador to the United Nations. Meanwhile, his academic research garnered great attention, and he occupied a professorship at Harvard University. In 1976, he was elected to the U.S. Senate from New York, serving until 2001. Senator Moynihan was a leader on the Greenspan Commission, which developed the Social Security reforms of 1983. He led legislation to establish Social Security as an independent government agency and is responsible for the annual statement of expected Social Security benefits that every working American now receives. Moynihan came to the belief that the program was not financially sustainable and that the Trust Fund was encouraging fiscal irresponsibility in Washington. So he attempted to recreate Social Security as a true pay-as-you-go system. In 1990, he proposed shrinking the Trust Fund by cutting the payroll tax, and he later supported reducing benefits to the level of incoming receipts. He raised the argument that the Consumer Price Index led to overly generous COLAs. In 1998, he cosponsored the first serious bill to create individual retirement accounts within Social Security. (He believed this would help poor Americans who did not have access to 401(k) and other tax-sheltered savings programs.) In 2001, President George W. Bush appointed him the cochair of the Commission to Strengthen Social Security, which endorsed a partial privatization of Social Security. It is his series of reform proposals that have set the terms of the contemporary debate over Social Security.

Robert J. Myers (1912–)

The long-time chief actuary of the Social Security program, Robert Myers was intimately involved in most of its major decisions and reforms. A quick way of seeing his importance is that the *Guinness Book of World Records* shows Myers to have testified before Congress more times than anyone else in history. Myers, trained as an actuary, was part of the 1934 Committee on Economic Security's technical staff. He then held a variety of actuarial positions in the new program before becoming the chief actuary of the Social Security Administration in 1947. Myers developed the program's cost estimates. The use of long-run cost estimates for the program was his innovation, and he began the publication of the long-range estimates of Social Security's actual balance now included in the annual Trustee's Report. Our knowledge of Social Security's future is based on his methods. In 1969, he devised the wage-indexing formula that has been added to Social Security. His authority and apparent nonpartisanship were important elements in the favorable reception accorded Social Security proposals on Capitol Hill during his 33 years as chief actuary. In 1970, he abruptly resigned when he believed the program's administrators were violating their obligation to be nonpartisan by pushing to expand the Social Security program far beyond the wishes of their nominal superior, the Nixon administration. Myers returned to Washington when he was appointed a Social Security commissioner by President Reagan. He resigned shortly thereafter to become the executive director of the Greenspan Commission, which developed the 1983 Social Security reforms. In later years he continued to speak and write on Social Security, favoring extending the life of the program by raising the retirement age. In 2005, Myers came out against President George W. Bush's efforts to partially privatize the program.

Francis Perkins (1882–1965)

As President Roosevelt's secretary of Labor, Francis Perkins was FDR's primary influence in developing the Social Security program. Perkins has the dual honor of being both the first woman cabinet member in American history and the longest serving Secretary of Labor in U.S. history. Though born in Boston, she made her career in New York. She did early work at Hull House and other prominent antipoverty organizations. Already secretary of the New York Consumer's League, a group dedicated to education about worker's rights, she saw the famous 1911 Triangle Shirt Waist Company fire, which killed more than 100 employees because illegally locked doors prevented their escape. This experience led to Perkins obtaining a position on the Factory Investigating Commission, a seat on the New York Industrial Board, and eventually a close association with New York Governor Al Smith, as she became his chief adviser on social issues. She continued this role with Franklin Roosevelt when he became governor of New York. In 1933, now President Roosevelt asked her to come to Washington as his secretary of Labor. She served in that position for 12 years. She began advocating a national old-age assistance plan shortly after arriving in Washington, well before FDR or his other advisers picked up the issue. She suggested forming a committee to study the issue. When Roosevelt agreed, in 1934, he named Perkins as its chair. She thus oversaw the drafting of the Social Security Act, even quasi-secretly consulting with Supreme Court Justice Harlan Stone for advice on how to make it withstand tests of constitutionality. This was but one of many pieces of social legislation she developed during the New Deal years. After resigning from her position following FDR's death, she served on the Civil Service Commission until 1953 and continued to lecture for years thereafter.

James Jerrell Pickle (1913–2005)

A long-serving Texas congressman, J. J. Pickle is the person most responsible for raising the retirement age of Social Security from 65 to 67. A close associate of Lyndon Johnson, Pickle held Johnson's former House seat from 1963 to 1995. Pickle became chair of the Ways and Means subcommittee responsible for Social Security in 1979. He was one of the first to recognize the coming exhaustion of the Trust Fund that would lead to the Greenspan Commission and the reforms of 1983. He believed that the solution was not to move to a full pay-as-you-go system but to increase the size of the fund. This could be done by encouraging Americans to stay longer in the workforce, both by ending the benefit penalty on those who continued to work after their retirement age and by increasing the age at which one could retire on a full pension. In 1981, he sponsored legislation to slowly raise the retirement age from 65 to 68. This failed, and the Speaker of the House (and fellow Democrat) Tip O'Neill demanded that he not renew his efforts lest it harm the Democrats' ability to campaign on Social Security. Yet Pickle continued. When the Greenspan

Commission reforms were brought to Congress, he insisted on an amendment to those reforms that would increase the retirement age (now to 67). The amendment passed. By the 1990s, Pickle was endorsing a further extension to age 70, along with the reduction of early retirement and spousal benefits, as the mechanisms to best keep the program healthy. He retired in 1995 and died of cancer a decade later.

José Piñera (1948–)

Probably the most important advocate of social security privatization in the world, José Piñera is the architect of the Chilean pension system. Born to a prominent Chilean family, he earned a doctorate in economics at Harvard University in 1974 and returned to teach in Chile. Four years later, he joined the cabinet of Augusto Pinochet as minister of Labor and Social Security. A strong advocate of free markets and small government, Piñera then led the design of a fully privatized pension program based upon private personal retirement accounts to replace the country's failing retirement system. It was the world's first such program. In 1980, he became minister of Mining but left the cabinet a year later to fight for Chile's return to democratic rule. In 1994, he founded an international center to promote the Chilean model of pension reform to other countries. He also joined the Cato Institute, a U.S. think tank that supports privatization. He has written many books and articles on the Chilean system and the privatization of social security.

Augusto Pinochet (1915–2006)

The Chilean dictator Augusto Pinochet is the unlikely founder of the world's most celebrated privatized retirement system. Pinochet was a career soldier who, by 1972, had risen to become the general chief of staff of the Chilean army. Not two years later, he participated in the military coup that removed the elected president of Chile, Salvador Allende. As leader of the largest branch of the military, Pinochet became the head of the junta that then took power. The coup was followed by months of savage repression against supporters of Allende and others identified as being on the political left. In 1980, Pinochet appointed himself president of Chile, and a year later he added to his list of titles that of captain general. Like most of those who participated in the coup, or supported it, Pinochet blamed the socialist Allende for perpetuating an overregulated dysfunctional economic system that stymied the development of the country. The dictator sought to reverse this situation by supporting free market policies that would revive the economy and develop personal responsibility and entrepreneurship among the Chilean people. Thus he strongly supported the efforts of his minister of Labor and Social Security, José Piñera, to develop a system of private personal accounts to replace the old Chilean pension system. After losing a referendum in 1988, Pinochet turned power over to an elected civilian government in 1990. However, he held his position as leader of the army until 1998. His own retirement was not peaceful. While visiting the United Kingdom, he was arrested under a Spanish warrant accusing him of human rights violations. After returning to Chile, he was removed from the Chilean Senate and later indicted first for tax evasion and then for the 1973 kidnapping and murder of aides of President Allende.

Walter Riester (1943–)

The German Riester Pension ("Riester-Rente") is named after its author, Walter Riester, a leader of the country's Social Democratic Party (SPD). Riester came from a labor background, rising to become deputy chair of IG Metal, the large (more than 2 million members) German industrial trade union, in 1993. He was also active in the SPD and joined the party's federal executive committee in 1988. He entered the government of Prime Minister Gerhard Schroeder in 1998 after a coalition of the SPD and the Green Party took power, serving as the minister of Labor and Social Affairs. The election of that year had turned on the country's economic difficulties, very much including the cost of its social welfare programs. The SPD had opposed benefits cuts desired by the outgoing parties, but it needed to offer a benefits reform of its own. Riester's job was to design this reform. He decided not to raise the contributions rate but to focus on a new calculation formula that would bring benefits payments in line with Germany's financial resources. Realizing that this would amount to a benefits cut in future years, he first argued for adding a system of compulsory individual retirement accounts to make up for this loss. German workers would place a percentage of their income into tax-advantaged accounts managed by private companies. However, this proposal aroused a storm of opposition, including his labor union base, and he retreated to an optional plan in which workers could deposit up to 4 percent of their income in a private individual account. This was combined with incentives to encourage them to do so. The resulting individual retirement accounts were soon dubbed Riester Pensions. In 2002, the German government eliminated the Ministry of Labor and Social Affairs, costing Riester his cabinet position. He took up a seat in the Bundestag, the German legislature, where he continues to serve.

Franklin Delano Roosevelt (1882–1945)

The 32nd president of the United States, Franklin Roosevelt is the father of the U.S. Social Security program. The contours of Roosevelt's life are well known. From a prominent New York family, Roosevelt was a rising star of the Democrat Party until stricken by polio in 1921. He was presumed to be politically finished. Instead, through almost unbelievable force of will, Roosevelt learned to overcome the total paralysis of his legs and reentered politics. He was twice elected governor of New York before his election to the presidency in 1932. There he began his famous New Deal to combat the Great Depression. In 1934, FDR and aides believed that the emergency of the Depression was over. Expecting a large victory in that year's elections, they felt it was time to move to a more ambitious and permanent set of social reforms, since labeled the "second New Deal." Roosevelt included in this reform package a program for unemployment benefits he called "economic security." But this program was greeted as too tepid by his supporters, and, under the pressure of the Townsend Plan and Huey Long's call to "Share the Wealth," Roosevelt decided to develop a larger plan that would include old-age pensions. He created a committee to develop such a plan and insisted that the program be one of monthly benefits to be paid from earlier worker contributions, so that it would neither appear to be welfare nor draw from the government's general revenues. He also pushed for the notion of a trust fund to hold the contributions. Social Security was passed by Congress primarily because of the president's unmatched political skills. He would go on to be elected four times to the office and serve as the U.S. leader in World War II.

Isaac Rubinow (1875–1936)

Perhaps the best claim to being the intellectual father of the U.S. Social Security program can be made by an immigrant from czarist Russia, Isaac Rubinow. Shocked by the poverty he discovered in his New York medical practice, Rubinow turned to the study of social reform. In 1913, he published *Social Insurance,* often cited as the first and most significant book in the development of Social Security. After studying the social insurance systems of Europe, Rubinow argued that the modern economy created problems, such as unemployment, health care, and financial support during old age, that were beyond the control of the individual. The government thus had the necessary role of creating programs to assist Americans through these difficulties. Since it was impossible to know in advance which individuals would have need of these programs, the assistance was best provided on insurance principles. All would pay, creating a universal fund from which those with needs could draw. These programs would effectively redistribute income to those who had the greatest need for it. Rubinow's ideas were enthusiastically adopted in the Progressive movement, and became part of the platform of Theodore Roosevelt's Bull Moose Party. Rubinow continued to promote his ideas for the next 20 years. When Franklin Roosevelt took office as president, Rubinow urged that social insurance be included as part of the New Deal. In 1934, he published a second important volume, *The Quest for Security,* publicizing his ideas. FDR is said to have been reading the book during the writing of the Social Security Act. Though in certain features that act deviated from Rubinow's stances—he preferred using the general revenues to dedicated worker contributions, and he favored the redistribution of money to the needy aged as opposed to universal old-age pensions—it is his general argument that motivates today's program.

David Stockman (1946–)

As President Reagan's budget director, David Stockman undertook the largest effort to date to reduce Social Security expenditures. This effort indirectly led to the program's major reforms of 1983 and directly led to the program becoming the "third rail" of American politics for the next generation. Stockman had a meteoric political career. In 1976, he was elected to the House of Representatives at the age of 30, and only four years later he was appointed the director of the Office of Management and Budget. Responsible for the new president's ambitious economic program, Stockman needed to find some $75 billion in government spending cuts to go with the major tax cuts the administration was proposing. Through a variety of small reforms, and one big one, he found half of the needed cuts in the Social Security program. The big reform was an immediate and permanent reduction in the early retirement benefit (from 80 percent to 55 percent of the full benefit). It was a political bombshell. Facing a bipartisan outcry, President Reagan disavowed the cuts. As political cover, the administration instead created the Greenspan Commission to examine the program. Stockman was an active participant, shaping the congressional reforms that followed. But the tremendous reaction to Stockman's proposals signaled the political dangers that awaited anyone wishing to change Social Security. The journalist William Greider later published an article in which Stockman shared his doubts about the soundness of the budget he had prepared. This comment sharply reduced his political influence, and he left the Reagan administration for Wall Street in 1985. He later became the CEO of an auto parts company. In 2007, he was arrested for fraud relating to its financial operations.

Margaret Thatcher (1925–)

Margaret Thatcher, known as "the Iron Lady," was among the most important prime ministers in British history. An ardent free marketeer, she pushed the partial privatization of the United Kingdom's pension system, one of the first such attempts in the world. Originally trained as a chemist, Thatcher later became a lawyer before being elected to Parliament in 1959. In 1961, she entered the Conservative government as the parliamentary secretary at the Ministry of Pensions and National Insurance. She became the leader of the Conservative Party in 1975 and prime minister after the elections of 1979. As prime minister, Thatcher took vigorous action to end the endemic British inflation, willingly suffering a major recession to do so. This course of action succeeded, and Thatcher went on to tackle an ambitious agenda that included breaking the power of the British trade unions, deregulating the British economy, and raising the international profile of the United Kingdom. Faced with funding difficulties similar to those in the United States at that time, she won approval of a social security act that changed the indexation formula for calculating pensions. It sharply reduced the size of British pensions. She then floated the idea of privatizing the British system by ending its State-Earnings-Related-Pension-Scheme (SERPS) program in favor of compulsory private retirement accounts. This proved too daring, and she settled for partial privatization through a 1986 parliamentary act that greatly boosted the incentives to opt out of the SERPS in favor of private personal accounts. After two more electoral victories (1983 and 1987), Thatcher became the longest serving British prime minister in nearly two centuries. Not until 1990 did an unpopular poll tax, economic difficulties, and disputes over the United Kingdom's relationship with the European Union combine to divide the Conservative Party and lead to her fall from power. For many years thereafter, she continued to speak in favor of free market economics and a muscular foreign policy in defense of Western interests.

Francis Townsend (1867–1960)

In 1934, Dr. Francis Townsend created the "Townsend Plan," the most politically important old-age pension proposal offered prior to Social Security. The plan, and the mass movement that followed, pressured President Roosevelt to develop and offer his own plan. Dr. Townsend was the assistant city health director in Long Beach, California, but lost his job during the Great Depression. Witnessing the poverty around him, Townsend developed an idea that he believed could end it. The federal government should place a sales tax on all commercial transactions. The tax would fund a monthly pension of $200 for every American over the age of 60. To receive the pension, the individual had to promise to completely retire from the workforce and to spend the entire amount of the monthly benefit within 30 days. Townsend believed that the resulting spending spree would lift the United States out of the Depression. His friend, a Long Beach real estate

agent, Robert Earl Clements, is mostly responsible for the attention
the plan gained. Clements "sold" it using methods he had learned
in his business. Together, the two organized Townsend Clubs
across the United States. These would ultimately have a combined
membership of some 5 million people. Townsend thought FDR
would adopt the plan, but Roosevelt, like mainstream economists,
believed it unworkable and financially unsound. The plan continued to be proposed in Congress throughout the 1930s, but it faded
in light of Roosevelt's alternative Social Security plan. Embittered,
Townsend broke with Clements and joined the far right. His influence largely ended with the poor showing by his allies in the 1936
elections. However, he maintained his organization for some years
thereafter. As late as 1958, he was writing President Eisenhower to
reconsider his plan.

Harry S Truman (1884 –1972)

President Harry Truman led the transformation of Social Security from essentially an old-age welfare program into a livable
pension for senior citizens. Truman rose from a Missouri
county judge to become a U.S. senator in 1935. His work on a
military preparedness committee gave him a national reputation, and he was nominated as President Roosevelt's vice president in 1944. He became the 33rd president upon Roosevelt's
death in 1945. His presidency was most marked by a series of
foreign policy crises, but Truman remained committed to Roosevelt's social policies. Social Security was then on the defen-
sive. Congress refused to raise benefits and struck workers
from the program's rolls. The Senate initiated a Social Security
Advisory Council to examine more reforms in 1947. In 1948,
Congress attempted to remove another 500,000 workers. But
Truman vetoed the bill and made it an issue in his famous
"whistle-stop" campaign that produced a stunning upset victory in the 1948 election. Newly energized, he developed a set
of social reforms he called "the Fair Deal." It included a national health care plan (which failed) and, using the Advisory
Council's recommendations, a vast immediate increase in Social Security benefits along with the extension of the program
to self-employed, farm, and domestic workers. At stake was
whether Social Security would be defined as a bare minimum

on which to survive, as conservatives argued, or as a full pension plan. Truman fought for the latter, and won. In 1950, Congress added 10 million workers to Social Security and increased the monthly benefit by an average of 77 percent. Social Security was now cast as a true old-age pension program. Truman followed with a second benefits increase in 1952.

Adrian Turner (1955–)

A self-described "technocrat," Adrian Turner is the primary author of the substantial reforms to the British pension system that were enacted in 2007. Turner has spent most of his life in the business world, becoming a partner in the McKinsey consulting firm and later the vice chairman of Merrill Lynch Europe. He was the director of the British Confederation of Industry from 1995 to 1999. Upon taking office in 1997, the victorious Labour Party was faced with growing problems in the country's complex retirement system. Prime Minister Tony Blair and Chancellor of the Exchequer Gordon Brown differed on how to proceed, and they compromised by establishing an independent commission to offer reforms to improve its operations. Turner, then close to Blair, was named the chair of the three-person Pension Commission. The commission delivered its first report, more than 400 hundred pages, in late 2004. Its reforms were primarily authored by Turner. He called for a higher state pension, relinking that pension to earnings and not to the rate of inflation, increasing the retirement age to 68, and creating an employer-sponsored add-on savings program. He also called for the system to be one from which workers must opt out, rather than a system in which they must opt in, the opposite of the Thatcher reforms of 20 years earlier. Though generally well received, Turner's report did apparently clash with the desires of Gordon Brown, who thought these reforms too expensive and preferred to use means testing as a method to increase pensions to the poorest retirees. But Blair and Brown reached a compromise largely favorable to the commission's recommendations. Its reforms were then mostly enacted into law by the British Parliament in 2007. Turner remained chair of the commission until its final report was issued in mid-2006. In 2007, he became the chair of the United Kingdom's Economic and Social Research Council. In 2005, Turner was elevated to the peerage as Baron Turner of Ecchinswell.

Arthur Vandenberg (1884–1951)

Michigan Senator Arthur Vandenberg was the surprising initiator of perhaps the single most important change in Social Security, from being a fully funded program to today's pay-as-you-go system. Vandenberg served in the U.S. Senate from 1928 to 1951. He became the Senate's Republican minority leader in 1935. A gifted orator, he was most known for his vociferous isolationism. Vandenberg had broken with many Republicans to vote for Social Security. With his small minority, Vandenberg's tactic was not to attack New Deal programs as such, but rather to find significant flaws in their operations. By 1937, as funds poured into the new Social Security reserve account, he claimed to find such a flaw. Benefits did not begin until 1942. Vandenberg pointed out that the gap in time from the collection to disbursement of funds would produce a huge surplus in the account. He estimated that it would grow to $47 billion by 1980, an unbelievable amount of money then. He argued that the government would find it politically impossible not to tap this fund and spend its resources recklessly on any number of social programs. He asked Social Security Chair Arthur Altmeyer to convene an advisory council to study the issue. To blunt Vandenberg's charges, that council recommended ending the reserve account, beginning increased benefits payments before 1942, and adding survivors' benefits. The effect was to create a largely pay-as-you-go program. Congress duly passed these changes. Vandenberg gained his greatest fame after World War II, when he changed his position from isolationism to internationalism and supported the foreign policies of presidents Roosevelt and Truman. His actions are credited with creating the bipartisan foreign policy that characterized much of the Cold War era.

Robert Wagner (1877– 1953)

Arguably the author of more significant social legislation than any other U.S. politician, Senator Robert Wagner (D-NY) was the congressional sponsor of the Social Security Act of 1935. A German immigrant, Wagner became the lieutenant governor of New York and a justice on its Court of Appeals before being elected to the first of his four terms in the Senate in 1926. A social progressive and ardent New Dealer, Wagner wrote or sponsored a list of important bills that is second to none. It includes the Federal Emergency Relief Administration Act and the National Industrial Recovery Act—the two centerpieces of the New Deal—the National Labor Relations Act (which gave labor the right to organize), and the Wagner-Steagall Act (which created the U.S. Housing Authority). In 1934, Wagner introduced both a national unemployment compensation plan and a government pension program for railway workers. The latter was very similar to the future Social Security program. It was declared unconstitutional in 1934, a decision of great concern to those writing the Social Security bill. Though Wagner was not directly involved in drafting the Social Security Act, his prestige, support, and position on the Labor Committee made him the act's obvious sponsor. He then played an active role in its passage. Wagner spent much of the following decade in an unsuccessful effort to add a national health care plan to Social Security. He later served on the U.S. negotiating team that devised the postwar international monetary order at the Bretton Woods conference before resigning from the Senate shortly before his death.

John Winant (1889–1947)

One of America's most distinguished public servants, John Winant was the first chair of the Social Security Board. Winant began his career as a teacher but, upon returning from World War I, entered the political arena and rose to become governor of New Hampshire. A lifelong Republican, Governor Winant became one of the nation's leading social reformers. During his terms in office, the state adopted a minimum wage, a limited workweek for women and children, and a series of Depression relief programs; in addition, the state became the first to fill its Civilian Conservation Corps enrollment quota. Often compared to President Abraham Lincoln, for both his policies and his personal appearance, Winant was a rumored GOP candidate for the presidency in 1936. In the eyes of President Roosevelt, Winant's party affiliation and record of reform made him the perfect person to head the new Social Security program. Winant performed ably in the first difficult decisions of the program, keeping Social Security operating in the face of a Huey Long filibuster and engaging in arduous negotiations with members of Congress who sought specific favors in exchange for support of its administrative funding. Winant then unexpectedly resigned in late 1936. The 1936 Republican presidential candidate, Alf Landon, was making his opposition to Social Security a centerpiece of his campaign. Winant wished to publicly defend the program but believed that, as long as he remained a nonpartisan public official, he could not do so. Roosevelt reluctantly accepted the resignation but went on to secure Winant's appointment as director of the International Labour Organization (1939–1941) and U.S. ambassador to the United Kingdom through World War II (1941–1946). Regrettably, Winant committed suicide in 1947.

Edwin Witte (1887–1960)

Economics professor and public official Edwin Witte has been called the "father of Social Security" because he wrote the initial report that developed the plan. Witte was a prominent academic at the University of Wisconsin. His primary interest was unemployment policy. Associated with the "Wisconsin School" of social reform, he was an author of that state's pathbreaking unemployment compensation program. Because of his prominence and technical expertise, he was chosen by President Roosevelt to be the executive director of the 1934 Committee on Economic Security, the group charged with creating the Social Security program. Over the six months of the committee's existence, Witte coordinated the shaping of the program and then wrote the committee report. Some participants felt that Witte was actually rather lukewarm in his support for old-age insurance and that his preference for a state-run pension program (like that of unemployment insurance) over a national plan lost to the views of the committee's technical experts. But Witte strongly intervened to support a contributions-based pension program as opposed to the more redistributive system preferred by Isaac Rubinow and the committee's other experts, which would have been based on the government's general revenues. After drafting the report, Witte was the first person to testify for Social Security before Congress. His work done, he returned to his position as professor. Later, he participated in the Advisory Council that produced the 1939 reforms. There he was a strong opponent of recreating Social Security as a pay-as-you-go system. He argued for keeping a large reserve fund to ensure that the program would always be adequately financed. He lost this argument. Again returning to the academy, in 1956 he was chair of the American Economics Association.

6

Data and Documents

This chapter includes excerpts from among the most important reports, speeches, and Supreme Court opinions that relate to the U.S. Social Security program. It also contains recent trustee reports on the financial status of Social Security. The chapter begins with a brief guide to the complex law that creates the Federal Old-Age, Survivors, and Disability Insurance Benefits program.

The Social Security Act

The foundation of the U.S. Social Security program is the Social Security Act of 1935. Title II of that act established the program that is today called the Old Age, Survivors, and Disability Insurance program, or more informally, Social Security. After more than 70 years of revisions and extensions, the Social Security Act (more technically, Subchapter II of Chapter 7 of Title 42 of the U.S. Legal Code) has grown to two printed volumes of great detail and complexity. One may read the law, in all of its complexity, as it appears in the compilation of the U.S. Code at the Web site of the U.S. Code (http://www.access.gpo.gov/uscode/title42/chapter7_subchapterii_.html) or in volume 22 of the printed U.S. Code (Washington: Government Printing Office, 2000). Alternatively, one may consult the Social Security Act in the "Compilation of the Social Security Laws" held at the Social Security Administration Web site (http://ssa.gov/OP_Home/ssact/comp-ssa.htm).

Note that the sections pertaining to the Old-Age, Survivors, and Disability Insurance Program are prefixed by a "2" in the Social Security

Act itself (section 201, 202, etc.) but by a "4" in the U.S. Code (section 401, 402, etc.). Otherwise, they correspond directly with each other.

The Preamble is not part of the U.S. Code, but it does offer the statement of purpose for the program, as well as an early defense of its constitutionality ("provide for the general welfare").

The Preamble to the Social Security Act of 1935

An act to provide for the general welfare by establishing a system of Federal old-age benefits, and by enabling the several States to make more adequate provision for aged persons, blind persons, dependent and crippled children, maternal and child welfare, public health, and the administration of their unemployment compensation laws; to establish a Social Security Board; to raise revenue; and for other purposes.

The Supreme Court Opinion: *Helvering v. Davis*

The Social Security program was almost immediately challenged on grounds of its constitutionality. Even President Franklin Roosevelt and his aides feared that the program would be annulled by the courts. The test came in the form of Helvering v. Davis. *A stockholder of the Edison Electric Company, George Davis, sued to prove that his company should not have to pay its half of the Social Security contribution on the grounds that the program was unconstitutional. Davis lost the case in U.S. District Court, but he won on appeal. IRS Commissioner Guy Helvering then asked that the case be taken up by the U.S. Supreme Court. The Supreme Court, in a decision written by Justice Benjamin Cardozo, found that Titles II and VIII of the Social Security Act (the titles that established and funded the old-age pension program) were indeed constitutional. This decision carefully explains why the program meets the test of constitutionality. In doing so, it also offers a good summation of how the program was to operate. The Court's decision did more than save Social Security; it allowed for the large expansion of the program in the years to follow.*

The decision is presented here in only slightly edited format. Most references to other cases and statutes have been deleted.

United States Supreme Court, October Term 1936

Guy T. Helvering, Commissioner of Internal Revenue, and William M. Welch, Collector of Internal Revenue, for the District of Massachusetts, The Edison Electric Illuminating Company of Boston, Petitioners vs. George P. Davis, Respondent.

On Writ of Certiorari to the United States Circuit Court of Appeals for the First Circuit.

Mr. Justice Cardozo delivered the opinion of the Court.

[May 24, 1937]

The Social Security Act . . . is challenged once again.

. . . In this case Titles VIII and II are the subject of attack. Title VIII lays another excise upon employers . . . It lays a special income tax upon employees to be deducted from their wages and paid by the employers. Title II provides for the payment of Old Age Benefits, and supplies the motive and occasion, in the view of the assailants of the statute, for the levy of the taxes imposed by Title VIII. The plan of the two titles will now be summarized more fully.

Title VIII, as we have said, lays two different types of tax, an "income tax on employees," and "an excise tax on employers." The income tax on employees is measured by wages paid during the calendar year. The excise tax on the employer is to be paid "with respect to having individuals in his employ," and, like the tax on employees, is measured by wages. Neither tax is applicable to certain types of employment, such as agricultural labor, domestic service, service for the national or state governments, and service performed by persons who have attained the age of 65 years. The two taxes are at the same rate. . . . The income tax on employees is to be collected by the employer, who is to deduct the amount from the wages "as and when paid." He is indemnified against claims and demands of any person by reason of such payment. The proceeds of both taxes are to be paid into the Treasury like internal-revenue taxes generally, and are not earmarked in any way. There are penalties for nonpayment.

Title II has the caption "Federal Old-Age Benefits." The benefits are of two types, first, monthly pensions, and second, lump sum payments, the payments of the second class being relatively few and unimportant.

The first section of this title creates an account in the United States Treasury to be known as the "Old-Age Reserve Account." No present appropriation, however, is made to that account. All that the statute does is to authorize appropriations annually thereafter, beginning with the fiscal year which ends June 30, 1937. How large they shall be is not known in advance. The "amount sufficient as an annual premium" to provide for the required payments is "to be determined on a reserve basis in accordance with accepted actuarial principles, and based upon such tables of mortality as the Secretary of the Treasury shall from time to time adopt, and upon an interest rate of 3 per centum per annum compounded annually." Not a dollar goes into the Account by force of the challenged act alone, unaided by acts to follow.

Section 202 and later sections prescribe the form of benefits. The principal type is a monthly pension payable to a person after he has attained the age of 65. . . . They are to be measured . . . by a percentage of the wages the percentage decreasing at stated intervals as the wages become higher. In addition to the monthly benefits, provision is made in certain contingencies for "lump sum payments" of secondary importance. . . . This suit is brought by a shareholder of the Edison Electric Illuminating Company of Boston, a Massachusetts corporation, to restrain the corporation from making the payments and deductions called for by the act, which is stated to be void under the Constitution of the United States. . . . The expected consequences are indicated substantially as follows: The deductions from the wages of the employees will produce unrest among them, and will be followed, it is predicted, by demands that wages be increased. If the exactions shall ultimately be held void, the company will have parted with moneys which as a practical matter it will be impossible to recover. Nothing is said in the bill about the promise of indemnity. The prediction is made also that serious consequences will ensue if there is a submission to the excise. The corporation and its shareholders will suffer irreparable loss, and many thousands of dollars will be subtracted from the value of the shares. The prayer is for an injunction and for a declaration that the act is void.

. . . The District Court held that the tax upon employees was not properly at issue, and that the tax upon employers was constitutional. It thereupon denied the prayer for an injunction, and dismissed the bill. On appeal to the Circuit Court of Appeals for the First Circuit, the decree was reversed, one judge dissenting. The court held that Title II was void as an invasion of powers reserved by the Tenth Amendment to the states or to the people and that Title II in collapsing carried Title VIII along with it. As an additional reason for invalidating the tax upon employers, the court held that it was not an excise as excises were understood when the Constitution was adopted. . . .

A petition for certiorari followed. It was filed by the intervening defendants, the Commissioner and the Collector, and brought two questions, and two only, to our notice. We were asked to determine: (1) "whether the tax imposed upon employers by Section 804 of the Social Security Act is within the power of Congress under the Constitution," and (2) "whether the validity of the tax imposed upon employees by Section 801 of the Social Security Act is properly in issue in this case, and if it is, whether that tax is within the power of Congress under the Constitution." The defendant corporation gave notice to the Clerk that it joined in the petition, but it has taken no part in any subsequent proceedings. . . .

First: Questions as to the remedy invoked by the complainant confront us at the outset.

. . . a majority of the court . . . find in this case extraordinary features making it fitting in their judgment to determine whether the benefits and the taxes are valid or invalid. . . . The ruling of the majority removes from the case the preliminary objection as to the nature of the remedy which we took of our own motion at the beginning of the argument. Under the compulsion of that ruling, the merits are now here.

Second: The scheme of benefits created by the provisions of Title II is not in contravention of the limitations of the Tenth Amendment.

Congress may spend money in aid of the "general welfare." Constitution, Art. I, section 8. There have been great statesmen in our history who have stood for other views. We will not resurrect the contest. It is now settled by decision. United States v. Butler, supra. The conception of the spending power advocated by Hamilton and strongly reinforced by Story has prevailed over that of Madison, which has not been lacking in adherents. Yet difficulties are left when the power is conceded. The line must still be drawn between one welfare and another, between particular and general. Where this shall be placed cannot be known through a formula in advance of the event. There is a middle ground or certainly a penumbra in which discretion is at large. The discretion, however, is not confided to the courts. The discretion belongs to Congress, unless the choice is clearly wrong, a display of arbitrary power is not an exercise of judgment. This is now familiar law. "When such a contention comes here we naturally require a showing that by no reasonable possibility can the challenged legislation fall within the wide range of discretion permitted to the Congress." . . . Nor is the concept of the general welfare static. Needs that were narrow or parochial a century ago may be interwoven in our day with the well-being of the nation. What is critical or urgent changes with the times.

The purge of nation-wide calamity that began in 1929 has taught us many lessons. Not the least is the solidarity of interests that may once have seemed to be divided. Unemployment spreads from state to state, the hinterland now settled that in pioneer days gave an avenue of escape. . . . Spreading from state to state, unemployment is an ill not particular but general, which may be checked, if Congress so determines, by the resources of the nation. If this can have been doubtful until now, our ruling today in the case of the Steward Machine Co. supra, has set the doubt at rest. But the ill is all one or at least not greatly different whether men are thrown out of work because there is no longer work to do or because the disabilities of age make them incapable of doing it. Rescue becomes necessary irrespective of the cause. The hope behind this statute is to save men and women from the rigors of the poor house as well as from the haunting fear that such a lot awaits them when journey's end is near.

Congress did not improvise a judgment when it found that the award of old age benefits would be conducive to the general welfare The President's Committee on Economic Security made an investigation and report, aided by a research staff of Government officers and employees, and by an Advisory Council and seven other advisory groups. Extensive hearings followed before the House Committee on Ways and Means and the Senate Committee on Finance. A great mass of evidence was brought together supporting the policy which finds expression in the act. Among the relevant facts are these: The number of persons in the United States 65 years of age or over is increasing proportionately as well as absolutely. What is even more important the number of such persons unable to take care of themselves is growing at a threatening pace. More and more our population is becoming urban and industrial instead of rural and agricultural. The evidence is impressive that among industrial workers the younger men and women are preferred over the older. In time of retrenchment the older are commonly the first to go, and even if retained, their wages are likely to be lowered. . . . With the loss of savings inevitable in periods of idleness, the fate of workers over 65, when thrown out of work, is little less than desperate. A recent study of the Social Security Board informs us that "one-fifth of the aged in the United States were receiving old age assistance, emergency relief, institutional care, employment under the works program, or some other form of aid from public or private funds; two-fifths to one-half were dependent on friends and relatives, one-eighth had some income from earnings; and possibly one-sixth had some savings or property. Approximately three out of four persons 65 or over were probably dependent wholly or partially on others for support."

. . . The problem is plainly national in area and dimensions. Moreover laws of the separate states cannot deal with it effectively. Congress, at least, had a basis for that belief. States and local governments are often lacking in the resources that are necessary to finance an adequate program of security for the aged. This is brought out with a wealth of illustration in recent studies of the problem. Apart from the failure of resources, states and local governments are at times reluctant to increase so heavily the burden of taxation to be borne by their residents for fear of placing themselves in a position of economic disadvantage as compared with neighbors or competitors. . . . A system of old age pensions has special dangers of its own, if put in force in one state and rejected in another. The existence of such a system is a bait to the needy and dependent elsewhere, encouraging them to migrate and seek a haven of repose. Only a power that is national call serve the interests of all.

Whether wisdom or unwisdom resides in the scheme of benefits set forth in Title II, it is not for us to say. The answer to such inquiries must come from Congress, not the courts. Our concern here as often is with power, not with wisdom. Counsel for respondent has recalled to us the virtues of self-reliance and frugality. There is a possibility, he says, that aid from a paternal government may sap those sturdy virtues and breed a race of weaklings. If Massachusetts so believes and shapes her laws in that conviction must her breed of sons be changed, he asks, because some other philosophy of government finds favor in the halls of Congress? But the answer is not doubtful. One might ask with equal reason whether the system of protective tariffs is to be set aside at will in one state or another whenever local policy prefers the rule of laissez faire. The issue is a closed one. It was fought out long ago. When money is spent to promote the general welfare, the concept of welfare or the opposite is shaped by Congress, not the states. So the concept be not arbitrary, the locality must yield. Constitution, Art VI, Par. 2.

Third: Title II being valid, there is no occasion to inquire whether Title VIII would have to fall if Title II were set at naught.

The argument for the respondent is that the provisions of the two titles dovetail in such a way as to justify the conclusion that Congress would have been unwilling to pass one without the other. The argument for petitioners is that the tax moneys are not earmarked, and that Congress is at liberty to spend them as it will. The usual separability clause is embodied in the act.

We find it unnecessary to make a choice between the arguments and so leave the question open.

Fourth: The tax upon employers is a valid excise or duty upon the relation of employment.

As to this we need not add to our opinion in Steward Machine vs. Davis, supra, where we considered a like question in respect of Title IX.

Fifth: The tax is not invalid as a result of its exemptions.

Here again the opinion in Steward Machine Co. v. Davis supra says all that need be said.

Sixth: The decree of the Court of Appeals should be reversed and that of the District Court affirmed.

Source: Helvering v. Davis 301 U.S 619(1937)

Principal Presidential Speeches and Messages

A handful of presidential addresses stand out for their importance to the development of the Social Security program. Below are excerpts from each.

Franklin Roosevelt: Message to Congress Reviewing the Broad Objectives and Accomplishments of the Administration, June 8, 1934

In the summer of 1934, President Roosevelt informed Congress of his intent to offer a government pension program. Here he presents his rationale and the basic principles that would guide his development of this program.

You are completing a work begun in March 1933, which will be regarded for a long time as a splendid justification of the vitality of representative government. I greet you and express once more my appreciation of the cooperation which has proved so effective. Only a small number of the items of our program remain to be enacted and I am confident that you will pass on them before adjournment. . . .

Next winter we may well undertake the great task of furthering the security of the citizen and his family through social insurance.

This is not an untried experiment. Lessons of experience are available from States, from industries and from many Nations of the civilized world. The various types of social insurance are interrelated; and I think it is difficult to attempt to solve them piecemeal. Hence, I am looking for a sound means which I can recommend to provide at once security against several of the great disturbing factors in life—especially those which relate to unemployment and old age. I believe there should be a maximum of cooperation between States and the Federal Government. I believe that the funds necessary to provide this insurance should be raised by contribution rather than by an increase in general taxation. Above all, I am convinced that social insurance should be national in scope, although the several States should meet at least a large portion of the cost of management, leaving to the Federal Government the responsibility of investing, maintaining and safeguarding the funds constituting the necessary insurance reserves. I have commenced to make, with the greatest of care, the necessary actuarial and other studies for the formulation of plans for the consideration of the 74th Congress.

These three great objectives the security of the home, the security of livelihood, and the security of social insurance—are, it seems to me, a minimum of the promise that we can offer to the American people. They constitute a right which belongs to every individual and every family willing to work. They are the essential fulfillment of measures already taken toward relief, recovery and reconstruction.

This seeking for a greater measure of welfare and happiness does not indicate a change in values. It is rather a return to values lost in the course of our economic development and expansion.

. . . The third factor relates to security against the hazards and vicissitudes of life. Fear and worry based on unknown danger contribute to social unrest and economic demoralization. If, as our Constitution tells us, our Federal Government was established among other things, "to promote the general welfare," it is our plain duty to provide for that security upon which welfare depends.

Source: Rosenman, Samuel I., ed. 1938. *Public Papers and Addresses of Franklin D. Roosevelt,* vol. III. New York: Random House, 1938.

FDR's speeches are also available online through the American Presidency Project at http://www.presidency.ucsb.edu/ws/.

Franklin Roosevelt: Message to Congress on Social Security, January 17, 1935

This is an excerpt of President Roosevelt's message introducing what would become the Social Security Act of 1935 to Congress. Of particular interest today are his final remarks, in which he appears to endorse a program of voluntary contributions in addition to the government-supported pensions. Was he urging the creation of a program of individual retirement accounts? There is much dispute over these words.

In addressing you on June eighth, 1934, I summarized the main objectives of our American program. Among these was, and is, the security of the men, women, and children of the Nation against certain hazards and vicissitudes of life. This purpose is an essential part of our task. In my annual message to you I promised to submit a definite program of action. This I do in the form of a report to me by a Committee on Economic Security, appointed by me for the purpose of surveying the field and of recommending the basis of legislation.

I am gratified with the work of this Committee and of those who have helped it: . . . It is my best judgment that this legislation should be brought forward with a minimum of delay.

. . . Three principles should be observed in legislation on this subject. First, the system adopted, except for the money necessary to initiate it, should be self-sustaining in the sense that funds for the payment of insurance benefits should not come from the proceeds of general taxation. Second, excepting in old-age insurance, actual management should be left to the States subject to standards established by the Federal Government. Third, sound financial management of the funds and the reserves, and protection of the credit structure of the Nation should be assured by retaining Federal control over all funds through trustees in the Treasury of the United States.

. . . In the important field of security for our old people, it seems necessary to adopt three principles: First, non-contributory old-age pensions for those who are now too old to build up their own insurance. It is, of course, clear that for perhaps thirty years to come funds will have to be provided by the States and the Federal Government to meet these pensions. Second, compulsory contributory annuities which in time will establish a self-supporting system for those now young and for future generations. Third, voluntary contributory annuities by which individual initiative can increase the annual amounts received in old age. It is proposed that the Federal Government assume one-half of the cost of the old-age pension plan, which ought ultimately to be supplanted by self-supporting annuity plans.

Source: Rosenman, Samuel I., ed. 1938. *Public Papers and Addresses of Franklin D. Roosevelt,* vol. IV. New York: Random House. FDR's speeches are also available online through the American Presidency Project at http://www.presidency.ucsb.edu/ws/.

Franklin Roosevelt: State of the Union Address, January 11, 1944

In 1944, President Roosevelt offered what has become known as his "Economic Bill of Rights." This speech became and remains the rallying cry of those who wish a more generous or expansive social security system in the United States.

We have come to a clear realization of the fact that true individual freedom cannot exist without economic security and independence. "Necessitous men are not free men." People who are hungry and out of a job are the stuff of which dictatorships are made.

In our day these economic truths have become accepted as self-evident. We have accepted, so to speak, a second Bill of Rights under which a new basis of security and prosperity can be established for all regardless of station, race, or creed.

Among these are:

The right to a useful and remunerative job in the industries or shops or farms or mines of the Nation;

The right to earn enough to provide adequate food and clothing and recreation;

The right of every farmer to raise and sell his products at a return which will give him and his family a decent living;

The right of every businessman, large and small, to trade in an atmosphere of freedom from unfair competition and domination by monopolies at home or abroad;

The right of every family to a decent home;

The right to adequate medical care and the opportunity to achieve and enjoy good health;

The right to adequate protection from the economic fears of old age, sickness, accident, and unemployment;

The right to a good education.

All of these rights spell security. And after this war is won we must be prepared to move forward, in the implementation of these rights, to new goals of human happiness and well-being.

America's own rightful place in the world depends in large part upon how fully these and similar rights have been carried into practice.

Source: American Presidency Project. http://www.presidency
.ucsb.edu/sou/php.

Harry S Truman: State of the Union Address, January 14, 1946

*It is often forgotten that Social Security remained a controversial pro-
gram for many years after its passage. By the late 1940s, Congress was
rejecting the schedule of Federal Insurance Contributions Act (FICA)
tax increases and the program remained narrow in size and coverage.
The expansion of Social Security into the program recognized by Americans today began with this speech by President Truman. Here he makes
clear that he will focus upon extending and revitalizing Social Security
to create a large program that would include all of American society. He
also announces what would be his unsuccessful effort to add national
health insurance to the Social Security system.*

To the Congress of the United States . . .

. . . Our Social Security System has just celebrated its tenth an-
niversary. During the past decade this program has supported the welfare and morale of a large part of our people by removing some of the
hazards and hardships of the aged, the unemployed, and widows and
dependent children.

But, looking back over 10 years' experience and ahead to the future, we cannot fail to see defects and serious inadequacies in our system
as it now exists. Benefits are in many cases inadequate; a great many persons are excluded from coverage; and provision has not been made for
social insurance to cover the cost of medical care and the earnings lost by
the sick and the disabled.

In the field of old-age security, there seems to be no adequate reason for excluding such groups as the self-employed, agricultural and domestic workers, and employees of nonprofit organizations. Since many
of these groups earn wages too low to permit significant savings for old
age, they are in special need of the assured income that can be provided
by old-age insurance.

We must take urgent measures for the readjustment period ahead.
The Congress for some time has been considering legislation designed to
supplement . . . compensation payments to the unemployed . . . it is
sound economic policy. A sustained high level of consumer purchases is
a basic ingredient of a prosperous economy.

. . . The need for a program that will give everyone opportunity for
medical care is obvious. Nor can there be any serious doubt of the Government's responsibility for helping in this human and social problem.

The comprehensive health program which I recommended on November 19, 1945, will require substantial additions to the Social Security

System and, in conjunction with other changes that need to be made, will require further consideration of the financial basis for social security. The system of prepaid medical care which I have recommended is expected eventually to require amounts equivalent to 4 percent of earnings up to $3,600 a year, which is about the average of present expenditures by individuals for medical care. The pooling of medical costs, under a plan which permits each individual to make a free choice of doctor and hospital, would assure that individuals receive adequate treatment and hospitalization when they are faced with emergencies for which they cannot budget individually. In addition, I recommended insurance benefits to replace part of the earnings lost through temporary sickness and permanent disability.

Even without these proposed major additions, it would now be time to undertake a thorough reconsideration of our social security laws. The structure should be expanded and liberalized. Provision should be made for extending coverage credit to veterans for the period of their service in the armed forces. In the financial provisions we must reconcile the actuarial needs of social security, including health insurance, with the requirements of a revenue system that is designed to promote a high level of consumption and full employment.

. . . The plain people of this country found the courage and the strength, the self-discipline, and the mutual respect to fight and to win, with the help of our allies, under God. I doubt if the tasks of the future are more difficult. But if they are, then I say that our strength and our knowledge and our understanding will be equal to those tasks.

Source: American Presidency Project. http://www.presidency .ucsb.edu/sou.php

Dwight Eisenhower: State of the Union Address, February 2, 1953

Though buried deep in his first State of the Union address, President Eisenhower's words on Social Security were of major importance. Since the program's enactment, large sections of the Republican Party had opposed it. President Eisenhower was the first Republican president to be elected after its passage. Would he support the program or, heeding calls from many in his party, work to reduce or eliminate it? Here he not only announces his full-fledged support for Social Security but he clearly calls for its expansion. This speech marks the end of any real political resistance to the U.S. old-age pension plan.

Mr. President, Mr. Speaker, Members of the Eighty-third Congress:

I welcome the honor of appearing before you to deliver my first message to the Congress.

. . . This administration is profoundly aware of two great needs born of our living in a complex industrial economy. First, the individual citizen must have safeguards against personal disaster inflicted by forces beyond his control; second, the welfare of the people demands effective and economical performance by the Government of certain indispensable social services.

In the light of this responsibility, certain general purposes and certain concrete measures are plainly indicated now.

There is urgent need for greater effectiveness in our programs, both public and private, offering safeguards against the privations that too often come with unemployment, old age, illness, and accident. The provisions of the old-age and survivors insurance law should promptly be extended to cover millions of citizens who have been left out of the social-security system. No less important is the encouragement of privately sponsored pension plans. Most important of all, of course, is renewed effort to check the inflation which destroys so much of the value of all social-security payments.

. . . There is, in our affairs at home, a middle way between untrammeled freedom of the individual and the demands for the welfare of the whole Nation. This way must avoid government by bureaucracy as carefully as it avoids neglect of the helpless.

. . . In this spirit must we live and labor: confident of our strength, compassionate in our heart, clear in our mind. . . .

Source: American Presidency Project. http://www.presidency .ucsb.edu/sou.php

William Jefferson Clinton: State of the Union Address, January 19, 1999

After an absence of many years, Social Security returned to the forefront of the presidential agenda in 1999. Recognizing increasing fears about the future of Social Security, President Clinton announced a set of proposed reforms in his State of the Union address. None became law, but they have profoundly influenced the course of the debate over reforming the program.

Mr. Speaker, Mr. Vice President, members of Congress, honored guests, my fellow Americans. Tonight, I have the honor of reporting to you on the State of the Union.

. . . So with our budget surplus growing, our economy expanding, our confidence rising, now is the moment for this generation to meet our historic responsibility to the 21st century. Our fiscal discipline gives us an unsurpassed opportunity to address a remarkable new challenge: the aging of America. With the number of elderly Americans set to double by 2030, the baby boom will become a "senior boom." So first and above all, we must save Social Security for the 21st century. Early in this century, being old meant being poor. When President Roosevelt created Social Security, thousands wrote to thank him for eliminating what one woman called the "stark terror of penniless, helpless old age." Even today, without Social Security, half our nation's elderly would be forced into poverty. Today, Social Security is strong. But by 2013, payroll taxes will no longer be sufficient to cover monthly payments. And by 2032, the trust fund will be exhausted, and Social Security will be unable to pay out the full benefits older Americans have been promised. The best way to keep Social Security a rock-solid guarantee is not to make drastic cuts in benefits; not to raise payroll tax rates; and not to drain resources from Social Security in the name of saving it. Instead, I propose that we make the historic decision to invest the surplus to save Social Security. Specifically, I propose that we commit 60 percent of the budget surplus for the next 15 years to Social Security, investing a small portion in the private sector just as any private or state government pension would do. This will earn a higher return and keep Social Security sound for 55 years. But we must aim higher. We should put Social Security on a sound footing for the next 75 years. We should reduce poverty among elderly women, who are nearly twice as likely to be poor as our other seniors—and we should eliminate the limits on what seniors on Social Security can earn. Now, these changes will require difficult but fully achievable choices over and above the dedication of the surplus. They must be made on a bipartisan basis. They should be made this year. So let me say to you tonight, I reach out my hand to all of you in both houses and both parties and ask that we join together in saying to the American people: We will save Social Security now. Now, last year, we wisely reserved all of the surplus until we knew what it would take to save Social Security. Again, I say, we shouldn't spend any of it, not any of it, until after Social Security is truly saved. First things first. . . . Third, we must help all Americans, from their first day on the job, to save, to invest, to create wealth. From its beginning, Americans have supplemented Social Security with private pensions and savings. Yet today, millions of people retire with little to live on other than Social Security. Americans living longer than ever simply must save more than ever. Therefore, in addition to saving Social Security and Medicare, I propose a new pension initiative for retirement security in the 21st century. I propose that we use a little over 11 percent of the surplus to establish universal savings accounts—USA accounts—to give all Americans the means to save. With these new accounts, Americans can invest as they choose, and receive funds to match a portion of their savings, with extra help for those least able to save. USA accounts will help all Americans to share in our nation's wealth, and to enjoy a more secure retirement. I ask you to support them.

. . . Saving Social Security and Medicare, creating USA accounts—this is the right way to use the surplus. If we do so—if we do so—we will still have the resources to meet critical needs in education and defense. And I want to point out that this proposal is fiscally sound. Listen to this: If we set aside 60 percent of the surplus for Social Security and 16 percent for Medicare, over the next 15 years that saving will achieve the lowest level of publicly held debt since right before World War I, in 1917. So With these four measures—saving Social Security, strengthening Medicare, establishing the USA accounts, supporting long-term care— we can begin to meet our generation's historic responsibility to establish true security for 21st century seniors.

. . . My fellow Americans, this is our moment. Let us lift our eyes as one nation, and from the mountaintop of this American century, look ahead to the next one, asking God's blessing on our endeavors and on our beloved country. Thank you, and good evening.

Source: American Presidency Project. http://www.presidency .ucsb.edu/sou.php

George Walker Bush: State of the Union Address, February 2, 2005

After his reelection in 2004, President Bush returned to the issue of reforming Social Security. In this address, he calls for the partial privatization of Social Security through creating private individual retirement accounts. Though initially unsuccessful, his words again framed the debate for the years to come.

Mr. Speaker, Vice President Cheney, members of Congress, fellow citizens:

As a new Congress gathers, all of us in the elected branches of government share a great privilege: we have been placed in office by the votes of the people we serve. . . .Two weeks ago, I stood on the steps of this Capitol and renewed the commitment of our nation to the guiding ideal of liberty for all. This evening I will set forth policies to advance that ideal at home and around the world.

. . . One of America's most important institutions—a symbol of the trust between generations—is also in need of wise and effective reform. Social Security was a great moral success of the 20th century, and we must honor its great purposes in this new century. The system, however, on its current path, is headed toward bankruptcy. And so we must join together to strengthen and save Social Security.

Today, more than 45 million Americans receive Social Security benefits, and millions more are nearing retirement—and for them the system is sound and fiscally strong. I have a message for every American who is 55 or older: Do not let anyone mislead you. For you, the Social Security system will not change in any way.

For younger workers, the Social Security system has serious problems that will grow worse with time. Social Security was created decades ago, for a very different era. In those days people did not live as long, benefits were much lower than they are today, and a half century ago, about 16 workers paid into the system for each person drawing benefits. Our society has changed in ways the founders of Social Security could not have foreseen. In today's world, people are living longer and therefore drawing benefits longer—and those benefits are scheduled to rise dramatically over the next few decades. And instead of 16 workers paying in for every beneficiary, right now it's only about three workers—and over the next few decades, that number will fall to just two workers per beneficiary. With each passing year, fewer workers are paying ever-higher benefits to an ever-larger number of retirees.

So here is the result: Thirteen years from now, in 2018, Social Security will be paying out more than it takes in. And every year afterward will bring a new shortfall, bigger than the year before. For example, in the year 2027, the government will somehow have to come up with an extra $200 billion to keep the system afloat—and by 2033, the annual shortfall would be more than $300 billion. By the year 2042, the entire system would be exhausted and bankrupt. If steps are not taken to avert that outcome, the only solutions would be drastically higher taxes, massive new borrowing, or sudden and severe cuts in Social Security benefits or other government programs.

I recognize that 2018 and 2042 may seem like a long way off. But those dates are not so distant, as any parent will tell you. If you have a 5-year-old, you're already concerned about how you'll pay for college tuition 13 years down the road. If you've got children in their 20s, as some of us do, the idea of Social Security collapsing before they retire does not seem like a small matter. And it should not be a small matter to the United States Congress.

You and I share a responsibility. We must pass reforms that solve the financial problems of Social Security once and for all.

Fixing Social Security permanently will require an open, candid review of the options. Some have suggested limiting benefits for wealthy retirees. Former Congressman Tim Penny has raised the possibility of indexing benefits to prices rather than wages. During the 1990s, my predecessor, President Clinton, spoke of increasing the retirement age. Former Sen. John Breaux suggested discouraging early collection of Social Security benefits. The late Sen. Daniel Patrick Moynihan recommended changing the way benefits are calculated.

All these ideas are on the table. I know that none of these reforms would be easy. But we have to move ahead with courage and honesty, because our children's retirement security is more important than partisan politics. I will work with members of Congress to find the most effective combination of reforms. I will listen to anyone who has a good idea to offer. We must, however, be guided by some basic principles. We must make Social Security permanently sound, not leave that task for another day. We must not jeopardize our economic strength by increasing payroll taxes. We must ensure that lower income Americans get the help they need to have dignity and peace of mind in their retirement. We must guarantee that there is no change for those now retired or nearing retirement. And we must take care that any changes in the system are gradual, so younger workers have years to prepare and plan for their future.

As we fix Social Security, we also have the responsibility to make the system a better deal for younger workers. And the best way to reach that goal is through voluntary personal retirement accounts. Here is how the idea works. Right now, a set portion of the money you earn is taken out of your paycheck to pay for the Social Security benefits of today's retirees. If you are a younger worker, I believe you should be able to set aside part of that money in your own retirement account, so you can build a nest egg for your own future.

Here is why personal accounts are a better deal. Your money will grow, over time, at a greater rate than anything the current system can deliver—and your account will provide money for retirement over and above the check you will receive from Social Security. In addition, you'll be able to pass along the money that accumulates in your personal account, if you wish, to your children or grandchildren. And best of all, the money in the account is yours, and the government can never take it away.

The goal here is greater security in retirement, so we will set careful guidelines for personal accounts. We will make sure the money can only go into a conservative mix of bonds and stock funds. We will make sure that your earnings are not eaten up by hidden Wall Street fees. We will make sure there are good options to protect your investments from sudden market swings on the eve of your retirement. We will make sure a personal account can't be emptied out all at once, but rather paid out over time, as an addition to traditional Social Security benefits. And we will make sure this plan is fiscally responsible, by starting personal retirement accounts gradually, and raising the yearly limits on contributions over time, eventually permitting all workers to set aside four percentage points of their payroll taxes in their accounts.

Personal retirement accounts should be familiar to federal employees, because you already have something similar, called the Thrift Savings Plan, which lets workers deposit a portion of their paychecks into any of five different broadly based investment funds. It is time to extend the same security, and choice, and ownership to young Americans. . . .

Source: American Presidency Project. http://www.presidency.ucsb.edu/sou.php

Reform Commission and Advisory Council Reports

For most of the history of Social Security, major program reforms were first developed and promoted through councils or commissions devised for that purpose. Until 1994, Advisory Councils were convened periodically within the Social Security system to examine the operations of the program. Based on their findings, changes were made for the improvement of the program. On occasion, outside groups of experts and political figures have been asked to meet and examine the Social Security system, with an eye to reform. These have typically been called "commissions." The most influential have been those organized by the president of the United States.

The current era of "saving Social Security" has seen the reports of three major bodies—two presidential commissions and one Advisory Council. They have to a significant degree set the agenda for later congressional legislation and for the societal debate over what (if any) reforms to make to the program. Below are excerpts from the final reports of three important bodies.

Report of the National Commission on Social Security Reform (The Greenspan Commission). January 1983

The commission was established on December 16, 1981, by President Ronald Reagan. It was composed of 15 members: eight Republicans and seven Democrats. Five members were selected by the president; five were selected by the senate majority leader, in consultation with the senate minority leader; and five were selected by the speaker of the House of Representatives, in consultation with the House minority leader. It was asked to examine the current and long-term financial condition of the Trust Funds, to identify problems with the operations of the Social Security system, and to offer recommendations to solve them.

. . . Findings and Recommendations

The National Commission has agreed that there is a financing problem for the OASDI program for both the short run, 1983–89 (as measured using pessimistic economic assumptions) and the long range, 1983–2056 (as measured by an intermediate cost estimate) and that action should be taken to strengthen the financial status of the program. The National Commission recognized that, under the intermediate cost estimate, the financial status of the OASDI program in the 1990s and early 2000s will be favorable (i.e., income will significantly exceed outgo). The National Commission also recognized that, under the intermediate cost estimate, the financial status of the HI program becomes increasingly unfavorable from 1990 until the end of the period for which the estimates are made. . . .

The National Commission makes the following recommendations unanimously:

(1) The members of the National Commission believe that the Congress, in its deliberations on financing proposals, should not alter the fundamental structure of the Social Security program or undermine its fundamental principles. The National Commission considered, but rejected, proposals to make the Social Security program a voluntary one or to transform it into a program under which benefits are a product exclusively of the contributions paid, or to convert it into a fully-funded program, or to change it to a program under which benefits are conditioned on the showing of financial need. (2) The National Commission recommends that, for purposes of considering the short-range financial status of the OASDI Trust Funds, $150–200 billion in either additional income or in decreased outgo (or a combination of both) should be provided for the OASDI Trust Funds in calendar years 1983–89.

(3) The National Commission finds that, for purposes of considering the long-range financial status of the OASDI Trust Funds, its actuarial imbalance for the 75-year valuation period is an average of 1.80% of taxable payroll . . .

The National Commission was able to reach a consensus for meeting the short-range and long-range financial requirements, by a vote of 12 to 3. . . .

The 12 members of the National Commission voting in favor of the "consensus" package agreed to a single set of proposals to meet the short-range deficit. . . . They further agreed that the long-range deficit should be reduced to approximately zero. The single set of recommendations would meet about two-thirds of the long-range financial requirements. Seven of the 12 members agreed that the remaining one-third of the long-range financial requirements should be met by a deferred, gradual increase in the normal retirement age, while the other 5 members agreed to an increase in the contribution rates in 2010 of slightly less than one-half percent (0.46%) of covered earnings on the employer and the same amount on the employee, with the employee's share of the increase offset by a refundable income-tax credit.

Provisions of "Consensus" Package

. . . The "consensus" package would provide an estimated $168 billion in additional financial resources to the OASDI program in calendar years 1983–89. This amount is very close to the midpoint of the $150–200 billion range stated in Recommendation No. 2. . . .

. . . The National Commission recommends that coverage under the OASDI program should be extended on a mandatory basis . . . to all newly hired civilian employees of the Federal Government. The National Commission also recommends that OASDI-HI coverage should be extended on a mandatory basis . . . to all employees of nonprofit organizations.

. . . The National Commission recommends that State and local governments which have elected coverage for their employees under the OASDI-HI program should not be permitted to terminate such coverage in the future—specifically, termination notices now pending would be invalid if the process of termination is not completed by the enactment date of the new legislation.

. . . The National Commission is concerned about the relatively large OASDI benefits that can accrue to individuals who spend most of their working careers in noncovered employment from which they derive pension rights, but who also become eligible for OASDI benefits as a result of relatively short periods in covered employment with other employers. Accordingly, the National Commission recommends that the method of computing benefits should be revised for persons who first become eligible for pensions from non-covered employment, after 1983, so as to eliminate "windfall" benefits.

. . . The National Commission recommends that, beginning with 1984, 50% of OASDI benefits should be considered as taxable income for income-tax purposes for persons with Adjusted Gross Income (before including therein any OASDI benefits) of $20,000 if single and $25,000 if married. The proceeds from such taxation, as estimated by the Treasury Department, would be credited to the OASDI Trust Funds under a permanent appropriation.

It is estimated that about 10% of OASDI beneficiaries would be affected by this provision. The National Commission noted that a "notch" is present in this provision in that those with Adjusted Gross Income of just under the limit of $20,000/$25,000 would have a larger total income (including OASDI benefits) than those with Adjusted Gross Income just over the limit. The National Commission points out the presence of this "notch" and trusts that it will be rectified in the legislative process.

. . . The National Commission recommends that the automatic cost-of-living adjustments of OASDI benefits should, beginning in 1983, be made applicable to the December benefit checks (payable early in January), rather than being first applicable to the June payments. The National Commission also recommends that the amount of the disregard of OASDI benefits for purposes of determining Supplemental Security Income payment levels should be increased from $20 a month to $50.

. . . The National Commission recommends that the following changes in benefit provisions which affect mainly women should be made:

(a) Present law permits the continuation of benefits for surviving spouses who remarry after age 60. This would also be done for (1) disabled surviving spouses aged 50–59, (2) disabled divorced surviving spouses aged 50–59, and (3) divorced surviving spouses aged 60 or over.

(b) Spouse benefits for divorced spouses would be payable at age 62 or over (subject to the requirement that the divorce has lasted for a significant period) if the former spouse is eligible for retirement benefits, whether or not they have been claimed (or they have been suspended because of substantial employment).

(c) Deferred surviving-spouse benefits would continue to be indexed as under present law, except that the indexing would be based on the increases in wages after the death of the worker (instead of by the increases in the CPI, as under present law).

(d) The benefit rate for disabled widows and widowers aged 50–59 at disablement would be the same as that for non-disabled widows and widowers first claiming benefits at age 60 . . . instead of the lower rates under present law. . . . Such change would not only be applicable to new cases, but would also be applicable to beneficiaries of this category who are on the rolls on the effective date of the provision.

. . . The National Commission recommends that the OASDI tax schedule should be revised so that the 1985 rate would be moved to 1984, the 1985–87 rates would remain as scheduled under present law, part of the 1990 rate would be moved to 1988, and the rate for 1990 and after would remain unchanged. . . .

. . . The National Commission recommends that the OASDI tax rates for self-employed persons should, beginning in 1984, be equal to the combined employer-employee rates. One-half of the OASDI taxes paid by self-employed persons should then be considered as a business expense for income-tax purposes (but not for purposes of determining the OASDI-HI tax).

. . . The National Commission recommends that the proposed OASDI tax rates should be allocated between the OASI and DI Trust Funds in a manner different from present law, in order that both funds will have about the same fund ratios.

. . . The National Commission recommends that the authority for inter-fund borrowing by the OASDI Trust Funds from the HI Trust Fund be authorized for 1983–87.

. . . The National Commission recommends that a lump-sum payment should be made to the OASDI Trust Funds from the General Fund of the Treasury for the following items:

(a) The present value of the estimated additional benefits arising from the gratuitous military service wage credits for service before 1957 (subject to subsequent adjustments if the experience deviates from the estimates).

(b) The amount of the combined employer-employee OASDI taxes on the gratuitous military service wage credits for service after 1956 and before 1983 . . . The payment would include interest, but would be reduced for any costs therefor which were paid in the past to the OASDI Trust Funds from the General Fund of the Treasury. In the future, the OASDI Trust Funds would be reimbursed on a current basis for such employer-employee taxes on such wage credits for service after 1982.

(c) The amount of uncashed OASDI checks issued in the past (which were charged against the trust funds at time of issue), estimated at about $300–400 million. (The problem of uncashed checks in the future has been corrected as a result of changed procedures of the Treasury Department with regard to checks which are uncashed for a long time.)

. . . The National Commission recommends that, beginning with 1988, if the fund ratio of the combined OASDI Trust Funds as of the beginning of a year is less than 20.0% . . . the automatic cost-of-living (COLA) adjustments of OASDI benefits should be based on the lower of the CPI increase or the increase in wages. If the fund ratio is 32.0% or more at the beginning of a year, payments will be made during the following year as supplements to monthly benefits otherwise payable to make up to individuals for any use of wage increases instead of CPI increases in the past, but only to the extent that sufficient funds are available over those needed to maintain a fund ratio of 32.0%.

[The fund ratio is the balance in the fund, exclusive of any outstanding loan from the HI Trust Fund, as a percentage of the estimated outgo from the fund in the year.]

This provision will serve as a stabilizer against the possibility of exceptionally poor economic performance over a period of time.

The increases in wages would be determined from the "SSA average wage index," the series used by the Social Security Administration in determining such elements of the program as the maximum taxable earnings base and the "bend points" in the formula for the Primary Insurance Amount. As an example, assuming that this new indexing method were applicable for 1995 (for the December checks), the COLA percentage would be the smaller of (1) the percentage increase in the CPI from the third quarter of 1994, to the third quarter of 1995 or (2) the percentage increase in the "SSA average wage index" from 1993 to 1994.

. . . The National Commission recommends that the Delayed-Retirement Credit should be increased from the present 3% (for persons who attained age 65 after 1981) to 8%, to be phased in over the period 1990–2010.

Under present law, persons who do not receive benefits after age 65 . . . receive increases in their benefit (and in their widowed spouse's benefit, but not in any other auxiliary benefit) at the rate of 3% for each year of delay in receipt of benefits from age 65 through age 71. Under the proposal, the Delayed Retirement Credit for months in 1990 would be at the rate of 3 1/4%, those for 1991 would be at the rate of 3 1/2%, etc. until an 8% rate would be reached in 2009 and after . . .

Source: Social Security Administration. 1983. *Report of the National Commission on Social Security Reform,* January. http://www.ssa .gov/history/reports/gspan.html.

Report of the 1994–1996 Advisory Council on Social Security

This is the last Advisory Council report. This council was charged with the examination of the long-term financing of Social Security and the development of a policy response.

Findings and Recommendations

While the Council has not found any short-term financing problems with the Old-Age, Survivors, and Disability (OASDI) program, there are serious problems in the long run. Because of the time required for workers to prepare for their retirement, and the greater fairnes of gradual changes, even long-run problems require attention in the near term.

The Council identified four major areas of concern.

[The] Long-Term Balance. Under their intermediate assumptions, the Trustees of the Social Security Funds estimated that income (the sum of the revenue sources plus interest on accumulated funds) will exceed expenses each year until 2020. The trust fund balances will then start to decline as investments are cashed in to meet the payments coming due. The Trustees estimated that although 75 percent of costs would continue to be met from current payroll and income taxes, in the absence of any changes full benefits could not be paid on time beginning in 2030.

The deficit over the traditional 75-year projection period was 2.17 percent of taxable payroll . . . Consequently, one of the three major tasks the Council set for itself in the area of financing was to make recommendations that would eliminate the 2.17 percent of taxable payroll deficit. All members of the Council agree that this should be done, though there are differences of opinion on how the goal should be met.

The second major problem with Social Security financing is the deterioration in the program's long-range balance that occurs solely because of the passage of time. Because of the aging of the U.S. population, whenever the program is brought into 75-year balance under a stable tax rate, it can be reasonably forecast that, without any changes in assumptions or experience, the simple passage of time will put the system into deficit . . . All members of the Council agree that it is an unsatisfactory situation to have the passage of time alone put the system into long-run actuarial deficit, though there are again differences on how the problem should be corrected.

The third area of concern for the Council arises from the fact that from now on many young workers and workers of future generations under present law will be paying over their working lifetimes employee and employer taxes that add to considerably more than the present value of their anticipated benefits. This is the inevitable result of a pay-as-you-go system such as the United States has had, and an aging population. Although the money's worth that workers get from Social Security is only one of many criteria for judging the value of the Social

Security system, the Council believes that the system should meet a test of providing a reasonable money's worth return on the contributions of younger workers and future generations, while taking account of the redistributive nature of the Social Security system.

The Council is breaking new ground by dealing so explicitly with money's worth issues. It does so because of concerns about equity from one generation to another. The Council feels that equity among generations is a serious issue and that it is important to improve the return on retirement saving for young people.

All members of the Council favor the objective of improving the money's worth given by Social Security to younger generations. There are again differences on how this objective should be achieved.

The final issue involves public confidence in the system. Polling data suggest that younger people have unprecedentedly low levels of confidence that Social Security benefits "will be there" for them when they retire. Polling data also suggest some erosion in public confidence in Social Security over time. While some of this skepticism runs well beyond issues the Council was dealing with, the Council does want to reassure people about the future viability and fairness of Social Security.

. . . In the past, efforts to deal with Social Security's financial difficulties have generally featured cutting benefits and raising tax rates on a pay-as-you-go basis. All Council members agree that the pay-as-you-go approach should be changed. But despite its best efforts, the Council was not able to agree on one single plan for dealing with Social Security's financial difficulties. Rather, Council members expressed interest in three different approaches to restoring financial solvency and improving money's worth returns.

One group of members favors an approach, labeled the Maintenance of Benefits (MB) plan, that involves an increase in income taxes on Social Security benefits, a redirection to the OASDI funds beginning in 2010 of the part of the revenue from taxes on OASDI benefits now going to the Hospital Insurance (HI) Trust Fund, coverage of newly hired State and local government workers not currently covered by Social Security, a payroll tax increase in 2045, and serious consideration of a plan allowing the Government to begin investing a portion of trust fund assets directly in common stocks indexed to the broad market. Historically, returns on equities have exceeded those on Government bonds (where all Social Security funds are now invested). If this equity premium persists, it would be possible to maintain Social Security benefits for all income groups of workers, greatly improving the money's worth for younger workers, without incurring the risks that could accompany individual investment.

Another group of members supports an approach, labeled the Individual Accounts (IA) plan, that creates individual accounts alongside the Social Security system. This plan involves an increase in the income taxation of benefits (though not the redirection of HI funds), State and local coverage, an acceleration of the already-scheduled increase in the age of eligibility for full benefits up to year 2011 and then an automatic increase in that age tied to longevity, a reduction in the growth of future Social Security that benefits is structured to affect middle- and high-wage workers the most, and an increase in employees' mandatory contribution to Social Security of 1.6 percent of covered payroll, which would be allocated to individual defined contribution accounts. These individual accounts would be held by the Government but with constrained investment choices available to individuals. If individuals were to devote the same share of their IA funds to equities as they now do for their 401(k) private pension funds, the combination of the annuity income attributable to their individual accounts and their scaled-back Social Security benefits would on average yield essentially the same benefits as promised under the current system for all income groups.

A third group of members favors an approach, labeled the Personal Security Accounts (PSA) plan, that creates even larger, fully-funded individual accounts which would replace a portion of Social Security. Under this plan, workers would direct 5 percentage points of the current payroll tax into a PSA, which would be managed privately and could be invested in a range of financial instruments. The balance of the payroll tax would go to fund a modified retirement program and modified disability and survivor benefits. When fully phased in, the modified retirement program would offer all full-career workers a flat dollar benefit (the equivalent of $410 monthly in 1996, the amount being automatically increased to reflect increases in national average wages prior to retirement) plus the proceeds of their PSAs. This plan also would involve a change in benefit taxation, State and local coverage, an acceleration of the already-scheduled increase from 65 to 67 in the age of eligibility for full retirement benefits, with the age increased in future years to reflect increases in longevity, a gradual increase from 62 to 65 in the age of eligibility for early retirement benefits (although workers could begin withdrawing the proceeds of their PSAs at 62), a reduction in future benefits for disabled workers, a reduction in benefits for women who never worked outside the home, and an increase in benefits for many elderly widows.

If individuals allocated the assets in their PSAs in the same proportion as they do for their 401(k) private pension plans, the combination of the flat benefit payment and the income from their PSAs would, on average, exceed the benefits promised under the current system for all income groups. There would be a cost associated with the transition to this new system equivalent to 1.52 percent of payroll for 72 years. This transition cost would be met through a combination of increased tax revenues and additional borrowing from the public.

All of these approaches have in common that they seek to achieve more advance funding of Social Security's long-term obligations. They would also result in a higher level of national saving for retirement, although the impact on the nation's overall retirement saving would differ under the plans. The two individual account plans would raise overall retirement and national saving much more than the MB plan in the early years of the forecast horizon through the mandatory contributions of the IA plan or the transition tax of the PSA plan. These two plans are then likely to generate higher national income in the 21st century.

While each of the proposals would increase investment in the stock market, one approach invests new Social Security funds directly into equities to realize a higher rate of return; another approach adds additional, mandatory saving on top of a scaled-back version of the existing benefit system; and the third approach moves from the current pay-as-you-go, largely unfunded system to one in which future benefits are more than 50 percent funded through PSAs. Each of these plans has different potential to create real wealth for retirement and provides for different ownership of that wealth. And each involves a very different vision for the future evolution of the U.S. retirement system.

Source: Social Security Administration. 1997. *Report of the 1994– 1996 Advisory Council on Social Security. Volume I: Findings and Recommendations.* Washington, D.C.: Government Printing Office. http://ssa.gov/history/reports/adcouncil/report/toc.htm.

The 2001 President's Commission to Strengthen Social Security (The Moynihan Commission). December 21, 2001

On May 2, 2001, President George W. Bush appointed a bipartisan panel of 16 individuals to study the future financing of Social Security. The commission was chartered with providing bipartisan recommendations to the president for modernizing and restoring fiscal soundness to the Social Security system according to the following principles: modernization must not change Social Security benefits for retirees or near retirees; the entire Social Security surplus must be dedicated to Social Security only; Social Security payroll taxes must not be increased; the government must not invest Social Security funds in the stock market; modernization must preserve Social Security's disability and survivors' components; and modernization must include individually controlled, voluntary personal retirement accounts, which will augment the Social Security safety net.

Final Report. "Strengthening Social Security and Creating Personal Wealth for all Americans."

From the first, Social Security was a work in progress. It remains so now. In 1939, just four years after enactment, the Administration and Congress added major provisions. FDR called for more. As he signed the

1939 Amendments he stated: "we must expect a great program of social legislation, as such as is represented in the Social Security Act, to be improved and strengthened in the light of additional experience and understanding." He urged an "active study" of future possibilities.

One such possibility – personal retirement accounts that would endow workers with a measure of wealth – has emerged as the central issue in the ongoing national debate over social insurance.

There are a number of reasons for this. The first is the most obvious, if perhaps the least commented upon: Social Security retirement benefits are no longer the bargain they once were. There is nothing sinister about this. Early retirees benefited from the fixed formula of retirement benefits. For years the Social Security Administration would distribute photographs of Ida May Fuller of Ludlow, Vermont, who having paid $24.75 in Social Security taxes lived to age 100 and collected $22,889 in benefits.

In Miss Fuller's time there were almost 42 covered workers for each Social Security beneficiary. We are now down to 3.4 workers per beneficiary. As a result, Social Security as a retirement measure has become a poor investment. It is, even so, an essential program. Widows and dependent children are very reliant on dependent benefits. For widows, widowers, singles and children, the monthly check can be a steady, stabilizing factor in life. That said, however, Social Security's [sic] actuaries estimate that, for a single male worker born in 2000 with average earnings, the real annual return on his currently-scheduled contributions to Social Security will be only 0.86 percent. This is not what sends savers to savings banks. For workers who earn the maximum amount taxed (currently $80,400, indexed to wages) the real annual return is minus 0.72 percent.

This should come as no surprise. Demography is a kind of destiny. The founders of Social Security always assumed it would be supplemented by individual forms of savings. (In his original Message to Congress, President Roosevelt envisioned pensioners owning annuities.) . . .

The post–World War II growth period was reflected . . . in the stock market. More important, a new form of investment, the mutual fund, was developed which enabled small savers to "pool" their investments over a range of stocks and bonds. . . .

The surge in mutual fund ownership began in the early 1980s. One of the more notable innovations was the development of a similar fund, the Thrift Savings Plan, as part of the retirement arrangements for Federal employees. . . . The results have been stunning. . . . Three funds were available, in whatever combination the employee chose. A "G" Fund is invested in short-term non-marketable U.S. Treasury securities specially issued to the TSP. An "F" Fund is invested in a commercial bond index; and a "C" Fund is invested in an equity index fund. The compound rates of return for the closing decade of the last century were as follows:

G Fund	6.7 percent
F Fund	7.9 percent
C Fund	17.4 percent

Actual trading is contracted out and administrative expenses are minimal. . . . As of September 2001, 86.6 percent of all Federal employees participated in the program. It is a singular success.

. . . The Social Security tax (F.I.C.A. for Federal Insurance Contribution Act) began at two percent and has been raised more than twenty times, reaching the present 12.4 percent. This is a regressive tax that is paid on the first dollar of income by rich and poor alike. In fact, as of 1997, 79 percent of American households paid more in payroll taxes than in income taxes.

One egregious failing of the present system is its effect on minorities with shorter life spans than the white majority. For black men age 20, only some 65 percent can be expected to survive to age 65. Thus, one of every three black youths will pay for retirement benefits they will never collect . . . because Social Security provides no property rights to its contributors – the Supreme Court has twice so ruled – a worker could easily work forty years then die and own not a penny of the contributions he has made for retirement benefits he will never collect . . . far too many never receive any retirement benefits and leave no estate.

Similarly, the present Social Security program can prove unjust to women, especially divorced women who too often share nothing of the benefits acquired by a previous spouse. It is time we addressed this matter. . . .

By the 1990s, the time had come for Personal Retirement Accounts . . . the task was feasible – the Thrift Savings Accounts were already in place – and the cost modest . . .

Personal retirement accounts within Social Security could be designed and financed in a number of ways, some of which are analyzed by the Commission in detail in the pages that follow. . . . The system is not sustainable as currently structured, . . . Regardless of how policymakers come to terms with the underlying sustainability issues, however, one thing is clear to us: the time to include personal accounts in such action has, indeed, arrived.

. . . Social Security will be strengthened if modernized to include a system of voluntary personal accounts. Personal accounts improve retirement security by facilitating wealth creation and providing participants with assets that they own and that can be inherited, rather than providing only claims to benefits that remain subject to political negotiation. By allowing investment choice, individuals would be free to pursue higher expected rates of return on their Social Security contributions. Furthermore, strengthening Social Security through personal accounts can add valuable protections for widows, divorced per-sons, low-income households and other Americans at risk of poverty in old age. Partial advance funding of Social Security should be a goal of any effort to strengthen the system. Advance funding within Social Security can best be accomplished through personal accounts rather than direct government investment. . . .

Personal accounts can also contribute towards the fiscal sustainability of the Social Security system. While there are multiple paths to fiscal sustainability that are consistent with the President's principles for Social Security reform, we have chosen to include three reform models in the report that improve the fiscal sustainability of the current system, are costed honestly, and are preferable to the current Social Security system. . . .

The Commission believes that no matter which approach is taken, personal accounts can increase expected benefits to future participants in the Social Security system.

Each of the three reform plans abides by the President's Principles for reform.

- The Commission has developed three alternative models for Social Security reform that feature personal accounts as a central component. Under all three reform plans, future retirees can expect to receive benefits that are at least as high as those received by today's retirees, even after adjusting for inflation. . . .

- Because the Commission believes that the benefits currently paid to low-wage workers are too low, it has included a provision in two of the three plans that would enhance the existing Social Security system's progressivity. This provision will raise even more of our low-income elderly – most of whom are women – out of poverty. Two of the three models also boost survivor benefits for below-average income widows and widowers. . . .

- All three reform models improve the fiscal sustainability of the program, though some move farther than others. Model 1 would require additional revenues in perpetuity in order to pay scheduled Social Security benefits under the plan. Model 3 prescribes an amount of additional revenues needed to pay scheduled benefits under the plan, an amount smaller than that required under Model 1. Model 2 does not require permanent additional funding.

- All three models also require transitional investments to move to a system that includes Personal Accounts. These transitional investments advance fund future benefits, thus substantially reducing the cost on future generations.

- All three models reduce the long-term need for general revenues as compared to the current, unsustainable system. In two of the three plans (Models 2 and 3), the system's cash flow needs are met so that the benefits promised by each plan can be paid as retirees need them.

- All three of the models are expected to increase national saving, though some would do so more than others.
- The Commission concludes that building substantial wealth in personal accounts can be and should be a viable component of strengthening Social Security. We commend our three models to the President, the Members of Congress and to the American public in order to enrich national understanding of the opportunities for moving forward.

[Plan 1.] Workers can voluntarily invest 2 percent of their taxable wages in a personal account

In exchange, traditional Social Security benefits are offset by the worker's personal account contributions compounded at an interest rate of 3.5 percent above inflation.

No other changes are made to traditional Social Security. . . .

Workers, retirees, and taxpayers continue to face uncertainty because a large financing gap remains requiring future benefit changes or substantial new revenues.

Additional revenues are needed to keep the trust fund solvent starting in the 2030s.

[Plan 2.] Workers can voluntarily redirect 4 percent of their payroll taxes up to $1000 annually to a personal account (the maximum contribution is indexed annually to wage growth). No additional contribution from the worker would be required.

In exchange for the account, traditional Social Security benefits are offset by the worker's personal account contributions compounded at an interest rate of 2 percent above inflation.

Workers opting for personal accounts can reasonably expect combined benefits greater than those paid to current retirees; greater than those paid to workers without accounts; and greater than the future benefits payable under the current system should it not be reformed.

The plan makes Social Security more progressive by establishing a minimum benefit payable to 30-year minimum wage workers of 120 percent of the poverty line. Additional protections against poverty are provided for survivors as well.

Benefits under the traditional component of Social Security would be price indexed, beginning in 2009. . . .

[Plan 3.] Personal accounts are created by a match of part of the payroll tax – 2.5 percent up to $1000 annually (indexed annually for wage growth) – for any worker who contributes an additional 1 percent of wages subject to Social Security payroll taxes.

The add-on contribution is partially subsidized for workers in a progressive manner by a refundable tax credit.

In exchange, traditional Social Security benefits are offset by the worker's personal account contributions compounded at an interest rate of 2.5 percent above inflation.

The plan makes the traditional Social Security system more progressive by establishing a minimum benefit payable to 30-year minimum wage workers of 100 percent of the poverty line. . . . This minimum benefit would be indexed to wage growth. Additional protections against poverty are provided for survivors as well.

Benefits under the traditional component of Social Security would be adjusted by

- adjusting the growth rate in benefits for actual future changes in life expectancy,
- increasing work incentives by decreasing the benefits for early retirement and increasing the benefits for late retirement, and
- flattening out the benefit formula (reducing the third bend point factor from 15 to 10 percent). . . .

New sources of dedicated revenue are added in the equivalent amount of 0.6 percent of payroll over the 75-year period, and continuing thereafter.

Additional temporary transfers from general revenues would be needed to keep the Trust Fund solvent between 2034 and 2063. . . .

Source: Commission to Strengthen Social Security. 2001. *Strengthening Social Security and Creating Personal Wealth for All Americans, the Final Report of the President's Commission to Strengthen Social Security.* Washington, D.C.: Government Printing Office. http://www.csss.gov/reports/.

Social Security Annual Trustees Report

Each year the trustees of the Social Security Board are required to issue a report outlining the operations of the Social Security programs and their funding. The report is usually released in the spring. It is this report that has become famous for announcing the predicted date at which the Trust Fund will be exhausted. Presented below is the published summary of the 2007 Annual Trustees Report *and the summary of the Social Security program contained in the report of the* Status of the Social Security and Medicare Programs. *The full reports, which run many pages and are issued each year, may be found at the Social Security Administration Web site (go to http://ssa.gov and type "trustee report" in the Web site's search engine).*

A Summary of the 2007 Annual Trustees Report

... The Old-Age, Survivors, and Disability Insurance (OASDI) program in the United States makes available a basic level of monthly income upon the attainment of retirement eligibility age, death, or disability by insured workers. The OASDI program consists of two separate parts which pay benefits to workers and their families-Old-Age and Survivors Insurance (OASI) and Disability Insurance (DI). Under OASI, monthly benefits are paid to retired workers and their families and to survivors of deceased workers. Under DI, monthly benefits are paid to disabled workers and their families.

The Board of Trustees was established under the Social Security Act to oversee the financial operations of the OASI and DI Trust Funds. The Board is composed of six members. Four members serve by virtue of their positions in the Federal Government: the Secretary of the Treasury, who is the Managing Trustee; the Secretary of Labor; the Secretary of Health and Human Services; and the Commissioner of Social Security. The other two members, John L. Palmer and Thomas R. Saving, are public representatives initially appointed by President William J. Clinton on October 28, 2000, and reappointed by President George W. Bush on April 18, 2006. The Deputy Commissioner of the Social Security Administration (SSA) is designated as Secretary of the Board.

The Social Security Act requires that the Board, among other duties, report annually to the Congress on the financial and actuarial status of the OASI and DI Trust Funds. This annual report, for 2007, is the 67th such report . . .

The report's major findings are summarized below.

In 2006

At the end of 2006, 49 million people were receiving benefits: 34 million retired workers and their dependents, 7 million survivors of deceased workers, and 9 million disabled workers and their dependents. During the year an estimated 162 million people had earnings covered by Social Security and paid payroll taxes. Total benefits paid in 2006 were $546 billion. Income was $745 billion, and assets held in special issue U.S. Treasury securities grew to $2.0 trillion.

Short-Range Results

The OASI and DI Trust Funds, individually and combined, are adequately financed over the next 10 years under the intermediate assumptions. The combined assets of the OASI and DI Trust Funds are projected to increase from $2,048 billion at the beginning of 2007, or 345 percent of annual expenditures, to $4,210 billion at the beginning of 2016, or 407 percent of annual expenditures in that year. Combined assets were projected in last year's report to rise to 344 percent of annual expenditures at the beginning of 2007, and 407 percent at the beginning of 2016.

Long-Range Results

Under the intermediate assumptions, OASDI cost will increase more rapidly than tax income between about 2010 and 2030, due to the retirement of the large baby-boom generation. After 2030, increases in life expectancy and relatively low fertility rates will continue to increase Social Security system costs relative to tax income, but more slowly. Annual cost will exceed tax income starting in 2017 at which time the annual gap will be covered with cash from redemptions of special obligations of the Treasury that make up the trust fund assets, until these assets are exhausted in 2041. Separately, the DI fund is projected to be exhausted in 2026 and the OASI fund in 2042. For the 75-year projection period, the actuarial deficit is 1.95 percent of taxable payroll, 0.06 percentage point smaller than in last year's report. The open group unfunded obligation for OASDI over the 75-year period is $4.7 trillion in present value, and is $0.1 trillion above the measured level of a year ago. In the absence of any changes in assumptions, methods, and starting values, the unfunded obligation would have risen to $4.8 trillion due to the change in the valuation date.

The OASDI annual cost rate is projected to increase from 11.21 percent of taxable payroll in 2007, to 16.59 percent in 2030, and to 18.55 percent in 2081, or to a level that is 5.20 percent of taxable payroll more than the projected income rate for 2081. In last year's report the OASDI cost for 2080 was estimated at 18.74 percent, or 5.38 percent of payroll more than the annual income rate for that year. Expressed in relation to the projected gross domestic product (GDP), OASDI cost is estimated to rise from the current level of 4.3 percent of GDP, to 6.2 percent in 2030, and to 6.3 percent in 2081.

Conclusion

Annual cost will begin to exceed tax income in 2017 for the combined OASDI Trust Funds, which are projected to become exhausted and thus unable to pay scheduled benefits in full on a timely basis in 2041 under the long-range intermediate assumptions. For the trust funds to remain solvent throughout the 75-year projection period, the combined payroll tax rate could be increased during the period in a manner equivalent to an immediate and permanent increase of 1.95 percentage points, benefits could be reduced during the period in a manner equivalent to an immediate and permanent reduction of 13.0 percent, general revenue transfers equivalent to $4.7 trillion in present value could be made during the period, or some combination of approaches could be adopted. Significantly larger changes would be required to maintain solvency beyond 75 years.

The projected trust fund deficits should be addressed in a timely way to allow for a gradual phasing in of the necessary changes and to provide advance notice to workers. Making adjustments sooner will allow them to be spread over more generations. Social Security plays a critical role in the lives of this year's (2007) 50 million beneficiaries and 163 million covered workers and their families. With informed discussion, creative thinking, and timely legislative action, we will work with Congress and others to ensure that Social Security continues to protect future generations.

Status of the Social Security and Medicare Programs. (Social Security Section).

The annual cost of Social Security benefits represented 4.2 percent of Gross Domestic Product (GDP) in 2006, is projected to increase to 6.2 percent of GDP in 2030, and then rise slowly to 6.3 percent of GDP in 2081. The projected 75-year actuarial deficit in the combined Old-Age and Survivors and Disability Insurance (OASDI) Trust Fund is 1.95 percent of taxable payroll, down from 2.02 percent in last year's report. This decrease is due primarily to revisions in key assumptions and to changes in methods. Although the program passes our short-range test of financial adequacy, it continues to fail our long-range test of close actuarial balance by a wide margin. Projected OASDI tax income will begin to fall short of outlays in 2017, and will be sufficient to finance only 75 percent of scheduled annual benefits in 2041, when the combined OASDI Trust Fund is projected to be exhausted.

Social Security could be brought into actuarial balance over the next 75 years in various ways, including an immediate increase of 16 percent in payroll tax revenues or an immediate reduction in benefits of 13 percent or some combination of the two. Ensuring that the system is solvent on a sustainable basis beyond the next 75 years would require larger changes. To the extent that changes are delayed or phased in gradually, larger adjustments in scheduled benefits and revenues would be required that would be spread over fewer generations. . . .

Conclusion

The financial difficulties facing Social Security and Medicare pose enormous, but not insurmountable, challenges. The sooner these challenges are addressed, the more varied and less disruptive their solutions can be. We urge the public to engage in informed discussion and policymakers to think creatively about the changing needs and preferences of working and retired Americans. Such a national conversation and timely political action are essential to ensure that Social Security and Medicare continue to play a critical role in the lives of all Americans.

Henry M. Paulsen, Jr.,
Secretary of the Treasury,
and Managing Trustee

Elaine L. Chao
Secretary of Labor,
and Trustee

Source: Social Security Administration. 2007. *Social Security Annual Trustees Report.* http://ssa.gov.

7

Directory of Organizations

The policy and politics of Social Security are of immense importance to a great many people. Thus it is not surprising that many groups and organizations are active in developing and influencing, or attempting to influence, today's Social Security program and the debates that surround it. Below are descriptions of the most important of these actors, summarizing who they are, where they came from, and their basic interest or perspective. The actors are divided into governmental institutions, lobbying groups, and think tanks active on this issue.

Institutions and Organizations of the U.S. Government

Congress

House of Representatives Committee on Ways and Means

By the rules of the House of Representatives, all legislation and matters pertaining to Social Security must be submitted to the Committee on Ways and Means. This committee investigates, holds hearings, and drafts legislation concerning Social Security. It is thus the fulcrum of Social Security's politics in Congress. It is no accident that the program is under the jurisdiction of this powerful committee, as the Ways and Means Committee is given oversight of all government programs that involve the raising of revenues, as is the case for Social Security. Every major reform or change of Social Security since its enactment in 1935 has gone through this committee, and the program has been extensively influenced by its desires. Because this is a committee of Congress, it can be intensely partisan. In surveying information from this committee, remember that its majority party controls the framing of the materials that it releases to the public. The committee has a Subcommittee on Social Security, a standing body to which it refers all legislation involving the program.

Web site: http://waysandmeans.house.gov/

Senate Committee on Finance

The Committee on Finance is the Senate analog of the House's Committee on Ways and Means. It has responsibility for all Social Security legislation in that body. The Committee on Finance has had great influence over Social Security, especially in recent years. However, it has generally been less decisive than the Ways and Means Committee because Senate committees tend to be less powerful than House committees and because a provision of the Constitution mandates that all revenue bills be first introduced in the House of Representatives. This mandate means that any changes in the financing of Social Security must start there.

Web site: http://www.senate.gov/~finance

Executive Branch

Office of Management and Budget

The Office of Management and Budget (OMB) began as the Bureau of the Budget in 1922. It has the task of drafting the presidential budget and coordinating the activities of all the federal agencies and organizations in developing and implementing that budget. It has therefore become the president's right arm in managing the federal bureaucracy and in drafting new programs that involve it. For this reason, the director of the OMB has more than once been a key actor in the Social Security debate. As seen in chapter 1, the most recent major changes in Social Security followed efforts by President Ronald Reagan's OMB director to reform the program. Because the OMB acts as a management tool for the president, its analyses and recommendations almost always reflect the views and priorities of that president. OMB reports should not be viewed as nonpartisan or objective, even though the analytic quality is generally quite high.

Web site: http://www.omb.gov

White House—Council of Economic Advisors

The President of the United States is, of course, a key actor in the politics and policy of Social Security. The president usually attempts to influence the debate by using the OMB or other cabinet departments, friendly members of Congress, or the White House staff. Important here is the Council of Economic Advisors (CEA). This is a group of experts, usually prominent academics, who analyze and develop policy prescriptions for the president. It is debatable whether this group independently influences the president or whether, instead, it primarily responds to the president's agenda and priorities, but in either case they can play a large role in developing the specifics of any program reforms that the president may wish to offer. The CEA annually publishes the Economic Report of the President, which often contains a discussion of the Social Security program. This document develops and defends the president's proposals at a level that is both very readable and quite sophisticated analytically.

Web site: http://whitehouse.gov

Social Security Administration

Obviously an important actor, the Social Security Administration manages all of Social Security's programs. Social Security has been reorganized several times since its creation in 1935. Originally, it was administered by a board of three members appointed by the president who in turn hired whatever staff they needed. But in 1946, the board was replaced by the Social Security Administration, a larger, more complex bureaucracy headed by a commissioner who was appointed by the president. In 1953, President Dwight Eisenhower did away with this structure and moved the Social Security program within the new cabinet department known as the Department of Health, Education and Welfare. The program thus fell under the domain of the secretary of that department. Following another cabinet reorganization under President Jimmy Carter in 1980, Social Security was placed in the Department of Health and Human Services. In 1983, the National Commission on Social Security Reform (also known as the Greenspan Commission), however, recommended that the government examine the possibility of returning Social Security to an independent status. A year later, a study endorsed this idea, and in 1994, the Social Security Administration was again made an independent federal agency with a commissioner nominated by the president and confirmed by Congress. That is the organization's status today.

The Social Security Administration currently employs more than 62,000 people in its central office (headquartered in Baltimore), 10 regional offices, six processing centers, and 1,300 field offices. Its employees and commissioner are enjoined to be nonpartisan. There has been some recent debate about whether the commissioner has shown favoritism toward proposals to privatize the system, but in general the administration in power has stayed out of the debate over the reform of Social Security. This was not always the case, as the first generation of Social Security Board members and commissioners were undoubtedly advocates for the expansion of the program. Within the Social Security system, Social Security Advisory Councils, which met irregularly, were given the task of examining reforms to the Social Security program. Advisory Councils were the one tool available to those inside the program who wished to influence the debates surrounding it. The last Advisory Council met from 1994 to 1996.

The Social Security Trust Funds (recall that there are separate trust funds for the retirement program and the disability program) have their own set of trustees, led by the secretary of the Treasury, that are responsible for their financial soundness. By law, the trustees must submit an annual report on the state of the Trust Funds. This report has become a major factor in current Social Security reform debates, because it includes estimated dates for when the Trust Funds will turn negative, and when they will be exhausted.

Web site: http://ssa.gov.

Social Security Advisory Board

This is a seven-member board that advises Congress, the president, and the Social Security Administration on matters relating to the operations of the Social Security program. The idea of the board was developed by the Greenspan Commission in 1983, but it was not created until 1994. The board, which meets monthly, is bipartisan and primarily takes an interest in technical matters involving the workings of the Social Security and the Supplemental Security Income programs. The board refrains from specific proposals to reform Social Security, but it repeatedly urges Congress and the president to take action to shore up the financing of the program.

Web site: http://ssab.gov.

Interest Groups and Lobbying Organizations

Until relatively recently, few groups actively attempted to influence or reform the operations or policies of the Social Security program. Today scores of organizations lobby Congress and mount public campaigns on this issue. Most of this growth has come in the past two decades, after fears about the future of Social Security first emerged. Many other groups joined the fray after President George W. Bush's effort to partially privatize the program in 2005. Currently, more than 100 registered lobbying organizations list Social Security as a program in which they have an active interest. For better or worse, Social Security has become bound with the growing left/right divide in the United States, as many organizations and interest groups connected to conservative issues and the Republican Party became active in support of efforts at privatization, while other groups connected to liberal concerns and the Democrats were equally motivated to enter the battle in opposition to this idea. The following groups and interests are among those with the greatest impact on the Social Security reform agenda and the politics that swirl around it.

AARP

When a question of Social Security arises, there is little doubt about which interest group has the highest political profile—it is the AARP. Formerly known as the American Association of Retired Persons, the organization boasts more than 35 million members and is often cited as one of the most powerful lobbying groups in Washington.

The AARP is open to all Americans over the age of 50 years. A member does not even have to be retired, hence the organization's name change in 1999. However, the average age of an AARP member is 65, so Social Security remains an issue of fundamental importance to its membership. The organization was founded in 1958, growing out of a smaller organization of retired teachers. It first focused on health insurance, but Social Security rose to the fore after the passage of Medicare in 1965. Senior citizens are attracted to join the organization by favorable insurance programs and a wide variety of member discounts on everything from magazine subscriptions to hotel rooms. The AARP maintains a significant presence in Washington, with a number of lobbyists and a formidable mail and fund-raising operation.

The organization's formal position on Social Security is that reform is needed before a funding crisis occurs and that it is prepared to accept significant reforms even if they are not the ones preferred by the AARP. But it strongly opposes efforts at privatization. It prefers instead to make a set of gradual reforms to the existing program. It is fair to say that the organization is more skeptical of reforms that would reduce existing benefits than it is of other proposed changes. The AARP also lobbies against any policy that would appear to penalize senior citizens for continuing to remain in the workforce. In addition, it argues that employers should be made to offer meaningful pensions and that all Americans should be encouraged, through government incentives, to save more for their retirement.

Web site: http://www.aarp.org

Alliance for Retired Americans

This is a newly active lobbying and campaign fund-raising group affiliated with the AFL-CIO and other labor unions. Founded in 2001, the Alliance for Retired Americans claims 3 million members, most of whom only obtained membership through the unions to which they belong. The Alliance vociferously opposes the Social Security reforms supported by President George W. Bush, and indeed any efforts at privatization. Its views are basically those of the organizations that sponsor it.

Web site: http://retiredamericans.org

Alliance for Worker Retirement Security

This umbrella group of 35 organizations that support private personal retirement accounts includes the National Association of Manufacturers, the U.S. Chamber of Commerce, and the National Federation of Independent Business. The conservative Cato Institute played a key role in the organization of the Alliance in 1998. The Alliance was created to push for personal retirement accounts, and it raises money and sponsors educational programs to that purpose. It is linked to CoMPASS (see below), and together the two groups claim to have raised between $50 million and $150 million to further their policy agenda.

Web site: http://retiresecure.org

American Academy of Actuaries

Somewhere between a professional organization and a lobbying group, the American Academy of Actuaries keeps a strong interest in Social Security due to the professional concerns of its membership. Formed in 1956, it is a presence in Washington, where its representatives frequently testify before Congress and other federal bodies. The organization's standing Committee on Social Insurance keeps an eye on Social Security as well as other retirement programs. This committee takes the position that "preventive maintenance" is needed for Social Security and that reform should come as soon as possible. However, it takes no public position on which reform is superior. Its reports are nonpartisan and often excellent introductions to the various reforms that are circulating around the Capitol.

Web site: http://actuary.org

American Council of Life Insurers

The life insurance industry has a big interest in retirement policies because of its stake in the market for pension annuities, the traditional mode of saving for one's retirement. Its powerful lobbying organization crosses party lines and includes prominent Democrats and Republicans. The primary focus of its efforts in the Social Security debate is the preservation of a favorable tax status toward annuities, but it has come out against personal retirement accounts because of the possible effects of an individual retirement account (IRA) program on annuities purchases.

Web site: http://www.acli.com

American Federation of Labor and Congress of Industrial Organizations (AFL-CIO)

The AFL-CIO is the largest labor union federation in the United States. Today it includes 55 member labor unions and some 10 million workers. It was created in 1955 by a merger of the AFL and the CIO. Since its origins, the AFL-CIO has been among the most active and influential players in the politics of Social Security. For a generation, it was perhaps the most powerful interest pushing for a more generous Social Security program. It was equally as or more responsible than any other actor for the addition of a disability program to Social Security in the mid-1950s. Its Social Security Committee of that era was a leader in both research and policy advocacy. The AFL-CIO continues to support a generous public pension program, but it is opposed to personal retirement accounts and other forms of privatization. In addition to its own activity, it funds a number of other organizations active in the Social Security issue.

Web site: http://www.aflcio.org

American Federation of State, County and Municipal Employees

An affiliate of the AFL-CIO, with its 1.4 million members the American Federation of State, County and Municipal Employees is itself a powerful labor organization in Washington. It shares the AFL-CIO's positions on Social Security and funds several umbrella groups that have organized to fight reforms that would privatize the Social Security system.

Web site: http://www.afscme.org

American Savings Education Council

A public interest coalition focused on raising interest in retirement planning, the American Savings Education Council's activities are focused on supporting efforts to educate the public and to create incentives that will lead Americans to save more outside of the Social Security system. The Council's membership includes a range of groups stretching from the AARP to Fidelity Investments to the American Institute of Certified Public Accountants. Generally, it works to support the creation and maintenance of tax incentives on monies saved for retirement.

Web site: http://www.asec.org

Americans United for Change

Formerly known as "Americans United to Protect Social Security," this is a coalition of some 200 left-of-center organizations that oppose private retirement accounts. It dates from 2005, when it was organized in response to President George W. Bush's Social Security plan. It has since expanded its activities to oppose a variety of the president's other policies.

Web site: http://www.americansunitedforchange.org

Campaign for America's Future/ Institute for America's Future

The Campaign for America's Future is a sister organization to Americans United for Change that was created during the debates over President George W. Bush's personal retirement account proposal. Politically on the left, it has been associated with the progressive Democrat Internet fund-raising group MoveOn .org and the AFL-CIO. It strenuously opposes the Bush Social Security plan.

Web site: http://home.ourfuture.org (the organization maintains a number of Web sites with similar URLs)

Century Foundation

Somewhere between a lobbying group and a think tank, the Century Foundation was initiated by department store baron Edward A. Filene in 1919. The Foundation was an active supporter of the Social Security Act of 1935 and continues to follow the program. Since 1997, it has sponsored the Social Security Network, which collects information about Social Security. Its perspective might be termed moderate left. It opposes privatization but calls for moderate reforms to the system. It is relatively close to the AARP in perspective, with the two organizations frequently linking their information to one another. A number of prominent researchers and academics are associated with the Foundation and its research activities.

Web sites: http://www.tcf.org/ and http://www.socsec.org/

Club for Growth

A rather high-profile conservative group, the Club for Growth is primarily a campaign fund-raiser for congressional candidates who support tax cuts and limits on government spending. It was founded in 1999 by Stephen Moore, a conservative activist formerly associated with the Cato Institute (see "Think Tanks" below). It has recently added Social Security choice to its concerns and has joined the battle in favor of personal retirement accounts within the Social Security system. Because of its success in raising campaign monies it is a significant force, particularly within the Republican Party.

Web site: http://www.clubforgrowth.org

Coalition for American Financial Security

Formed in early 2000, this is an umbrella organization of banks and life insurance companies that support the partial privatization of Social Security. (Many other banks and life insurance companies do not, or take no position; the industry is divided.) The Coalition supports political candidates that take this position. Because the Coalition is close to the GOP, the candidates it supports are usually Republicans.

Web site: none

Coalition for the Modernization and Protection of America's Social Security

Created in 2002 with support from the National Association of Manufacturers, the Business Roundtable, and the Cato Institute, this group, also known as CoMPASS, was apparently organized with the sole purpose of providing support for President George W. Bush's initiative to create personal retirement accounts. It has worked fairly closely with the Bush White House in campaigning for the passage of a Social Security personal retirement account program.

Web site: http://www.generationstogether.net.

Coalition to Preserve Retirement Security

Another specialized lobbying organization, the Coalition to Preserve Retirement Security is composed of state and local government employee groups that oppose the mandatory participation of all government workers in the Social Security system. Recall that this was a reform suggested by the Greenspan Commission in 1983. The leadership of the group is almost entirely drawn from state employee and local teachers unions.

Web site: http://www.retirementsecurity.org

Committee for Economic Development

The Committee for Economic Development (CED) is a 65-year-old organization of business leaders and educators. Again somewhere between a think tank and an advocacy organization, the CED is placed here as an interest group because the organization does take a formal stand on the issues of the day, including Social

Security. The defined mission of the organization is to work for programs that would increase economic growth and productivity in the United States, support an open global economy, and provide greater opportunity for all Americans. The CED's board is studded with present or retired university presidents and chief executive officers of major corporations, and it is backed by a staff of prominent academics. Its stance on Social Security is that the current program needs changes in its benefits and coverage structures, and a second program of add-on personal retirement accounts needs to be added to the current program to maintain its financial viability.

Web site: http://www.ced.org

Concord Coalition

A public information organization, the Concord Coalition was created in 1992 by former senators Paul Tsongas (D-Mass.) and Warren Rudman (R-NH), along with former Commerce Secretary Peter Peterson. It was established in the wake of the unusually large federal deficits that began in the mid-1980s in the belief that these deficits were unsustainable and needed to be ended. Social Security is the U.S. government's most expensive program, so it not surprising that the organization soon took an interest in reforms that would restore the financial footing of the program. The Concord Coalition argues that reform is necessary but will be painful. It has not supported efforts at privatization, including the program developed by President George W. Bush, because it believes that this will not restore Social Security's finances. It instead has supported ideas such as mandatory add-on private accounts or changes in indexing formulas. The prominence of the organization's leaders gives the group significant media access.

Web site: http://www.concordcoalition.org

FreedomWorks

FreedomWorks dates from 2004, following a merger of two conservative organizations, Citizens for a Sound Economy, headed by former House Majority Leader Dick Armey, and Empower America, headed by Jack Kemp, the Republican vice presidential candidate in 1996 and a leading "supply sider" (supply siders argue that reducing taxes will actually increase government revenues and lower the budget deficit). Though primarily interested

in lowering taxes, it has endorsed personal retirement accounts and lobbies in favor of Social Security privatization.
Web site: www.freedomworks.org

Gray Panthers

Listed here more for reasons of historical interest than because of its political power, the Gray Panthers was organized in 1970 by five progressive (or left wing) activists in the New York City area. The group was dubbed the "gray panthers" because its radical agenda and style brought comparisons to the Black Panthers and other revolutionary groups of the 1960s. It has since relocated to Washington, D.C., where it operates in support of progressive policies for elders. Its stance on Social Security is that it must fight to preserve existing Social Security benefits and to prevent "destructive changes" to the program.
Web site: http://graypanthers.org

Institute for Policy Innovation/ Alliance for Retirement Prosperity

The Institute for Policy Innovation (IPI) was founded in 1987 in Lewisville, Texas, by future House Republican Majority Leader Dick Armey (R-Texas). In 2004, it created the Alliance for Retirement Prosperity as its arm for its Social Security efforts. The IPI pushes for a major overhaul of Social Security that would place half of worker Social Security contributions into personal retirement accounts. The organization terms itself a think tank and includes a small staff of economists. The leadership of the group is also tied to FreedomWorks (see above).
Web site: http://www.ipi.org

Investment Company Institute

Representing close to 10,000 investment funds with assets of more than $11 billion, the Investment Company Institute (ICI) is something of an elephant in the closet when it comes to the Social Security debate. Founded in 1940, the ICI works to advance the interests of the mutual fund industry, which has an immense stake in U.S. retirement policies. It lobbies in support of 401(k) and other retirement vehicles. To date, this powerful group has not developed a public stance on Social Security reform, but it has recently hired additional lobbyists known to be favorable to personal retirement accounts. This move may herald a change of direction that would be of some importance to the constellation of forces in Washington given the financial clout of the membership of this organization.

Web site: http://www.ici.org

MoveOn.org

Organized in 1998 to fight the impeachment of President Bill Clinton, MoveOn's great success at Internet fund-raising has made it a significant force in U.S. politics. In 2005, MoveOn added Social Security to its priorities, primarily through its financial support of the Americans United to Protect Social Security. Closely linked to the Democratic Party, MoveOn can be expected to oppose Social Security reform efforts that are identified with the Republicans.

Web site: http://moveon.org

National Center for Policy Analysis

The National Center for Policy Analysis dates from 1983 and, though officially nonpartisan, is generally aligned with conservatives on issues such as lower taxes and less government regulation. It is one of the few organizations headquartered outside of Washington (it is in Dallas). Its members include a mix of academics and (mostly Republican) politicians. Its formal goals are to find private alternatives for government regulations and programs. As might be expected, it is a strong supporter of personal retirement accounts as a way to reform Social Security. Because the organization formally advocates this position and generally does not develop new research, it is placed in this section rather than under the "Think Tanks" section.

Web site: http://www.ncpa.org and http://www.mysocial-security.org

National Committee to Preserve Social Security and Medicare

A public interest group, the National Committee to Preserve Social Security and Medicare was founded by James Roosevelt, President Franklin Roosevelt's oldest son, in 1982, as controversy swirled around the efforts of the Reagan administration to trim Social Security benefits. It was organized to oppose Reagan's plans. Today it mostly lobbies and raises funds to oppose Social Security reforms that involve privatization. It is currently headed by Barbara Kennelly, a former Democratic member of Congress from Connecticut, and, not surprisingly, is linked to the leadership of the Democratic Party. Its positions are in accordance with those leaders.

Web site: http://www.ncpssm.org

National Federation of Independent Business

The National Federation of Independent Business (NFIB) is one of Washington's most effective lobbying organizations. Formed in 1943, it is the largest organization that represents small and independent businesses. Not surprisingly, it takes pro-business positions on issues that are of concern to its members. Only in the last decade has it become interested in Social Security, where it now strongly supports Social Security reform and personal retirement accounts. Its particular concern is the impact on payroll taxes of any changes in the Social Security program. In recent years the NFIB has usually been closely associated with congressional Republicans.

Web site: http://www.nfib.com

National Organization for Women

The National Organization for Women (NOW) claims to be the largest feminist organization in the United States. It is certainly the most prominent. Founded in 1966, it now has 500,000 individual members. In the wake of the privatization issue, NOW entered the Social Security debate by taking a position opposing personal retirement accounts and any cuts of benefits.

Web site: http://www.now.org

Progress for America

Progress for America is an organization developed in 2001 to support the policies of George W. Bush. It is closely connected to the Bush White House and the Republican Party. It has spent more than $30 million to support President Bush's personal account plan. The group attracted some controversy when Thomas R.

Saving, one of the seven trustees of the Social Security Administration, joined the Progress for America as an adviser. Some accused him of a conflict of interest and accused the White House of potentially politicizing the Social Security Administration.

Web site: http://progressforamerica.org (note that the site contains only a statement relating to a Federal Elections Commission settlement with the group)

ProtectYourCheck.org

Recently organized by former Clinton officials and other Democrats, the group is related to Americans United for Change. ProtectYourCheck.org specifically opposes President Bush's privatization plan. The organization is close to the Democratic Party.

Web site: http://www.protectyourcheck.org

Securities Industry and Financial Markets Association

The Securities Industry and Financial Markets Association is a well-heeled and influential lobbying group that focuses upon issues of concern to bankers and Wall Street. For retirement issues, it has mostly focused on congressional actions that affect IRA programs, but it has recently, if mutedly, announced its opposition to personal retirement accounts. It argues that the fees earned by this industry in managing these accounts would likely be less than the fees currently earned through managing mutual funds. Therefore, if individuals responded to the new IRAs by taking savings out their mutual funds, the industry would stand to lose.

Web site: http://www.sifma.org

60 Plus Organization

An institution that claims to be a conservative counterpart of the AARP, the 60 Plus Organization was formed by former Republican members of Congress and staffers. The group boasts 500,000 members and offers insurance programs and discounts similar to those of the AARP. Its primary lobbying issue is the abolition of the estate tax, but it also promotes reforming Social Security to include personal retirement accounts.

Web site: http://www.60plus.org

USA Next

USA Next is perhaps most known for its close ties to the "Swift Boat" campaign against Senator John Kerry in the 2004 presidential election. Its forerunner was founded in 1991 by conservative fund-raising whiz Richard Viguerie. It can fairly be considered an organization that supports the positions of the Republican Party.

It has recently taken up the cudgel of personal retirement accounts. The organization is linked to United Seniors Associates, which is chaired by retired television personality Art Linkletter. The United Seniors Associates is rather like the conservative mirror image of the AARP. It offers discounts and other member benefits similar to the AARP (or its fellow conservative 60 Plus Organization) while attacking the policy positions of that organization. United Seniors Associates, too, supports reforming Social Security into a personal retirement account program.

Web site: http://www.unitedseniors.org

U.S. Chamber of Commerce

This well-known organization was founded in 1912 and presently includes more than 3 million businesses that are organized into some 3,000 local chambers. It has long been a powerful presence in Washington, lobbying for legislation and regulation favorable to business interests. It, too, has only recently become involved in the Social Security issue (though it did oppose the plan 60 years ago). It now includes Social Security reform, including the support for personal retirement accounts, as one of its policy priorities. It favors program reforms that preserve Social Security's viability with "as little impact on taxes and benefits as possible."

Web site: http://www.uschamber.com

Think Tanks

"Think tanks" are institutions, formally nonpartisan, that engage in the research and analysis of public policy issues. Most are staffed by academics, retired government officials, and other policy experts. They regularly publish working papers, policy papers, or journals and other research materials. Their members frequently testify before Congress and are seen on television news programs. Because these individuals are recognized for their expertise, they often can have a significant impact on public debate. These individuals are also very frequently the originators of specific reform ideas and plans. They engage in the "politics of ideas" that goes alongside the "politics of interest" explored above. Most think tanks emerged after World War II. Beginning in the late 1970s, when Social Security reemerged on the public agenda, many of these institutions began to take an interest in the issue. That interest has greatly expanded in recent years following the privatization debate. Below are the most significant think tanks that participate in the Social Security debate.

American Enterprise Institute for Public Policy Research

Dating from 1943, the American Enterprise Institute (AEI) is today one of the most influential think tanks in the United States, and it is considered by many to be the most influential conservative think tank. It is a large organization, with more than 50 full-time researchers on staff, and it is often the home of retired conservative members of Congress. In recent years it has been linked with the neoconservative movement. As indicated by its name, the AEI attempts to promote the free enterprise system and opposes large government programs. AEI research is often of high quality, the equal of work that appears in refereed journals. In the area of Social Security, AEI researchers have been reliable supporters of personal retirement accounts. Martin Feldstein, a professor of economics at Harvard University and perhaps the most prominent academic in support of this reform, has published a good portion of his work through this organization.

Web site: http://www.aei.org

Brookings Institution

Probably the best known and most influential of the think tanks, as well as the oldest, the Brookings Institution was formed in 1927 through a merger of several older institutions. Critics have dubbed it "the Democratic Party government-in-exile," but it is politically more centrist, though perhaps leaning a bit to the left. A number of the leading Social Security researchers work at, or have published through, the Brookings Institution. Though they have developed a variety of reform plans, and one cannot associate any one perspective to the organization, Brookings' researchers generally support modest reforms to the benefits structure, contribution ceilings, or indexing formulas in preference to major changes to the Social Security system. Few support privatization of the system (though some do urge mandatory add-on personal accounts). Research published through Brookings is reliably of very high quality.

Web site: http://www.brook.edu

Cato Institute

A prominent think tank, the Cato Institute was founded in 1977. Its basic perspective is libertarian, reflecting the view that private markets are almost always superior to government action in the provision of goods and services. Cato's founders were previously active in the Libertarian Party. The name comes from "Cato's Letters," a set of pamphlets written around the time of the American Revolution that argued against the need for a strong government. The Cato Institute has a "project on social security choice" that conducts research on this issue. Not surprisingly, the Institute and its members argue for a fully privatized Social Security system. They advocate a model something along the lines of the current Chilean system. If a study bears the Cato imprint, one can usually expect a well-argued defense of letting private markets handle the retirement needs of U.S. senior citizens.

Web site: http://www.cato.org

Center for American Progress

Founded by President Clinton's former chief of staff, John Podesta, in 2003, the Center for American Progress remains closely connected to the Clinton family. Podesta aimed to create a counter to the Heritage Foundation, and the Center sports a lineup of experts that is moderately left of center. However, this new think tank is nowhere near the size of those described above. Researchers at the Center for American Progress have tended to focus on raising the ceiling on earned income subject to the Federal Insurance Contributions Act (FICA) tax as a solution to the Social Security problem. The Center is linked to the Center for American Progress Action Fund, a political fund-raising organization.

Web site: http://www.americanprogress.org

Center on Budget and Policy Priorities

The Center on Budget and Policy Priorities (CBPP) think tank was founded in 1981 to analyze federal budget priorities. It focuses upon the impact of budget choices on low-income Americans. Surveys of members of Congress and of federal officials have found that the CBPP is among the most respected and influential think tanks currently operating. Most research that comes out of the Center is politically in the center or perhaps on the moderate left. Most of its researchers endorse gradual reforms of Social Security, including benefit changes and increased revenues, to maintain the program's financial soundness. The researchers are often quite distinguished academics and retired federal officials, many of whom are also linked, or have been linked, to the Brookings Institution. In fact, Web links found on the Center's Web site often go to the Brookings Web site.

Web site: http://www.cbpp.org

Center for Economic and Policy Research

The Center for Economic and Policy Research (CEPR) was established in 1999 by several economists but today has grown to have an advisory board of some of America's most illustrious economists, including two Nobel Prize winners. The CEPR publishes high-quality research on a variety of public policy issues. They are generally from a somewhat left-of-center perspective. In the area of Social Security, its lead researcher is its cofounder, Dean Baker, who has written a book in which he argues that Social Security can be saved by making but modest reforms. He vigorously opposes privatizing the system. This is the typical perspective of research that issues from the CEPR. However, some of its researchers do endorse add-on personal accounts.

Web site: http://www.cepr.net

Economic Policy Institute

The Economic Policy Institute (EPI) was created in 1986. It is largely funded by labor unions, and its research takes a pro-union perspective on most issues. Its stated purpose is to include the interests of low- and middle-income workers in any discussion of economic policy. The EPI generally favors governmental action and expanded social programs. For Social Security, this means opposition to private accounts or other forms of privatization along with a defense of existing benefit levels.

Web site: http://www.epi.org

Employee Benefit Research Institute

The Employee Benefit Research Institute (EBRI) is the only organization dedicated to providing data and research on employee retirement and benefit programs. Created in 1978, it has provided research on Social Security since 1982. The EBRI has developed a large computer model through which one can calculate the effects of proposed changes to Social Security on its performance. EBRI researchers provide economic analyses of the costs and operations of the Social Security system and of the reforms offered to alter it. The Institute also offers public surveys and other information. It is nonpartisan and does not endorse any particular reform or set of reforms.

Web site: http://www.ebri.org

Heritage Foundation

A reliably conservative think tank, the Heritage Foundation originated in 1973 and was funded by major conservative figures such as Joseph Coors (of the Colorado-based beer company by the same name). The Heritage Foundation subscribes to a philosophy of public policies based on "free enterprise, limited government, individual freedom, traditional American values, and a strong national defense." Its position on Social Security is similar to that of the AEI, with the Heritage Foundation's researchers more likely to endorse full privatization of the system. Though the two organizations share a similar philosophy, the AEI's list of fellows and academic researchers is more prominent than is the Heritage Foundation's.

Web site: http://www.heritage.org

National Academy of Social Insurance

The National Academy of Social Insurance was created by long-time Social Security official and advocate Robert M. Ball. It is financed by a wide range of corporations, labor unions, private foundations, medical groups, and the AARP. It currently has some 750 experts affiliated with it. Its mission is to provide nonpartisan information about social insurance programs and their operations. Much of its attention is devoted to Social Security. It offers analyses of the current system and its future, as well of proposed reforms. Though the Academy takes no formal positions on the reform proposals that have been advanced, its research typically defends the existing system. This was certainly the perspective of its founder. Most of the Academy's work favors Social Security reforms other than the provision of personal retirement accounts.

Web site: http://www.nasi.org

Urban Institute

The Urban Institute dates from 1968, after a commission of civic leaders recommended to President Lyndon Johnson that an independent research center be established to analyze the problems facing U.S. cities. Since then, the Urban Institute has expanded its interests to other areas, such as Social Security. It has created the Income and Benefits Policy Center, which studies Social Security, among other issues. The Urban Institute sponsors numerous studies and meetings on the topic, and its research has a very solid reputation. Politically it is moderate to moderate-left in orientation and has been the home to more prominent Democrats than Republicans. But its publications are nonpartisan and do not all hew to the same policy positions.

Web site: http://www.urban.org

8

Resources

There are innumerable sources of information about the U.S. Social Security program and the pension programs of other governments. There is also a wealth of material on the issues and the problems of national public retirement programs in general. This chapter gives the citations and references that were used in writing this book, along with additional materials that will enable you to begin your own further research on this topic. The chapter first presents the Internet sites of the major American and international public agencies that collect information and analyses on Social Security. They are increasingly becoming the best place to seek initial information on this issue. Presented next are particularly good Web sites compiled and maintained by two news journals and several television networks. That section is followed by Web sites from which recent academic research on the Social Security program can be obtained.

The number of books and articles on Social Security must be numbered in the thousands. Those included here are among the most current, important, and detailed.

Note that because of the rapid evolution of program reforms and debates, much of this material is in the form of pamphlets and policy briefings. These materials are divided into those that pertain to the history of the program and those that pertain to the current debate on Social Security's future.

Finally, there is bibliography of works relating to the other major government retirement programs discussed in chapter 3. This list is organized by country, beginning with that country's national pension program Web site(s). The bibliography also includes entries for Mexico and Japan, two countries with interesting pension systems well worthy of study, although they were not included in this volume. In all cases, where a Web link to the material is available, the URL is provided. Note that many materials are published by think tanks and other participants in the Social Security debate. Please refer back to chapter 7 to review the orientations and ideological predilections of these publishers.

Public Agencies

U.S. Government: Federal Agencies

Social Security Administration

The first and best source of information about Social Security is found on the Web pages of the agency that administers the program. The Social Security Web site is a treasure trove of information. The main pages detail the operations of today's Social Security system. You can also retrieve your own Social Security statement and calculate your likely Social Security retirement pension. The Web site contains the full text of the Social Security Act (http://www.ssa.gov/OP_Home/ssact/comp-ssa.htm) as well as the text of all legislation relating to Social Security that has been passed since 1987. You will find on the site the annual report of the Social Security trustees. This report, usually released in April, details the financial operations of the program and estimates its future, including forecasts of the year that the Trust Fund will be exhausted.

The history pages (http://www.ssa.gov/history/history .html) contain a remarkable collection of oral histories, articles, speeches, biographies, and other materials relating to the passage of the Social Security Act of 1935 and its subsequent development. These pages also give a full administrative history of the Social Security Administration, as well as the earlier Social Security Board. Video and audio clips relating to Social Security's history are held here as well.

Also to be found on the site is the *Social Security Bulletin* (http://www.ssa.gov/policy/docs/ssb/). This is a quarterly publication that includes articles about the history and administration of Social Security as well as discussions of proposed reforms to the program.

The research pages (http://www.ssa.gov/policy/research .html) contain a variety of often quite technical analyses of various aspects relating to the economics, demographics, program financing, and other issues important to the operations of the program. Here you can also find a monthly update of changes and reforms that have occurred in other pension systems around the world (http://www.ssa.gov/policy/research_sub50.html).

In short, this is the logical place to start for anyone interested in pursuing more information about Social Security.

General Social Security Web site: http://www.ssa.gov/

Council of Economic Advisors

The Council of Economic Advisors (CEA) is located in the White House. It offers the president advice on economic policy. It also serves as the in-house think tank for developing economic policies desired by the president. Every year, it publishes *The Economic Report of the President.* Though the topics covered in this document vary annually, very often there is a chapter on Social Security. In years where the president has offered a major proposal on Social Security, there will invariably be a detailed discussion of the Social Security system and the president's proposed legislation. As an arm of the presidency, the CEA's discussion in this document will reflect the perspective of the White House. Past editions of the *Economic Report of the President* are archived on the Web site of the Government Printing Office (GPO).

CEA Web site: http://www.whitehouse.gov/cea/

GPO Web site: http://www.gpoaccess.gov/eop/download.html

U.S. Government: Congress
House of Representatives Committee on Ways and Means

The Ways and Means Committee has jurisdiction over all Social Security legislation in the House. Its Web site thus contains information about current hearings and legislation that involve the program. This information is located under the Ways and Means Subcommittee on Social Security. Note that the party that controls the House also controls this committee, and the policies and programs favored by that party are given the lion's share of favorable attention.

Ways and Means Committee Web site: http://waysandmeans.house.gov/

Senate Finance Committee
The Finance Committee is the Senate counterpart to the House Ways and Means Committee. It has jurisdiction over Social Security in that body. Senate hearings and legislation that involve Social Security is found here. As with the House, the information is posted to put the party in power in the best possible light.

Senate Finance Committee Web site: http://www.senate.gov/~finance/

Congressional Budget Office
The CBO was established as part of the new federal budget process that was created in 1974. Its task is to develop unbiased analyses of the cost and impact of federal programs, or proposed federal programs, in order to aid Congress in its task of developing an annual federal budget. Today, it is generally believed to be the most objective of the various governmental bodies charged with delivering budget estimates and program analyses. In the CBO's work, it frequently addresses the issue of Social Security. On its Web site you will find many statements, analyses, and testimonies before Congress that relate to Social Security: its cost, its future, as well as estimates of the effects of proposed reforms

CBO Web site: http://cbo.gov/publications/bysubject.cfm?cat=11

Government Accountability Office
The GAO (formerly the General Accounting Office) is an investigative arm of Congress, created in 1921, that evaluates and audits federal programs. Generally, its reports are in response to official requests by Congress. Today it produces more than 1,000 reports a year. Because of its mandates, it produces a wide variety of reports relating to the Social Security program and proposed changes to it. Its search mechanism is a little clumsy. A suggestion upon entering its Web site is to click "Reports and Testimony," then "Agency," and then "Social Security Administration." This will lead to its collection of reports on Social Security.

GAO Web site: http://www.gao.gov/index.html

Library of Congress
The Library of Congress's Thomas database was established by Congress in 1995. It is a searchable record of every piece of legis-

lation that has been introduced in Congress since that date. Researchers can discover the fate of any individual piece of Social Security legislation, obtain a detailed history of the hearings and debate that surrounded it, or learn which members of Congress voted for or against it.

Library of Congress Thomas Web site: http://thomas.loc .gov/home/abt_thom.html

International Organizations

Organization for Economic Cooperation and Development

The OECD is an international organization of 30 countries, including the United States, that researches and analyzes economic and social policies around the world. Founded in 1961 and located in Paris, it is sometimes called the "Rich Country Club" because its member states are the world's high-income countries. Its Web site features statistics, comparisons, and analyses of the retirement demographics, pension programs, and old-age security issues of its member nations. You can locate the "browse" tab and click "by topics" to access this material.

OECD Web site: http://www.oecd.org/home/

International Bank for Reconstruction and Development

The World Bank, as this organization is more commonly called, has been a major player in global debates over Social Security and pension reform. As part of its interest in global economic development, it has offered policy advice to and has analyzed pension programs in some 80 countries over the past decade. The "Pensions" area of its Web page offers a compilation of pension legislation from around the world (though focusing especially on the developing world) as well as a huge holding of World Bank publications and seminars on pension systems and retirement issues. It has tended to recommend fully funded pension systems over pay-as-you-go financed systems.

World Bank Web site: http://www.worldbank.org/

International Labour Organization

The International Labour Organization (ILO), created in 1919, has the charge of monitoring working conditions around the world. As part of this effort, its Social Security Department compiles statistics on global social security expenditures. They are found on the site's "statistical knowledge base."

ILO Web site (for Social Security): http://www.ilo.org /public/english/protection/secsoc/areas/stat/ssi.htm

Media and Press Sites

Recent events and developments in Social Security are, of course, most easily followed through the the news media.. In addition to the major daily newspapers and weekly news magazines, the following specialized media cover the politics and policies of Social Security in great detail.

National Journal and *Congressional Quarterly Weekly Report*

Both are weekly publications and provide in-depth analysis. Each is primarily focused on Congress, and on the course of legislation that has been introduced in Congress, but also offers coverage of the Executive Branch, the budget, and other topics of concern to Social Security. They are excellent resources to "catch up" on the politics and policy of Social Security. Both have Web sites, but they do not offer a great deal beyond the information contained in their core print publications.

National Journal Web site: http://nationaljournal.com
Congressional Quarterly Web site: http://cq.com

CNN

In conjunction with *Money* and *Fortune* magazines, the CNN network maintains a Social Security Web page that contains recent news, commentary, and other archived materials on the Social Security system.

CNN Web site: http://money.cnn.com/news/specials /socsec/

C-SPAN

Created in 1979 as a public service to provide televised access to congressional debates and other political activities, C-SPAN maintains a Social Security Web page. Though most of the print materials are available elsewhere, the site holds the videos of recent Social Security events that have appeared in its programming.

C-SPAN Web site: http://www.c-span.org/

National Public Radio

National Public Radio (NPR) frequently runs news stories and interviews about Social Security and its proposed reforms. It maintains an audio archive of this material.

NPR Social Security Web site: http://www.npr.org /templates/topics/topic.php?topicId=1083

Internet Research Sites

Among the many organizations that post analyses and research of research, two of the foremost are the Public Agenda and the National Bureau for Economic Research. The former site contains numerous materials on various aspects of Social Security and the debate over its reform. It is resolutely nonpartisan and oriented to the general reader. The latter is far more analytically high powered. Many articles are quite technical, but they are also the cutting edge of academic research.

Public Agenda Web site: http://www.publicagenda.org /issues/frontdoor.cfm?issue_type=ss

National Bureau for Economic Research Web site: www .nber.org/papers

Books and Articles

General History

Achenbaum, W. Andrew. 1986. *Social Security: Visions and Revisions*. New York: Cambridge University Press. 320 pages.

An authoritative history of Social Security in the 1970s, the years when the program encountered its first crisis after the implementation of the cost-of-living adjustment (COLA).

Altman, Nancy. 2005. *The Battle for Social Security: From FDR's Vision to Bush's Gamble.* **New York: John Wiley. 362 pages.**

A history of the politics that have surrounded the passage of Social Security and subsequent efforts at reform, the book is sharply critical of efforts to privatize the program.

Altmeyer, Arthur J. 1966. *The Formative Years of Social Security.* **Madison, WI: University of Wisconsin Press. 314 pages.**

An insider's history of the beginnings of Social Security, written by one of the program's early leaders.

Amenta, Edward. 2006. *When Movements Matter: The Townsend Plan and the Rise of Social Security.* **Princeton, NJ: Princeton University Press. 336 pages.**

This is the best single history of Dr. Francis Townsend's pension plan and the politics that surrounded it.

Arnold, Douglas R., Michael Graetz, and Alicia H. Munnell. 1998. *Framing the Social Security Debate: Values, Politics, and Economics.* **Washington, D.C.: Brookings Institution. 200 pages.**

This book is a hodge-podge of information about the politics of Social Security, albeit a hodge-podge written at a very high level. It includes a discussion of how economists view Social Security versus political scientists, how to use public opinion polls in evaluating support for Social Security, and the political feasibility of reforming the system, among other topics.

Ball, Robert M., with Thomas N. Bethell. 1998. *Straight Talk about Social Security.* **New York: Century Fund/Twentieth Century Fund. 79 pages.**

Long-time advocate and Social Security official Robert Ball provides a vigorous defense of the program, opposing major reforms to it, but he also offers interesting historical vignettes about Social Security as it developed in its first decades.

Beland, Daniel. 2005. *Social Security: History and Politics from the New Deal to the Privatization Debate.* **Studies in Government and Public Policy. Lawrence, KS: University Press of Kansas. 252 pages.**

Another history of the politics that have shaped Social Security, this volume is a bit more academic and focuses on the interaction of deeply held American beliefs with the institutions of government in the creation and evolution of the program.

Benavie, Arthur. 2003. *Social Security under the Gun: What Every Informed Citizen Needs to Know about Pension Reform.* **New York: Palgrave MacMillan. 160 pages.**

Somewhere between a history and user's guide for those receiving or about to receive Social Security benefits, this book also vigorously argues that the present system will survive and attacks efforts at privatization.

Berkowitz, Edward. 1995. *Mr. Social Security: The Life of Wilbur J. Cohen.* **Lawrence, KS: University Press of Kansas. 416 pages.**

A rare biography of a major figure in the history of Social Security. Berkowitz is perhaps the leading historian of the Social Security program.

Berkowitz, Edward. 1991. *America's Welfare State: From Roosevelt to Reagan.* **Baltimore: Johns Hopkins University Press. 240 pages.**

Though beginning to date a bit, this remains the standard history of the Social Security program. It is perhaps the easiest to read of the many histories, though readers may detect the author's critical position toward most conservative politicians.

Berkowitz, Edward. 2003. *Robert M. Ball and the Politics of Social Security.* **Madison, WI: University of Wisconsin Press. 455 pages.**

A bookend with Berkowitz's biography of Wilbur Cohen. Ball was perhaps the leading figure in Social Security's history over the second half of the 20th century.

Berkowitz, Edward, and Kim McQuaid. 1998. *Creating the Welfare State: The Political Economy of Twentieth Century Reform.* **New York: Praeger. 272 pages.**

The authors reject an earlier consensus that U.S. business opposed Social Security and other government programs. They show how business was in fact critical to its creation. They also place Social Security's history within the larger history of the construction of the post–New Deal American welfare state.

Cates, Jerry R. 1983. *Insuring Inequality: Administrative Leadership in Social Security: 1934–1954.* **Ann Arbor, MI: University of Michigan Press. 200 pages.**

This study of the first years of the Social Security Board, the initial federal agency that managed the program, is critical of the decisions that the board took in developing the program.

Derthick, Martha. 1979. *Policymaking for Social Security.* **Washington, D.C.: Brookings Institution Press. 460 pages.**

A recognized classic in the field of public policy, Derthick's volume offers a first-rate analysis of how the Social Security program was developed and administered in the years after World War II. This may be the definitive account of the policies and politics of the program's first four decades.

Derthick, Martha. 1990. *Agency Under Stress: The Social Security Administration in American Government.* **Washington, D.C.: Brookings Institution. 245 pages.**

Another often-cited work, here Derthick analyzes why the Social Security Administration performed so poorly in administering program changes in the 1970s and 1980s. It is an account of why it is so difficult to manage this huge program.

Elmendorf, Douglas W., Jeffrey B. Liebman, and David W. Wilcox. 2002. "Fiscal Policy and Social Security Policy During the 1990s," 61–138. **In Jeffrey A. Frankel and Peter R. Orszag, eds.,** *American Economic Policy in the 1990s.* **Cambridge, MA: MIT Press. 1,119 pages.**

The best single account of Social Security policy, and the debates surrounding it, during the Clinton presidency. It is written by former administration officials and includes commentary from a panel of experts.

Epstein, Abraham. 1938. *Insecurity: A Challenge to America.* **New York: Random House. 939 pages.**

A leading figure in the development of Social Security defends national unemployment and retirement pension programs against its early critics.

Glasson, William H. 1918. *Federal Military Pensions in the United States.* **Oxford: Oxford University Press. 305 pages.**

The U.S. pension system was originally tied to military service. Admittedly an obscure volume, this is the history of that system, the forerunner to the Social Security program.

Greider, William. 1986. *The Education of David Stockman and Other Americans.* **New York: Dutton. 161 pages.**

A bombshell in its day, Greider reported the inside story of the making of the first Ronald Reagan budget. It includes much information about that administration's initial plans for Social Security reductions. These plans eventually produced the National Commission on Social Security Reform (the Greenspan Commission).

Hacker, Jacob S. 2002. *The Divided Welfare State: The Battle Over Public and Private Social Benefits in the United States.* **New York: Cambridge University Press. 464 pages.**

Why is part of the U.S. retirement program public (Social Security) and part private (employer pensions), and what difference does it make? Hacker addresses this in the first section of this book.

Light, Paul. 1985. *Artful Work: The Politics of Social Security Reform.* **New York: Random House. 256 pages.**

A public policy analyst examines the politics of Social Security reform through the era of the Greenspan Commission. While it is very complete, some old Social Security hands found it sensationalistic in its conclusions.

Leff, Mark H. 1983. "Taxing the Forgotten Man: The Politics of Social Security Finance in the New Deal." *Journal of American History* **70 (3): 359–381.**

Now that the program's financing is again controversial, it is interesting to compare the politics over the same issue at the time of the program's founding. This is the definitive article on that subject.

Livingston, Steven G. 2002. *Student's Guide to Landmark Congressional Laws on Social Security and Welfare.* Westport, CT: Greenwood Press. 258 pages.

The book provides a brief legislative history of each major reform to the U.S. Social Security system, as well as edited extracts from the relevant legislation that was enacted.

Marmor, Theodore R., Jerry L. Mashaw, and Philip L. Harvey. 1990. *America's Misunderstood Welfare State: Persistent Myths, Enduring Realities.* New York: Basic. 292 pages.

As the title indicates, this book argues that most Americans do not understand how their own country's social programs operate and that much of the criticism of these programs comes from this lack of knowledge. The book offers a slightly dated history of the major social programs, including Social Security, to rectify this.

Mommsen, Wolfgang J., ed. 1981. *The Emergence of the Welfare State in Britain and Germany: 1850–1950.* London: Croom Helm. 443 pages.

An accessible study of how the world's first social security programs were developed.

Myers, Robert J. 1970. *Expansionism in Social Insurance.* London: Institute of Economic Affairs. 31 pages.

A brief, revisionist history of Social Security by a long-time official. Myers argues that, contrary to what other officials might have been saying, the program was structured for inexorable growth in benefits and cost. That is what agency officials wanted from the start. Obviously controversial.

Quadagno, Jill. 1988. *The Transformation of Old-Age Security: Class and Politics in the American Welfare State.* Chicago: University of Chicago Press. 268 pages.

An academic study of the origins of Social Security. At times controversial, the author attempts to show the impact of class, race, and region on the creation of the program.

Rubinow, I. M. 1913. *Social Insurance, with Special Reference to American Conditions.* New York: Henry Holt. 525 pages.

Perhaps of limited analytic interest today, it is included here because this work had a greater impact on the development of the U.S. Social Security system than did any other publication.

Rubinow, I. M. 1934. *The Quest for Security.* **New York: Henry Holt. 638 pages.**

A second volume primarily of historical interest. Rubinow argued, in mid-Depression, that the American worker was the most insecure of any in the world owing to the lack of unemployment or old-age policies. President Roosevelt is believed to have read this book while he was initiating his plan for Social Security.

Schlabach, Theron. 1969. *Edward E. Witte: Cautious Reformer.* **Madison, WI: State Historical Society of Wisconsin. 290 pages.**

A biography of the author of the government report that led to the Social Security program.

Schlesinger, Arthur M., Jr. 1988. *The Age of Roosevelt: The Coming of the New Deal.* **Boston: Houghton Mifflin. 669 pages.**

The classic account that positions Social Security within the context of Franklin Roosevelt's New Deal.

Skocpol, Theda. 1992. *Protecting Soldiers and Mothers.* **Cambridge, MA: Harvard University Press. 736 pages.**

The best history and analysis of the U.S. government pension programs that preceded Social Security.

Solomon, Carmen D. 1986. "Major Decisions in the House and Senate Chambers on Social Security." *CRS Report for Congress.* **Congressional Research Service, Library of Congress. Washington, D.C.: Government Printing Office. 117 pages.**

This is a useful guide to all major legislative decisions taken by the U.S. Congress during the first 50 years of Social Security.

Stevens, Robert B., ed. 1970. *Statutory History of the United States: Income Security.* **New York: Chelsea House. 919 pages.**

A compilation of laws that includes the full texts of the initial Social Security Act and its amendments up to 1970.

Van Atta, Dale. 1998. *Trust Betrayed: Inside the AARP.* **Washington, D.C.: Regnery. 208 pages.**

The author takes a very dim view of the political influence and operations of the largest interest group interested in Social Security. Though very critical, this is probably the most detailed of several books about the AARP.

Vandenberg, Arthur H. 1937. "The $47,000,000,000 Blight." *Saturday Evening Post* **209 (43): 5–7.**

This article by Senator Vandenberg initiated the 1939 amendments and the conversion of Social Security into a pay-as-you-go program.

Weaver, Carolyne L. 1996. "Birth of an Entitlement: Learning from the Origins of Social Security." *AEI Online,* **May. http://www.aei.org/publications/pubID.6500/pub_detail.asp.**

Originally written for a libertarian magazine (*Reason*), this is a brief but very informative history of the initial design of the Social Security program and the issues surrounding it. The author links those issues to her own preference that the system now be privatized.

Wise, David A., Richard G. Woodbury, and Rudolph Penner. 1995. "Policy Toward the Aged," 741–794. In Martin Feldstein, *American Economic Policy in the 1980s.* **National Bureau of Economic Research Conference Report. Chicago: University of Chicago Press. 834 pages.**

The most complete evaluation of Social Security policy during the Reagan and early George H. W. Bush presidencies. A panel of experts offers commentary on the policy making of this era.

Witte, Edwin. 1963. *Development of the Social Security Act.* **Madison, WI: University of Wisconsin Press. 239 pages.**

An inside history of the Social Security Act of 1935 written by one of the program's pioneers.

Current Issues

Below are listed, alphabetically, works that address particular Social Security reform proposals or other issues that are currently in debate.

Demographics

Clark, Robert L., Richard V. Burkhauser, Marilyn Moon, Joseph F. Quinn, and Timothy M. Smeeding. 2004. *The Economics of an Aging Society.* Malden, MA: Blackwell. 376 pages.

The issues around Social Security ultimately rest upon the changing demographics of the United States. This book is a recent, up-to-date survey and analysis of those demographics.

Kotlikoff, Laurence J., and Scott Burns. 2004. *The Coming Generational Storm: What You Need to Know about America's Economic Future.* Cambridge, MA: MIT Press. 274 pages.

The authors claim that an aging population will play havoc with most U.S. social programs. To save Social Security, they suggest moving to a system of government-managed private accounts.

Krugman Paul. 2005. "America's Senior Moment." *New York Review of Books* 52 (4): 6–8.

The economist and *New York Times* columnist argues that demographic trends will actually have but a modest effect on America's ability to finance its social programs. (This article is a review of Kotlikoff and Burns, *The Coming Generational Storm.*)

Peterson, Peter. 1999. *The Gray Dawn: How the Coming Age Wage Will Transform America—And the World.* New York: Random House. 288 pages.

An interesting and passionate (for Social Security) discussion of the impact of the large growth in senior citizens that is expected in the coming years. Peterson compares the effects across policies and across countries.

Solow, Robert M. 1999. "On Golden Pond." *New York Review of Books* 46: 8.

Nobel Prize–winning economist Solow argues that the demographic situation, while undoubtedly a coming cause of financing problems for Social Security, is not as dire as some claim (the article is a review of Peterson's *The Gray Dawn*).

The Rate of Return Question

Beach, William W., and Gareth G. Davis. 1998. *Social Security's Rate of Return.* Washington, D.C.: Heritage Foundation.

An argument that Social Security offers a poor rate of financial return for many Americans. Controversially, it asserts that African Americans and low-income earners do particularly poorly under the current system.

Furman, Jason. 2005. *Would Private Accounts Provide a Higher Rate of Return than Social Security?* Washington, D.C.: Center on Budget and Policy Priorities. http:/www.cbpp.org. 14 pages.

The author concludes no, they would not.

Orszag, Peter R. 1999. *Individual Accounts and Social Security: Does Social Security Really Provide a Lower Rate of Return?* Washington, D.C.: Center on Budget and Policy Priorities. http:/www.cbpp.org. 47 pages.

Presented as an argument against an individual retirement account (IRA) carve-out, Orszag attempts to demonstrate that reforms to Social Security would not affect its rate of return.

Overviews of Reform Proposals and Debates
Anders, Susan B., and David S. Hulse 2006. "Social Security: The Past, the Present, and Options for Reform." *Online CPA Journal*, May. http://www.nysscpa.org/cpajournal/2006/506/infocus/p20.htm.

Written for accountants, this article is an excellent survey of the impact of demographics on the future of Social Security. It clearly explains how the Trust Fund operates and why it will vanish.

Concord Coalition. 2005. "Automatic Cost Growth Drives the Problem" Social Security Series, Issue No. 7. http://www.concordcoalition.org/issues/.

Though written as an advocacy piece, this brief online exposition nicely explains why Social Security becomes more costly over time

Concord Coalition. 1998. *Saving Social Security: A Framework for Reform. Volume 2: Options for Reform.* http://www.concordcoalition.org/issues/. 36 pages.

A second useful piece by the Concord Coalition. After arguing that reform is necessary, this work gives a careful overview of many of the reform proposals that have been made and summarizes the pros and cons of each.

Diamond, Peter. 2002. *Social Security Reform.* **New York: Oxford University Press. 100 pages.**

This is a relatively brief explanation of how Social Security reform is bound with the operations of the U.S. labor and capital markets. This sounds quite complex, but the book is presented at a nontechnical level by one of the issue's leading analysts.

Gebhardtsbauer, Ron. 2000. "Understanding Social Security. How Social Security Works, Social Security's Long-Range Financial Problem, and Pros and Cons of Social Security Reform Proposals." Washington, D.C.: American Academy of Actuaries. http://www.actuary.org/pdf/socialsecurity/ss_speech0800.pdf. 43 pages.

Though presented to an audience of insurance actuaries and most attentive to insurance issues, this presentation is admirably clear in introducing and summarizing many of the reforms to Social Security that have been developed. The author frequently works through the likely results of given reforms.

Graetz, Michael, and Jerry L. Mashaw. 1999. *True Security: Rethinking American Social Insurance.* **New Haven, CT: Yale University Press. 369 pages.**

Placing Social Security in historical context as part of a larger U.S. social insurance system, the authors offer recommendations for building a more complete, and more affordable, system for all Americans.

Kingson, Eric R., and James H. Schulz. 1997. *Social Security in the Twenty-First Century.* **New York: Oxford University Press. 313 pages.**

This edited volume features articles on a number of major issues, including the economic impact of Social Security, whether the program ought to be means tested, and whether the system is fair to women. The authors are diverse in their perspectives on the Social Security program.

Nuschler, Dawn. 2006. "Social Security Reform." *CRS Issue Brief for Congress.* Congressional Research Service, Library of Congress. Washington, D.C.: U.S. Congress. 19 pages

This is a brief survey of recent issues and debates over Social Security. It includes information on public opinion polling and legislation that has been proposed in recent sessions of Congress. This publication is available at a number of sites over the Internet. Because it is occasionally updated, and not all sites follow the updates, it is perhaps best to search for the article. It was originally prepared for use by members of Congress and their staffs.

Schaviro, Daniel. 2000. *Making Sense of Social Security Reform.* Chicago: University of Chicago Press. 185 pages.

Though written before the most recent privatization debates, this volume is a basic primer on the economics behind Social Security and balanced discussion of many of the proposals to reform it.

Shieber, Sylvester, and John B. Shoven. 1999. *The Real Deal: The History and Future of Social Security.* New Haven, CT: Yale University Press. 450 pages.

This is a remarkably complete examination of how Social Security has developed and the options for its reform. The authors present their own plan for reforming Social Security, which they call "personal security accounts."

U.S. Government Accountability Office. 2005. *Social Security Reform: Answers to Key Questions.* GAO-05-193SP (May). Washington, D.C.: Government Printing Office. 69 pages. http://www.gao.gov/index.html.

A very good survey of the potential impact of proposed reforms. The material is presented as answers to a long list of questions that one might have about Social Security.

Pay-as-You-Go Financing

Congressional Budget Office. United States Congress. 2004. "How Pension Financing Affects Returns to Different Generations." *Long-Term Fiscal Policy Brief* 12. Washington, D.C.: Congressional Budget Office. http://www.cbo.gov. 6 pages.

This is a relatively accessible synopsis of a difficult but important issue: as the demographics of a society change, how does the rate of return on the Social Security contributions vary across different generations?

Feldstein, Martin. 1974. "Social Security, Induced Retirement, and Aggregate Capital Accumulation." *Journal of Political Economy* **82 (5): 905–926.**

A bit technical, but an initial argument against pay-as-you-go financing. It is written by one of the major scholars of the Social Security program.

Gramlich, Edward M. 1998. *Is It Time to Reform Social Security?* **Ann Arbor, MI: University of Michigan Press. 120 pages.**

The chair of the 1994–1996 Advisory Commission on Social Security offers his thoughts on reform. He believes the program should move to greater reliance on the advance funding of benefits, as opposed to the current pay-as-you-go structure.

Viard, Alan D. 2002. "Pay-as-You-Go Social Security and the Aging of America: An Economic Analysis." *Economic and Financial Policy Review* **1 (4): 1–25.**

A thorough discussion of how pay-as-you-go financing operates and how demographic changes will affect a social security system that is so financed. The author presents an objective analysis; no policy recommendations are made.

Changing the Benefits Formula
American Academy of Actuaries. 2004. "Social Security Reform: Changes to the Benefit Formula and Taxation of Benefits." *Issue Brief* **(May). 8 pages. http://www.actuary.org.**

Making no recommendations, this article explores the possibilities of reforming Social Security through making these two changes.

Thompson, Lawrence H. 2004. "Social Security Reform and Benefit Adequacy." *Retirement Project, Brief Series,* **17. New York: Urban Institute. 7 pages. http://www.urban.org/.**

Thompson argues that too many retirees cannot afford to see their benefits reduced. He provides a great deal of information about the distribution of Social Security benefits in the United States.

Changes in Indexing

Congressional Budget Office. Congress of the United States. 2003. "The Future Growth of Social Security: It's Not Just Society's Aging." *Long Range Fiscal Policy Brief* 9 (July). Washington, D.C.: Congressional Budget Office. http://www.cbo.gov. 4 pages.

This brief enables one to understand the effects of wage indexing on the future cost of the Social Security program.

Congressional Budget Office. Congress of the United States. 2005. *Projected Effects of Various Provisions on Social Security's Financial and Distributional Outcomes.* (May 25), 23 pages. http://www.cbo.gov.

This is an objective analysis of exactly how various changes in index or benefits formulas would affect the Trust Fund and the finances of Social Security generally.

Greenstein, Robert. 2005. *So-Called Price Indexing Proposal Would Result in Deep Reductions over Time in Social Security Benefits.* Washington, D.C.: Center on Budget and Policy Priorities. 11 pages. http://cbpp.org.

This is a response to a proposal by President George W. Bush of shifting from wage to price indexing in the Social Security benefits calculation.

Johnson, Richard W., Joshua H. Goldwyn, and Melissa M. Favreault. 2004. "Social Security COLA Reductions Would Weaken Financial Security for the Oldest and Poorest Retirees." Retirement Project, *Brief Series,* 18. New York: Urban Institute (September). 9 pages. http://www.urban.org/.

As indicated by the title, this article shows that proposed COLA reductions would sharply reduce the incomes of the poorest retirees.

Munnell, Alicia H., and Mauricio Soto. 2005. "What Does Price Indexing Mean for Social Security Benefits?" *Just the Facts on Retirement Issues,* 14 (January). Boston: Center for Retirement Research, Boston College. http://crr.bc.edu/index.php. 5 pages.

A primer on how price and wage indexing operate, and the difference between the two.

Investing in the Stock Market

Aaron, Henry J., and Robert D. Reischauer. 1998. *Countdown to Reform: The Great Social Security Debate*. New York: Century Foundation Press.

An argument for incremental reform of the Social Security system, including placing a portion of the Trust Fund into the stock market, by two of the leading scholars on Social Security.

Baker, Dean. 2002. *The Stock Market Bubble and Investing Social Security in the Stock Market*. Washington, D.C.: Center for Economic and Policy Research. http://www.cepr.net/publications/social_security_2002_07.htm.

This article makes the argument that investing in the stock market will harm the economy and reduce the wealth of U.S. stock investors.

Congressional Budget Office. Congress of the United States. 2003. *Evaluating and Accounting for Federal Investment in Corporate Stocks and Other Private Securities*. Washington, D.C.: Congressional Budget Office. http://www.cbo.gov. 36 pages.

The Congressional Budget Office studies the effects of investing Social Security funds in the stock market on the U.S. economy and government finances generally. It discusses the trade-offs of such investment on other policy goals.

Individual Retirement Accounts

Concord Coalition. 2005. "Personal Retirement Accounts: Should They Be Voluntary or Mandatory?" *Social Security Reform* 8. http://www.concordcoalition.org/issues/. 7 pages.

True to its focus on increasing Americans' savings, the Concord Coalition presents the case for mandatory IRAs as a part of Social Security.

Congressional Budget Office. Congress of the United States. 2005. *Congressional Budget Office Cost Estimate: H.R. 3304, Growing Real Ownership for Workers Act, as Introduced on July 14, 2005*. Washington, D.C.: Congressional Budget Office. http://www.cbo.gov. 56 pages.

A detailed analysis of the financial costs and impact of H.R. 3304, a bill that provides for diverting a portion of Social Security contributions into IRA-type accounts. This bill is very similar to the proposal for Social Security reform made by President George W. Bush.

Cordes, Joseph J., and C. Eugene Steurele. 1999. "A Primer on Privatization." Retirement Project, *Occasional Paper* No. 3. New York: Urban Institute. http://www.urban.org/. 18 pages.

This careful study covers many issues, including investing in the stock market, but focuses on the effects of partial privatization. The authors do not oppose privatization but argue that it is no panacea to the problems of the current system.

Furman, Jason. 2005. *Evaluating Alternative Social Security Reforms.* **Washington, D.C.: Center for Budget and Policy Priorities. http://cbpp.org. 21 pages.**

This is Furman's prepared testimony to the House Ways and Means Committee. He is an opponent of President George W. Bush's privatization proposal, but here he offers a useful summary of the differences between carve-out and add-on individual retirement accounts.

Horney, James, and Richard Kogan. 2005. *Private Accounts Would Substantially Increase Federal Debt and Interest Payments.* **Washington, D.C.: Center on Budget and Policy Priorities. http://cbpp.org. 43 pages.**

An argument that privatization would have severe effects on the federal budget, and thus should be opposed.

John, David C. 2004. "How to Fix Social Security." *Backgrounder* 1811 (November 17). Washington, D.C.: Heritage Foundation. http://heritage.org. 16 pages.

John concludes that Social Security IRAs are the only realistic reform for Social Security.

Orszag, Peter R., and Robert Greenstein. 2001. *Voluntary Individual Accounts for Social Security: What Are the Costs?* **Washington, D.C.: Center on Budget and Policy Priorities. http://cbpp.org. 16 pages.**

Leading analysts explain their opposition to IRA carve-outs.

Privatization

Aaron, Henry J., and John B. Shoven. 1999. *Should the United States Privatize Social Security?* Cambridge, MA: MIT Press. 190 pages.

This book is an excellent primer on privatization. It features one chapter written by a prominent proponent of partial privatization, and a second chapter written by an equally prominent opponent. These chapters are followed by responses from a number of leading economists.

Aaron, Henry J., and Robert Reischauer. 1998. *There When You Need It: Saving Social Security for Future Generations of Americans.* Washington, D.C.: Brookings Institution. 195 pages.

This is a general guide to Social Security reform proposals, but it also contains a chapter that makes the case against privatizing the system.

Feldstein, Martin, ed. 1998. *Privatizing Social Security.* Chicago: University of Chicago Press. 488 pages.

Feldstein, the most academically prominent supporter of privatization, and his colleagues explore in a favorable light how the U.S. Social Security program might be turned into a program of private, individual retirement accounts. Chapters are devoted to the experiences of individual countries with privatization.

Kotlikoff, Lawrence J. 1996. "Privatization of Social Security: How It Works and Why It Matters." National Bureau of Economic Research Working Paper No. 5330 (October).

One of the first systematic examinations of Social Security privatization, this paper outlines how a privatized retirement system would operate and how it would differ from today's Social Security.

Shoven, John, ed. 2000. *Administrative Costs and Social Security Privatization.* Chicago: University of Chicago Press.

What sounds like a particularly trivial topic is actually of great importance, as the returns to any pension program, but most particularly to a privatized program, depend to a significant extent upon its administrative costs. Estimates of whether privatization

will or will not outperform other forms of Social Security reform
often turn on the assumptions about its administrative costs.

Tanner, Michael D., ed. 2004. *Social Security and Its Discontents: Perspectives on Choice.* **Washington, D.C.: Cato Institute.
386 pages.**

The Cato Institute is a leading proponent of Social Security privatization. This book is a well-regarded defense of that position.

Raising the Retirement Age
Burtless, Gary. 1998. **Increasing the Eligibility Age for Social
Security Pensions: Testimony before the Senate Special Committee on Aging, July 15. Washington, D.C.: Brookings Institution.   http://www.brookings.edu/views/testimony/burtless
/19980715.htm.**

Burtless's Senate testimony clearly outlines the issues surrounding raising the Social Security retirement age.

Response to Detailed Reform Plans
Diamond, Peter, and Peter R. Orszag. 2005. "Saving Social Security." *Journal of Economic Perspectives* 19 (2): 11–32.

A synopsis of the plan offered in the book by Diamond and
Orszag (below), it also provides an interesting overview of the
current debate on Social Security.

Diamond, Peter, and Peter R. Orszag. 2003. *Saving Social Security: A Balanced Approach.* **Washington, D.C.: Brookings Institution. 287 pages.**

The authors, experts on Social Security, present their own plan for
saving it. The plan is a mix of privatization along with changes in
existing operation.

Diamond, Peter, and Peter R. Orszag. 2002. *Reducing Benefits
and Subsidizing Individual Accounts: An Analysis of the Plans
Proposed by the President's Commission to Strengthen Social
Security.* **New York: Century Foundation; Washington, D.C.:
Center on the Budget and Policy Priorities. http://cbpp.org. 41
pages.**

A very negative response to the recommendations of the Moynihan Commission report (below).

Report of the President's Commission on Social Security (Daniel Moynihan and Richard Parsons, co-chairs). 2001. *Strengthening Social Security and Creating Personal Wealth for All Americans.* **Washington, D.C.: Government Printing Office. 256 pages.**

This is an authoritative and comprehensive examination of the current Social Security program. However, it is most noted for its support of a partial privatization program, and this report was the basis for the Social Security reform that President George W. Bush then offered.

World Bank. 1994. *Averting the Old Age Crisis.* **Oxford: Oxford University Press. 402 pages.**

This is an initial volume of recommendations from the World Bank's program on global pension programs. It argues of the dangers of large trust funds and pay-as-you-go financing. It is in this volume that the World Bank advances a "tri-pillar" strategy for Social Security: each country should provide a minimum public pension that is not linked to earnings, insist upon a second pension to be provided by employers, and then offer a third voluntary pension program that is financed through individual contributions. This is the standard advice that the World Bank now gives to its member countries.

Ending Social Security Altogether

Aaron, Henry, and Robert D. Reischauer. 1999. "Should We Retire Social Security? Grading the Reform." *Brookings Review,* 6–11.

Two respected analysts argue that Social Security remains an effective retirement system. Reforms must be made, they claim, but the system should not be ended.

Ferrara, Peter J. 1980. *Social Security: The Inherent Contradiction.* **San Francisco: Cato Institute.**

A fierce argument in favor of ending the Social Security program altogether.

Murray, Charles. 2006. *In Our Hands: A Plan to Replace the Welfare State.* **Washington, D.C.: American Enterprise Institute Press. 230 pages.**

An audacious plan to end federal social programs and replace them with annual grants of $10,000 to every American over the age of 21. Murray is known for his provocative, right-of-center ideas, and in that department this book does not disappoint.

Standing Pat: Not Yet Time for Reform?
Baker, Dean. 1998. "Nine Misconceptions about Social Security." *Atlantic Monthly* 282 (1): 34–39.

This article argues that most Social Security reforms are misguided. The implicit argument is that the system should be kept as it is.

Foreign Social Security Systems

Below are English-language materials for further research of the programs presented in chapter 3. They are organized by country. Also included are some materials on Japan and Mexico, two countries with recently reformed retirement programs that space precluded from coverage in chapter 3. They may also be of interest.

Cross-Country Comparisons
In addition to the *Social Security Bulletin,* the *International Social Security Review* and the *British Actuarial Journal* regularly feature articles on the operations, difficulties, and reforms of pension systems around the world.

Blackburn, Robin. 2002. *Banking on Death or, Investing in Life: The History and Future of Pensions.* New York: Verso Press. 550 pages.

Separate chapters are devoted to the British and U.S. retirement systems, while additional chapters survey the global history of pension systems. The perspective is from the left, with clear and detailed discussions of how different pension systems operate.

Congressional Budget Office. United States Congress. 1999. *Social Security Privatization: Experiences Abroad.* Washington, D.C.: Congressional Budget Office. 101 pages.

Very detailed, with chapters on individual countries.

Feldstein, Martin, and Horst Siebert, eds. 2001. *Social Security Pension Reform in Europe.* National Bureau of Economic Research Conference Report. Chicago: University of Chicago Press. 500 pages.

The National Bureau of Economic Research, located in Cambridge, Massachusetts, is one of the premier collections of economic research in the United States. It compiles edited books, such as this one, and working papers on a variety of economic topics. It regularly publishes compendiums of articles on Social Security systems around the world. These may sometimes be highly technical, but they often give unparalleled understanding into the operations and problems of foreign pension programs.

Gruber, Jonathan, and David A. Wise. 1999. *Social Security and Retirement Around the World.* National Bureau of Economic Research Conference Report. Chicago: University of Chicago Press. 496 pages.

This is an edited volume that looks at how retirement systems have affected labor force participation across numerous countries. The book chapters offer thumbnail descriptions of many foreign retirement programs.

James, Estelle. 1998. "New Models for Old-Age Security: Experiments, Evidence, and Unanswered Questions." *World Bank Research Observer* 13 (2): 271–301.

This article compares the "Latin American model," reform through privatization, to the "OECD model" of reform (referring to the model developed by the Organisation for Economic Co-operation and Development) that does not touch the pay-as-you-go financing of the pension system. The bibliography includes sources for information on pension systems not otherwise considered in this book.

James, Estelle. 2005. *Reforming Social Security: Lessons from Thirty Countries.* NCPA Policy Report, 277. Dallas: National Center for Policy Analysis. http://ncpa.org/pub/st/st277. 39 pages

Shows how exact questions of program design can have a huge impact on the performance of a public pension system.

Organisation for Economic Co-operation and Development. 2007. *Pensions at a Glance: Public Policies across OECD*

Countries. Paris: Organisation for Economic Co-operation and Development. 204 pages. http://www.oecdbookshop.org /oecd/display.asp?CID=&LANG=EN&SF1=DI&ST1=5L4S6T KVJ30P.

Published annually, this is a survey and comparison of retirement policies across the 30 OECD member states. It includes brief summaries of the pension system of each country along with a great deal of statistical information.

Turner, John. 2005. *Social Security Privatization Around the World.* **Washington, D.C.: AARP. 33 pages.**

The AARP has long opposed privatization, but this relatively up-to-date survey simply and relatively objectively describes the major privatization efforts that have been taken around the world over the past two decades.

Urban Institute. 2006. Transcript of "An International Conference on Social Security Reform in Selected OECD Countries." Washington, D.C.: Urban Institute. 96 pages.

This is a very interesting panel discussion that took place February 24, 2006. Panelists presented overviews of how the retirement systems of many of the major developed countries operate (Canada, Japan, Germany, Sweden, United Kingdom, Italy) and the recent reforms that have occurred in each. Discussants then comment upon the presentation, and questions from the audience are entertained. A great way to quickly get up to speed on many of the major pension topics and issues.

Valdes-Prieto, Salvador, ed. 1997. *The Economics of Pensions: Principles, Policies, and International Experiences.* **New York: Cambridge University Press. 377 pages.**

Written before many of the reforms have been made, this volume is of more interest in its discussion of the pension problems that were facing most countries in the 1990s. Chapters are devoted to the experiences of a number of individual countries.

Canada

The government of Canada maintains several Web sites that explain the operations of its pension system. These are the places to start for a serious investigation of how this system operates.

Because the Canadian program is divided into the old-age security plan and the Canadian pension plan, there are several sites to examine.

The Web site for the old-age security plan:

http://www1.servicecanada.gc.ca/en/isp/oas/oastoc.shtml

The Web site for the Canada Pension Plan:

http://www.hrsdc.gc.ca/en/isp/cpp/cpptoc.shtml

The latter site includes fact sheets, benefits information, and a variety of other materials.

The Web site for details on the 1998 Canadian reforms:

http://www.hrsdc.gc.ca/en/isp/cpp/cppchanges.shtml

The Web site for the Canadian Pension Plan annual reports: http://www.hrsdc.gc.ca/en/isp/pub/cpp/pubcpptoc.shtml#annual

The investment board that manages the pension plan funds maintains its own site. The investments, investment strategies, and investment returns are discussed in detail.

The Web site for the Canadian Pension Plan funds:

http://www.cppib.ca/

The Canadian government produces financial reviews of the soundness of its pension programs. They are available at http://www.fin.gc.ca/cpp/indexe.html.

The Canadian Department of Human Resources and Social Development also provides a number of articles and fact sheets on the Canadian retirement system.

http://www.hrsdc.gc.ca/en/gateways/topics/cpr-gxr.shtml

Baker, Michael, Jonathan Gruber, and Kevin Milligan. 2004. "Income Security Programs and Retirement in Canada," 99–154. In Jonathan Gruber and David Wise, eds., *Social Security Programs and Retirement Around the World: Microestimation*. Chicago: University of Chicago Press.

Much of this paper is technical, focusing on the factors that encourage workers to retire, but part II is a very good history of the development of the Canadian pension system.

Battle, Kenneth, and Edward Tamagno. 2007. "Public Pensions in a Development Context: The Case of Canada." *Social Policy and Development Programme Paper, 31.* United Nations Research Institute for Social Development. http://www.unrisd.org/unrisd /website. 36 pages.

This article covers the recent reforms to the Canadian Pension Plan, and the politics that surrounded them. It takes a favorable view of the results.

Béland, Daniel. 2006. "The Politics of Social Learning: Finance, Institutions, and Pension Reform in the United States and Canada." *Governance: An International Journal of Policy, Administration, and Institutions* 19 (4): 559–583.

Generally a theoretical account of "learning," but the middle sections of this piece trace the history of the recent Canadian reforms and compare that history to Social Security debates in the United States.

Béland, Daniel, and John Myles. 2005. "Stasis Amidst Change: Canadian Pension Reform in an Age of Retrenchment," 252–273. In Giuliano Bonoli and Toshimitsu Shinkawa, eds., *Ageing and Pension Reform Around the World: Evidence from Eleven Countries.* Cheltenham, UK: Edward Elgar.

A basic description of the new Canadian pension system, positioning its adoption in the context of the increasing costs of public pension programs that all countries now face.

Finkel, Alvin. 2006. *Social Policy and Practice in Canada: A History.* Waterloo ON: Wilfred Laurier University Press. 396 pages.

An up-to-date history of the Canadian welfare state generally, but with attention to the development of its national retirement system. The author presents a "centrist" history, arguing that Canadian programs and reforms have been neither as left-wing nor as right-wing as often projected.

Guest, Dennis. 1997. *The Emergence of Social Security in Canada.* Vancouver, BC: University of British Columbia Press. 303 pages.

Though superseded by later reforms, this volume remains the best history of the development of the Canadian pension program. While the author clearly believes in an expansive program, his account is comprehensive and complete.

Sarney, Mark, and Amy Prenata. 2001/2002. "The Canada Pension Plan's Experience with Investing Its Portfolio in Equities." *Social Security Bulletin* **64 (2): 46–56.**

A discussion of the Canadian reforms' most controversial aspect.

Sass, Stephen A. 2006. "Reforming the Canadian Retirement System: Investing Social Securities Assets in Equities." *Global Issues in Brief* **5 (April). Boston: Center for Retirement Research, Boston College. http://crr.bc.edu/index.php. 13 pages.**

A guarded but positive overview and account of the recent Canadian reforms.

Australia

Because the Australian pension system has several components, there are several official Web sites. The Australian Age Pension program is carefully outlined at the following site. Much of the information, of course, is directed at Australians interested in obtaining their benefits from the program.

The Web site for the Age Pension program:

http://www.centrelink.gov.au/internet/internet.nsf/payments/age_pension.htm

The Web site for the superannuation program:

http://www.australia.gov.au/70

Australia also provides another user friendly Web site that explains the program: http://www.understandingmoney.gov.au/content/consumer/financialliteracy/superannuation/.

To gather information on financing issues, the Australian taxation office is helpful: http://www.ato.gov.au/super. Lastly, the government provides information to Australians about how to choose a superannuation fund: http://www.superchoice.gov.au/default.asp.

Commonwealth Treasury of Australia. 2001. "Towards Higher Retirement Incomes for Australians: A History of the Australian Retirement Income System since Federation." *Treasury*

Economic Roundup Centenary Edition 2001. Canberra: Australian Treasury Department. http://www.treasury.gov.au /contentitem.asp?ContentID=110&NavID=.

A recent and good official history of the development of the Australian pension system.

Department of Social Security of Australia. 1996. "Australian Age Pension." *Older Australia at a Glance,* **vol. 20. Canberra: Commonwealth of Australia.**

A brief description of the Age Pension and how it operates.

Bateman, Hazel, and John Piggott. 2001. "Australia's Mandatory Retirement Saving Policy: A View from the New Millennium." *Working Paper No. 23160.* **Washington, D.C.: World Bank. http://siteresources.worldbank.org/SOCIALPROTECTION/Res ources/SP-Discussion-papers/Pensions-DP/0108.pdf. 46 pages.**

A primer on the Australian system and how it is operating. The article judges that system in the context of the World Bank's preference for systems that are composed of a combination of public, individual, and employer financing.

Carney, Terry, and Peter Hanks. 1994. *Social Security in Australia.* **Oxford: Oxford University Press[A1]. 352 pages.**

Dated, but a good source to follow the development of the Australian welfare state, including its retirement system.

Heavey, Jerome F. 2006. "Superannuation and Social Security in Australia and the United States." *Journal of Australian Political cal Economy* **53: 191–207.**

This work is admittedly in a rather specialized journal, but it offers a clear explanation of superannuation and a useful comparison between the U.S. and Australian retirement systems.

Mitchell, Daniel, and Robert P. O'Quinn. 1997. "Australia's Privatized Retirement System: Lessons for the United States." *Backgrounder* **1149 (December 8). Washington, D.C.: Heritage Foundation. http://www.heritage.org/research/socialsecurity/.**

Though from the Heritage Foundation's pro-privatization perspective, this provides a good overview of how Australia developed its superannuation program.

Sass, Stephen A. 2004. "Reforming the Australian Retirement System: Mandating Individual Accounts." *Global Issues in Brief* 2 (April). Boston: Center for Retirement Research, Boston College. http://crr.bc.edu/index.php. 15 pages.

A relatively brief summary of the Australian program focusing on superannuation and individual retirement accounts.

Germany

The English-language portions of the German pension Web site are not particularly informative. However, the Web site does give an overview of the German system.

The English-language Web Site for the German Pension system:

http://www.bmas.bund.de/Englisch/Navigation/pensions.html
Those who can read German should access the German language pages, as more information is available there.

Börsch-Supan, Axel H., and Christina B. Wilke. 2006. "Reforming the German Public Pension System." Paper prepared for the 2006 Annual Meeting of the American Economic Association. 33 pages. http://www.rand.org/labor/aging/rsi/rsi_papers/2006_axel1.pdf.

Discusses the 2001 and 2004 reforms. It also has a useful bibliography. Börsch-Supan is the most prominent English-language commentator upon the German system. This is his most recent publication.

Capretta, James C. 2006. "Building Automatic Solvency into U.S. Social Security: Insights from Sweden and Germany." *Brookings Institution Policy Brief*, 151. Washington, D.C.: Brookings Institution. http://www.brook.edu. 8 pages.

A very good explanation of Germany's "sustainability factor."

U.S. Government Accountability Office. 2003. *Social Security Reform: Information Concerning Using a Voluntary Approach to Individual Accounts*. GAO-03-309 (March). Washington, D.C.: Government Printing Office. http://www.gao.gov/index.html. 72 pages.

Appendix III discusses the German experience with individual pension accounts.

Sweden

Sweden's official pension pages are, helpfully, almost all available in English. There is not a great deal of information on the Web pages themselves; it is best to look for the articles and publications available to be downloaded. The primary site is called "Financial Security in Old Age," maintained by the Ministry of Health and Social Affairs.

The English-language Web site for the Swedish pension system:

http://www.sweden.gov.se/sb/d/3829

You may recall that Sweden has an add-on individual retirement account program.

The Web site for the Premium Pension Fund: http://www.ppm.nu/tpp/infodocument/1:1;201469,201304,201475,201481

Körnberg, Bo, Edward Palmer, and Annika Sundén. 2003. "The NDC Reform in Sweden: The 1994 Legislation to the Present," 449–466. In Robert Holzman and Edward Palmer, eds., *Pension Reform: Issues and Prospects for Non-Defined Financial Contribution Schemes*. Washington, D.C.: World Bank.

Covers the politics behind the creation of the new Swedish system as well as an overview of how that system now operates.

Kruse, Agnata, and Edward Palmer. 2006. "The New Swedish Pension System-Financial Stability and the Central Government Budget." Paper presented at the Urban Institute International Conference on Social Security, February 24, 2006. 23 pages.

This is a background paper written for the Urban Institute conference described above (under Cross-Country Comparisons).

Lundberg, Urban. 2006. "Social Democracy Lost: The Social Democrat Party in Sweden and the Politics of Pension Reform, 1978–1998." In Lena Erikson and Eero Carroll, eds. *Welfare Politics Cross-Examined: Eclecticist and Analytical Perspectives in Sweden and the Developed World*. New Brunswick, NJ: Transaction Books. 334 pages.

Written for an audience more interested in academic theory, but still the best article on the politics behind pension reform in Sweden.

Palme, Joakim. 2003. "Pension Reform in Sweden and the Changing Boundaries between Public and Private." In Gordon L. Clark and Noel Whiteside, eds. *Pension Security in the 21st Century: Redrawing the Public-Private Debate.* New York: Oxford University Press. 308 pages.

A discussion of the Swedish pension system, and how its notional system blurs traditional understandings of the difference between pay-as-you-go and private defined contribution systems.

Palme, Mårten, and Ingemar Svensson. 1999. "Social Security, Occupational Pensions, and Retirement in Sweden," 355–402. In Jonathan Gruber and David Wise, eds. *Social Security and Retirement Around the World.* Chicago: University of Chicago Press.

This paper actually focuses on how the pension system has actually influenced the pattern of retirements in Sweden, but in doing so, it presents a full overview of the Swedish pension system.

Socialdepartementet. Ministry of Health and Social Affairs/ Riksförsäkringsverket. National Social Insurance Board. Government of Sweden. 2003. *The Swedish National Pension System.* http://www.sweden.gov.se/sb/d/2028/a/24221;jsessionid=aU absLHkduo8. 25 pages.

A government publication that carefully explains the Swedish system.

Swedish Social Insurance Agency. 2006. *The Orange Report: The Annual Report of the Swedish Pension System, 2006.* Stockholm: Swedish Social Insurance Agency. 94 pages. http://www .forsakringskassan.se/sprak/eng/.

An extraordinarily useful compendium of information about the Swedish system and pension programs generally. It is published annually.

Weaver, R. Kent. 2005. "Social Security Smorgasbord? Lessons from Sweden's Individual Pension Accounts." *Brookings Institution Policy Brief,* 140. Washington, D.C.: Brookings Institution. http://www.brookings.edu. 8 pages.

A survey of Sweden's experience with its add-on personal accounts.

World Bank. 2001. *Notional Accounts: Notional Defined Contribution Plans as a Pension Reform Strategy.* **Washington, D.C.: World Bank. http://siteresources.worldbank.org/INTPENSIONS /Resources/395443–1121194657824/PRPNoteNotionalAccts.pdf. 8 pages.**

An introduction to notional accounts, the reform that is at the heart of the new Swedish system.

United Kingdom

The British Department for Work and Pensions keeps the primary information site for the United Kingdom's various pension schemes and reforms. It features pension calculators and other features, similar to the U.S. Social Security Web site.

http://www.dwp.gov.uk/lifeevent/penret/

The Pension Service itself, located within that department, also has a Web site. The information here is directed particularly to British citizens who are or will be drawing a retirement pension, but there is much additional information, too.

The Web site for the Pension Service:

http://www.thepensionservice.gov.uk/

Not surprisingly, given the complexity of the British system, there is a special Web site that explains the coming reforms to the British pension program:

http://www.dwp.gov.uk/pensionsreform/

For those interested in the finances of the British programs, and national insurance contribution rates that must be paid into them, that information is found at:

http://www.hmrc.gov.uk/rates/nic.htm

The state broadcasting company of the United Kingdom, the British Broadcasting Company (BBC) also maintains a Web site on retirement pension programs. It fully covers the pension debate and the recent reforms in the United Kingdom, but there is also coverage of a number of retirement systems across the globe.

The BBC Web site:

http://news.bbc.co.uk/1/hi/in_depth/business/2005/turner_report/default.stm

Beer, Alex. 2006. "UK Pensions and Pension Reform." Paper presented at the Urban Institute International Conference on Social Security, February 24, 2006. 22 pages.

This is a background paper written for the Urban Institute conference described above (under the Cross-Country Comparisons section).

Blake, David. 2002. "The United Kingdom Pension System: Key Issues." Discussion Paper PI-0107. London: Pensions Institute, Birkbeck College, University of London.

Already a little dated, but this brief paper outlines the major issues that confront the British retirement system.

Sass, Stephen A. 2004. "Reforming the UK Retirement System: Privatization Plus a Safety Net." *Global Issues in Brief No. 3.* Boston: Center for Retirement Research, Boston College. 16 pages. http://crr.bc.edu/index.php.

A review of the impossibly complex British retirement system, current through 2003. Sass notes how difficult it is to predict the future operations or impact of the British programs.

Government of the United Kingdom. Financial Services Authority. 2007. "The Second State Pension: Should You Be Contracted Out?" *FSA Factsheet* (May). 6 pages. http://moneymadeclear.fsa.gov.uk.

The Financial Services Authority is an independent agency of the British government. This brief survey clearly explains the Second State Pension and how it operates.

United Kingdom. Department for Work and Pensions. Pensions Service. 2005. *A Guide to State Pensions.* 113 pages. http://thepensionsservice.gov.uk.

Everything you wanted to know about the operations of Britain's State Pensions. Still the best overview, but now parts are superseded by the reforms of 2007.

United Kingdom. Department for Work and Pensions. Pensions Service. 2006. *Personal Accounts: A New Way to Save. Executive Summary* (December). 44 pages. http://dwp.gov.uk /pensionsreform.

An explanation of the reforms passed by Parliament in 2007.

United Kingdom. Department for Work and Pensions. Pensions Service. 2007. "Implementing a National Pension Savings Scheme." *A New Pensions Settlement for the Twenty-first Century* 354–403. http://thepensionsservice.gov.uk.

Can be read as a supplement to the above to bring the reader up to date.

United States Government Accountability Office. 2003. *Social Security Reform: Information Concerning Using a Voluntary Approach to Individual Accounts.* GAO-03-309. Washington, D.C.: Government Printing Office. 72 pages. http://www.gao.gov /index.html.

Appendix I discusses the British experience with individual pension accounts.

Whiteside, Noel. 2003. *Constructing the Public-Private Divide: Historical Perspectives and the Politics of Pension Reform.* In Gordon L. Clark and Noel Whiteside. Pension Security in the 21st Century: Redrawing the Public-Private Divide. Oxford: Oxford University Press. 308 pages.

Good on the politics behind the frequent reforms in Britain.

Chile

Chile has an excellent Web site for its pension system. However, it is almost all in Spanish. An exception is the Web edition of "The Chilean Pension System," a very complete and useful survey of all aspects of Chile's pension program. It is available in English as well as Spanish.

The Web site for La Superintendencia de Administradoras de Fondos de Pensiones:

http://www.safp.cl/sist_previsional/index.html

The Web site of the English language edition of "The Chilean Pension System":

http://www.safp.cl/sischilpen/english.html

Diamond, Peter, and Salvador Valdés-Prieto. 1994. "Social Security Reforms." In Barry P. Bosworth, Rudiger Dornbusch, and Raul Lában, eds. *The Chilean Economy: Policy Lessons and Challenges.* **Washington, D.C.: Brookings Institution. 441 pages.**

A relatively early narrative of the history of the Chilean policy reforms.

Gill, Indermit, Truman Packard, and Juan Yermo. 2005. *Keeping the Promise of Social Security in Latin America.* **Palo Alto, CA: Stanford University Press. 341 pages.**

Many Latin American nations have followed the Chilean example with major pension reforms of their own. This volume studies the success of these various reforms.

James, Estelle. 2004. *Private Pension Annuities in Chile.* **NCPA Policy Report, 271. Washington, D.C.: National Center for Policy Analysis (December). 39 pages. http://www.ncpa.org.**

Though a bit technical, this paper includes a very good discussion of the Chilean system with emphasis upon how Chileans actually respond to the choices that are offered in this privatized system. A useful bibliography is included as well.

Pension Research Council. 2006. *Lessons from Pension Reform in the Americas.* **Pension Research Council Working Paper, 2006–8. Wharton School, University of Pennsylvania. 38 pages. http://prc.wharton.upenn.edu/prc/prc.html.**

This is a summary of a Federal Reserve Bank of Atlanta conference on this topic. It includes a discussion of how knowledgeable Chileans are of their new pension program, and what difference that knowledge makes to their retirement planning.

Tamborini, Christopher. 2007. *Social Security: The Chilean Approach to Retirement.* **CRS Research Report for Congress. Congressional Research Service. United States Congress. 33 pages.**

An objective assessment of the success of the Chilean program.

Japan

Japan has the oldest population in the world, and hence the most precarious government pension system. It has attempted reforms, most recently in 2004, that in some respects mirror the reforms made in Germany. Here are several readings that introduce the Japanese system. The Japanese Pension Bureau, which manages the system, has a limited Web page in English. However, if one follows the "Links to Related Documents," one will find a number of English-language materials available for download.

The Web site for the Japanese Pension Bureau:

http://www.mhlw.go.jp/english/org/policy/p36-37.html

Kabe, Tetsuo. 2006. "Japan's Public Pension Reforms." Paper presented at the International Conference on Social Security Reform(February 2006). New York: Urban Institute. 19 pages.

This paper discusses debates over the Japanese retirement system that are, in many ways, similar to those that are occurring in Germany.

National Institute of Population and Social Security Research. 2007. *Social Security in Japan.* Tokyo: Government of Japan. 51 pages. http://www.ipss.go.jp.

An up-to-date brief description of the Japanese retirement system, with some emphasis on its demographic underpinnings.

Sakamoto, Junichi. 2005. *Japan's Pension Reform.* SP Discussion Paper, 0541. Washington, D.C.: World Bank (December). 76 pages.

Focuses on the reforms of 2004 and Japan's effort to develop an automatic balancing mechanism, along similar lines as that of Germany.

Takayama, Noriyuki. 2003. "Pension Arrangements in the Oldest Country: The Japanese Case," 185–217. In Noriyuki Takayama, ed. *Taste of the Pie: Searching for Better Pension Provisions in Developed Countries.* Tokyo: Maruzen.

This chapter looks at the great difficulties Japan has faced in reforming its pension system under very unfavorable demographic conditions.

Takayama, Noriyuki. 2001. "Japanese Social Security Pensions in the Twenty-first Century." Paper presented at the International Conference on Pensions (March 2001), Tokyo. http://www.ier.hit-u.ac.jp.

Mexico

Mexico has also undertaken a major recent reform of its pension system. It drew heavily from the Chilean example, but with several of its own unique features. The readings below offer an introduction to the new Mexican system. The Web site of the Mexican pension regulatory agency, CONSAR, is exclusively in Spanish.

The Web site of CONSAR:

http://www.consar.gob.mx/

Espinosa-Vega, Marco A., and Tapin Sinha. 2001. "A Primer and Assessment of Social Security Reform in Mexico." *Economic Review* **1–23.**

This article is the best single introduction to the Mexican pension system.

Grandolini, Gloria, and Luis Cerda. 1998. *The 1997 Pension Reform in Mexico: Genesis and Design Features.* **Washington, D.C.: World Bank. 42 pages.**

More focused on the details of the new program than is Espinosa-Vega and Sinha (2001) (mentioned above).

Rodriguez, L. Jacobo. 1999. "In Praise and Criticism of Mexico's Pension Reform." *Policy Analysis,* **No. 340. Cato Institute. 15 pages.**

A survey of Mexico's reforms from the perspective of those who believe in full privatization.

Sandeval, Héctor. 2004. "Analysis of the Pension Reform in Mexico." Actuarial Research Clearing House. Society of Actuaries. http://www.soa.org. 52 pages.

The author examines the Mexican system, in particular the impact of its Chilean style reforms.

Glossary

Add-on   An individual retirement account that would supplement the benefits from Social Security. Add-ons could be voluntary or mandatory. They would not change the operations of the Social Security system.

Annuity   A contract that guarantees a series of payments to a retired person in exchange for an original lump-sum purchase or investment. Annuities are typically purchased from life insurance companies. Social Security is not an annuity program, though it was designed to look like one.

Average Indexed Monthly Earnings (AIME)   When an individual retires, her or his past monthly earnings are adjusted to account for the rise in average earnings that has occurred since that time. The Social Security Administration uses an "average wage index" to make this adjustment. The resulting AIME is used to calculate the amount of the Social Security benefit.

Carve-out   An individual retirement account (IRA) that would replace a portion of the benefits from Social Security. Typically, a portion of the worker's Federal Insurance Contribution Act (FICA) contributions would go into the IRA, not into Social Security. Accordingly, at the time of retirement, the benefit from Social Security would be smaller.

Clawback   A rebate demanded from upper-income retirees against their anticipated pension benefits. Above a set income threshold, a retiree must pay back a portion of his or her benefits to the government, reducing the pension benefit that will be received. The Canadian clawback, for example, demands a repayment of 15 percent of all benefits above the established threshold.

Consumer Price Index (CPI)   A measure of the average increase (or decrease) over time in the prices paid by an individual or family for a basket of consumer goods and services. The Social Security program uses the U.S. Department of Labor's CPI for Urban Consumers to make its annual cost-of-living adjustment.

261

Cost-of-Living Adjustment (COLA) Each January, Social Security benefits are automatically increased to offset inflation. The increase is based on the rise of the Consumer Price Index. The annual Social Security COLAs began in 1975.

Covered Worker, Covered Employment Occupations for which one must pay the Social Security contribution, and for which one gains the Social Security benefit.

CPP/QPP The Canada Pension Plan/Quebec Pension Plan. One of Canada's two major old-age pension programs.

Credits, Social Security Credits A worker typically needs 40 credits to be eligible for Social Security benefits. A credit is accrued each time the worker reaches a stipulated level of earnings (this level changes every year). A worker may accrue four credits per year. "Social Security credit" is essentially synonymous with the older terms "quarter" or "quarter of coverage."

Defined-Benefit versus Defined-Contribution Pension Plans In a defined-contribution plan, an individual contributes to the retirement system. The contributions are used to buy financial assets (typically bonds or stocks). Upon retirement, the individual's retirement benefits are based upon the rate of return of the assets that had been purchased over the course of the individual's working life. For example, assume that an individual had contributed $500,000 to the system during her or his working years and that, at the time of retirement, this investment had grown to $1,000,000. The individual's pension would then be drawn from this $1,000,000. In a defined-benefit pension plan, there is no necessary connection between the contributions paid in and the benefits paid out. In a defined-benefits plan, an individual contributes to the retirement system, but the benefits that she or he will receive at retirement are based not upon the returns to the contributions that were made but upon a contract or formula that stipulates the size of the benefit. The U.S. Social Security program is a defined-benefit plan, with each retiree's monthly pension amount set by law, not by the level of contribution.

Dependency Ratio The number of individuals who may draw from Social Security divided by the number who contribute to it. This is usually calculated as the number of Americans over the age of 65 divided by the number of Americans between the ages of 20 and 64. (Some authorities prefer to use ages 15 and 64).

Early Retirement Workers may opt to retire and collect Social Security benefits as early as age 62. If they do so, they will receive a lower monthly benefit than if they had waited until their full retirement age.

Entitlement Program A program of government benefits to which an individual has a legal right, provided that that individual meets the eligibility requirements specified in the law that authorizes the program. The amount of the benefits is not decided at the discretion of Congress; it is stipulated in the law itself. Social Security is an entitlement program.

Federal Insurance Contributions Act (FICA) The payroll tax that funds Social Security and Medicare, FICA was enacted in 1939. The tax is currently 12.4 percent of covered income. One-half of the FICA tax is directly paid by the worker; the other half is paid by the employer.

Fully Funded A retirement program for which sufficient money is put aside each year to pay for all of the future benefits is called a fully funded program. Defined-contribution plans are fully funded.

General Revenues Government receipts collected from income, excise, luxury, and other taxes, tolls, or customs that are not dedicated by law to any certain purpose are placed in the General Fund of the Treasury. Congress may appropriate these revenues, at its discretion, for any constitutional purpose.

Individual Retirement Account (IRA) Generally, IRAs are tax-advantaged investment plans into which individuals can place their own savings during their working years. The funds can be withdrawn at the time of their retirement. The choice of how to invest the monies in the IRA is left to the worker. IRAs have been proposed, under innumerable plans, to supplement or replace the traditional Social Security monthly benefit payment. These plans are often called plans to "privatize" Social Security.

Means Testing An administrative or investigative process to determine if an individual is eligible to receive money from a government program. The "test" usually is a requirement that the individual has an income or financial assets below a stipulated level. Social Security has no such process or requirement and hence is not a means-tested program.

Notional Defined Contributions A pay-as-you-go pension system in which each worker is given an individual account into which his or her retirement benefits accrue. These are termed "notional" because the account does not contain that worker's actual contributions. It is simply an accounting device that records the claims held on the system's assets by each worker. At retirement, the worker receives that claim, distributed over annual or monthly increments. Sweden was the first country to develop a pension system based on this principle.

Old Age Security (OAS) Canada's oldest pension program. It is universal and funded from the general revenues.

Old-Age, Survivors, and Disability Insurance (OASDI) The official name of the U.S. Social Security program. It includes the Disability Insurance program and the Retirement and Survivors Insurance program.

Pay as You Go A social security system that is funded by collecting taxes from workers and then making direct payments to retired persons from those taxes. The U.S. Social Security system has followed this principle since 1939.

Payroll Tax A tax on a worker's earnings. The tax may be paid directly by the worker, or indirectly by the worker's employer (see Federal Insurance Contribution Act).

Ponzi Scheme A Ponzi scheme involves convincing individuals that they will receive a great investment return on money they give to the organizer of the scheme. That organizer then convinces additional investors to give money; that money is paid to the old investors, meeting the promises made to them. The scheme collapses when no more new investors can be found, and the organizer then has no money with which to continue paying on the promises made.

Prefunding A policy of increasing the revenues going into the Social Security Trust Fund before its anticipated date of exhaustion. Enacting such a proposal would enable the Social Security program to continue to pay its promised benefits to each worker for many more years, if not indefinitely.

Price Indexation A method of revising an earlier year's or month's financial or monetary figure to account for the rise in prices (i.e., inflation) that has occurred since that time. The Consumer Price Index is the most commonly used index for this purpose. It is used to index the Social Security COLA.

Primary Insurance Amount The formal title for the monthly Social Security benefit paid to a retired (or disabled) worker. It is calculated from the worker's average indexed monthly earnings.

Progressive, Progressivity A tax or benefits system in which the rate of taxation increases (or of benefits decreases) as one's income rises. Under such a system, wealthier individuals either pay a larger percentage of their income than do poorer individuals or receive relatively lower benefits than do poorer individuals. The purpose of progressive taxation is to redistribute wealth or program benefits to those with the lowest incomes. The U.S. income tax system is progressive, as higher tax brackets are imposed on larger incomes. The Social Security system is progressive as well, as higher benefits (as a percentage of monthly earnings) are paid to those with lower earnings.

Rate of Return The gain or loss from an investment, such as common stocks or bonds, over a specific period of time. The annual rate of return is the gain or loss over a period of one year.

Retirement Earnings Test For most of the history of Social Security, the monthly benefit was reduced for those individuals who continued to work after their retirement age. Currently, only workers who take early retirement and continue to earn more than a stipulated amount see their monthly benefits reduced.

Social Security Administration (SSA) Headquartered in Baltimore, with 1,300 field offices and more than 60,000 employees, the SSA manages the Social Security program. It issues Social Security numbers, manages the Trust Funds, and administers the Disability Insurance program and the Supplemental Security Income program in addition to the Retirement and Survivors Insurance program.

Social Security Reserve Account In the original Social Security program, worker contributions were paid into this fund. The fund invested the contributions in U.S. Treasury securities and then returned the contributions, with interest, to the worker in the form of monthly payments at the time of his or her retirement. The fund was eliminated in the 1939 amendments to the Social Security Act.

Social Security Trust Fund There are two Social Security Trust Funds, one for the Old-Age and Survivors Program and a second for the Disability Program. Each is primarily an accounting device to keep track of the contributions to Social Security and the benefits paid out. The existence of the funds allows the Social Security Administration to pay benefits without the need for specific legislation to do so. Monies that remain after benefits have been paid are invested in Treasury securities. Note that, in spite of the name, the Social Security Trust Fund is neither legally nor in its operations anything like a private trust fund. It does not hold or manage a stock of financial assets.

Steady State Financing The level of taxation necessary to guarantee that the pension system can pay all the benefits that have been guaranteed to retirees and future retirees.

Superannuation The name of the Australian principle that all employers must offer pension programs for their employees.

Survivor, Survivor's Benefits If a recipient of Social Security dies, certain family members continue to receive benefits. With exceptions, these include the spouse of the deceased, children under age 18, and parents (if the deceased provided for their support).

Sustainability Factor An automatic reduction of pension benefits that occurs should the dependency ratio of workers to retirees decline. It is a principle of the German retirement system.

Index